Advance Praise for
BRUJO

"Congratulations on your success!"
—*Tony Hillerman*

"This masterfully plotted thriller hooked me on page one and took me on an unforgettable journey. The minute I finished it, I was on the phone—optioning the movie rights!"
>—*Martin Markinson*
>*Producer\Theatre Owner*
>*Helen Hayes Theatre, New York*

"A vivid and entertaining page t
— *Judith Van Geiso*

D1571900

"I loved this story so much that I c........u a ⊔uropean vacation to star in the movie version!"
>—*Suzanne Somers*

"*SENSATIONAL!* Once *BRUJO* gets hold of you, it doesn't let go! A first-rate thriller!"
>*It's A Wrap*
>—*New Mexico Entertainment Industry*
>*Quarterly*

"Jann Arrington Wolcott extracts new lifeblood from the Gothic thriller genre in this steamy page-turner! She combines a deep-rooted knowledge of New Mexico with a passion for the exotic and a flair for the dramatic."
>—*Jon Bowman*
>*Editor, New Mexico Magazine*

BRUJO
Seduced By Evil

Jann Arrington Wolcott

Route 66
Publishing, Ltd.

Brujo; *Seduced by Evil*

Published by Route 66 Publishing, Ltd. P.O. Box 25222,
Albuquerque, NM 87125
1. Arrington , Jann Wolcott
2. Fiction
ISBN 0-9644293-0-6
Library of Congress Catalog Card Number 95-67555

Cover illustration by Julie Tompkins

Printed in the United States of America

Acknowledgments:

Many people helped me in the writing of this book. First of all, I am indebted to the late Karl Nordling, a talented editor and good friend, for convincing me that I should and could write *BRUJO*. Secondly, without the support and encouragement of my husband, John, it would have been a most difficult task. Last but not least, I want to thank all the tireless and terrific people at Route 66 Publishing, Ltd., for making my dream come true.

In addition to my family, many dear friends offered unofficial editing and emotional support. They include: Bliss Kelly-Loree, Arny and Judy Katz, Dr. Stephen Blumberg, Wendy Wolff Blumberg, Hans and Ann Kresny, Jim Gautier, Suzanne Crayson, Dan McBride, and the talented and supportive group known as "Writers At Elaine's."

I also wish to acknowledge my agent, Manfred Mroczkowski of InterLicense, Ltd., as well as the following people for their special contributions: Charmian Lindsay Shaw, who is no longer in body, but with me always in spirit; Bobette Perrone, for the integrity of her approach to research, writing, and life; Brenda Katz, Melanie Costanzo, and P. J. Liebson, for their tactful editing skills; and those healers and "magical" practitioners who shared their traditions and knowledge with me but asked not to be named.

Special thanks goes to my wise and good friend, Arlena Markinson, for helping me to understand, on a soul level, the story that I was writing; to White Eagle, Pipe Carrier, and Medicine Person in the Bear Clan of the Tsalagi (Cherokee) Nation; to Dancing Shadow for teaching me what I needed to know; and especially to Wakanda, whose guidance keeps me on path.

*In Memory of Tom Loree,
who believed in this story and,
no matter how busy, always found the time.*

BRUJO

Seduced By Evil

Chapter 1

She climbed through the darkness along a narrow path that wound close to the cliff's edge. At the top of the mesa, she rested, leaning on her walking stick and gazing out across the moonlit canyon far below. Her heart felt heavy. There was much to do and time was short.

Something small dashed through the thick brush off to her left. A rabbit. They were fat and plentiful this year. Tomorrow she would set her trap and make a stew, using the sweet roots and herbs that grew around the women's lodge. The thought made her mouth water. She was tired from the long climb and had not eaten since early morning.

A familiar boulder stood near the cliff's edge a short distance ahead. Shaped like a crouching bear, it was carved with symbols sacred to the Grandmothers. The lodge lay just beyond.

A tall figure stepped suddenly from the shadows to block her path. He moved swiftly toward her, the night wind lifting his long black hair. Cold fury radiated from

1

*his body. Perched on his shoulder was an enormous
raven.*

*She froze, her throat constricting in terror. There
was no escape. Even if her crippled foot would allow it,
there was nowhere to run. He had broken an ancient
and powerful taboo by coming here. The high mesa was
forbidden to all men. His motive was clear.*

*"You dare to come to this place?" Her voice
shattered the silence. He stared at her for a long
moment. Although his face remained expressionless, she
saw the grief in his eyes. Suddenly, he clapped his
hands together. Once. The sound ripped through her
heart like an obsidian blade.*

*With a savage screech, the bird flew at her face. She
stumbled backward, shielding her eyes with her hands.
For a moment, strong arms protected her as the man
rushed forward and seized her, crushing her to his chest.
She felt his lips graze her forehead. Then in an abrupt,
brutal motion, he shoved her away.*

*The ground disappeared beneath her feet. She flung
her arms forward, clawing empty air as she reached for
him. The night sky tilted. She screamed his name, the
sound drowning out the croaking of the raven as great
jagged rocks rushed up to meet her.*

* * *

"Lee, wake up!" Nick turned on the bedside lamp.
"Honey! You're having a nightmare."

She sat up in bed, staring at her husband. "What?
Oh, God, it was so real."

"It must have been. You're shaking like a leaf."

"It was one of those terrible dreams I've had for
years. I was falling, I think from a cliff. But this time,
there was more to it. Someone pushed me. A wild-
looking man with long black hair. He had a bird, a huge
black bird, that attacked me. Slashed my face." She
touched her cheek, half-expecting to feel a bloody tear.

"Good lord," Nick stifled a yawn. "It must have been
those chile rellenos you had for dinner."

"The most bizarre thing about the dream was that the

man was so familiar. He had a strange name. In fact, I was screaming his name as I fell. I can almost remember it—but then it slips away." She shuddered and pulled the covers up over her shoulders. "I know it sounds silly, but it was terrifying."

"Well, it was just a dream. Try to forget it, and go back to sleep."

"I don't think I can. It was so realistic. The man was wearing some kind of leather outfit. I felt it against my cheek when he grabbed me. And necklaces. He was wearing several unusual necklaces. I think they were made of shells. And the bird, it must have been a raven—"

"Babe," Nick interrupted, "fascinating though your nocturnal adventures might be, I need some sleep. I have an important meeting first thing in the morning." He turned off the light and rolled over.

"Well, excuse me for disturbing you, Doctor Lindsay. I'll try to keep my 'nocturnal adventures' to myself." She moved as far away from him as possible.

"Oh, come on. Don't get mad. I didn't mean to hurt your feelings. But it is the middle of the night."

Much to her surprise, Lee started to cry.

"I don't believe this," Nick said, snapping the light back on. "Honey, what's the matter with you? You had a bad dream. That's no reason to carry on like this."

"I don't know what's the matter with me! I was just so frightened. I was certain I was going to die in that dream. And then I felt myself falling. It just left me feeling so...sad." She reached for a tissue and blew her nose. "Go back to sleep. I'm okay."

"You sure?"

Lee nodded, and Nick turned out the light. Soon he was snoring softly. She lay awake for much of the night, staring into the darkness and wondering why the dream had shaken her so deeply.

* * *

When the alarm went off at six-thirty the next morning, Lee felt as though she had just gotten back to sleep. She forced herself up and into the shower. Half an hour later, still feeling groggy and out of sorts, she was dressed for work and in the kitchen.

Nick soon joined her, briefcase in hand. Tall and trim, he still resembled the handsome graduate student he had been when she met him twenty years ago. Only the deep lines between his eyes and strands of silver in his hair hinted at middle age. At forty-four, Nick was an attractive and vigorous man. He gave Lee a quick kiss on the cheek before pouring himself a cup of coffee. "Morning, gorgeous."

"Good morning," she said, setting out several varieties of cold cereal.

"How're you feeling? You had a pretty rough night."

Lee thought about the nightmare that had shattered her sleep—vague memories of sharp talons and dark wings flying into her face. With an effort, she pulled herself back to the present. "I'm okay. Sorry I disturbed your sleep."

"I wasn't sleeping all that well anyway. Couldn't stop worrying about next week's rocket shot." He fixed himself a bowl of cereal before sitting down at the snack bar with the morning paper.

Lee poured two glasses of orange juice. "Is it an important experiment?"

Nick was studying the weather section of the paper. "Hmmm?"

"I asked if this is an important experiment."

"It's critical. We're ready to launch that electron accelerator. That is, if bad weather doesn't add more delays." He glanced at his watch, then hurriedly ate his cereal while reading the sports page. His attention was still focused on the box scores when he added, "I have to leave for Fairbanks on Friday morning."

"What? You're leaving for Alaska this Friday?"

He nodded, continuing to read while he drank his juice. "Afraid so. I'll need the weekend to get the station set up."

"But what about the Buchanans' party Saturday night? I explained to you that this is important to the magazine. They're our biggest advertisers."

He looked up at her with a puzzled frown that quickly dissolved into chagrin. "Uh oh. That completely slipped my mind."

"Oh, Nick," Lee said in an exasperated voice. "You promised you'd be home this weekend. Damn it, I'm sick of going to social functions by myself."

He stood up and walked around the snack bar. "I'm sorry, babe," he said, putting his arms around her. "Ray was scheduled to get the equipment set up, but he begged off. Out-of-town company or something. So I volunteered—"

"Of course, you volunteered. As usual."

"I agreed to leave a few days early," he continued, "in order to get things ready. Someone has to do it, and it has to be done right. You understand, don't you?"

"Would it make any difference if I didn't?"

"Come on, babe, don't make a big deal out of this. I said I was sorry, and I promise I'll make it up to you when I get back." He gave her a quick hug and released her.

"When will that be?"

"A couple of weeks."

"That long?"

"Like I said, this is a big experiment. Our funding for next year may depend on the it."

"I see." She turned her back to him and poured a cup of coffee.

"What's on your agenda for today?" he asked, obviously eager to change the subject.

"I'm going into the office for an hour or so to get some editing out of the way before my interview."

"Who are you interviewing?"

"Someone in a little village north of town."

"Really? How come?"

"I need some local history for an article I'm writing for the January issue. I talked to a man yesterday who gave me a lead..." Her voice trailed off as she saw Nick glance at his watch and reach for his briefcase. "Never mind. Go on, I'll tell you about it tonight."

"Where's Sara? I haven't seen her this morning."

"She's still asleep. There's a teacher's conference at the high school today, so classes are cancelled. I'm going to meet her downtown for lunch."

Lee gave Nick a perfunctory wave as he left the house a few minutes later. After clearing the snack bar, she hurried up the stairs to finish dressing. She ran a brush through her stylishly cut blond hair and peered critically into the mirror. I look tired, she thought, her mind again returning to her nightmare. She shook her head, attempting to dislodge the disturbing memory. Then she smoothed a little makeup under her slightly puffy eyes and applied a quick coat of mascara to her lashes. That would have to do. She was running late.

Grabbing her purse, she crossed the hall and opened Sara's bedroom door. "Sweetie?" She gently shook her sleeping fifteen-year-old daughter's shoulder. "I'm leaving now. Wendy's mom is dropping you girls off downtown later this morning, right?"

"Uh huh." Sara's voice was muffled with sleep.

"Okay. I'll meet you on the plaza about one-thirty. Then we'll go somewhere special for lunch. Don't forget to lock the front door when you leave. Oh, and please feed Mister. He's outside stalking lizards. There's an open can of cat food in the fridge."

"Okay. Bye." Sara rolled over, her long brown hair fanning across the pillow.

* * *

Lee pulled out of the driveway and headed down the dirt road toward her office, located two blocks west of the downtown plaza. As she drove, her thoughts returned to the Buchanans' party. She wasn't surprised that it had conveniently slipped Nick's mind. He hadn't really wanted to go. It would be the kind of thing that she enjoyed and he merely suffered through—an eclectic gathering of artists, writers, and colorful Santa Fe personalities. The "artsy-fartsy crowd," as he jokingly referred to her circle of friends and business acquaintances.

Oh, well, she thought, I'm used to attending parties alone. I'll just go for an hour or so. At least put in an appearance. Whether Nick realized it or not, occasional socializing with advertisers was part of the magazine business. And the Buchanans owned one of the most successful art galleries in town.

Lee pulled into the **Santa Fe Today** parking lot at eight o'clock sharp, noting that Annabel's car was already there. Annabel Garrett, her partner of almost ten years, was a hard worker and a good editor. The only problem was Annabel's nosiness. She was a busybody, there was no getting around it. But she had a good heart. And, all things considered, they made a darned good team. They had succeeded in building the once floundering magazine into a thriving business with a full-time staff of six and a sizeable pool of free-lance writers. Lee was proud of what they had accomplished. It hadn't been easy.

Carrying her purse and bulging briefcase, she walked into the remodeled adobe building. Annabel, her stocky figure stuffed into a rhinestone-studded denim jumpsuit, was bent over the front desk, shuffling through a pile of papers.

"Hi," Lee said.

Annabel jumped. "I didn't expect you in this morning," she said. "Aren't you interviewing some guy out in the boonies?"

"Not until eleven. I thought I'd edit a few articles first. Is Julie coming in?"

"As far as I know. I was just checking her 'in' box. I see there's a letter here from her lawyer." She held it up to the light. "I can't believe that girl's going through another divorce. How many does this make so far?"

"I haven't been counting."

"I think it's at least five. Let's see, there was that flamenco guitar player—he didn't last long, did he? Then there was the bald guy who turned out to be gay. I heard

7

that he—"

"Annabel," Lee interrupted, losing her patience, "Julie is the best receptionist we've ever had. She practically runs this office. As long as it doesn't interfere with her work, I really don't think her love life is any of our business."

"My, my. You're a bit testy this morning."

Lee sighed. "I guess I am. Sorry."

"What happened? A fight with Nick?"

"No. I'm just tired. I woke up in the middle of the night and couldn't get back to sleep. Listen, I want to get these articles ready for the typesetter. I'll talk to you later." She hurried into her office.

* * *

Two hours later, Lee was driving north. The day was brisk and clear, perfect weather to take a break from the busy office. She passed the sweeping roof of the Santa Fe Opera and began the descent into the wide *piñon*-dotted Española valley. As always, she was struck by the grandeur of the northern New Mexico landscape. It had a timeless, mystical quality that never failed to move her. Distant mesas loomed in the background like huge sacrificial platforms. And beyond, thirty miles to the west, rose the magnificent Jémez Mountains, the forested remnants of an ancient volcano. At their base, perched on a seven-thousand-foot-high plateau, sat Los Alamos, home of the world's first atomic weapons and the famed Los Alamos National Laboratories—Nick's employer since he had earned his Ph.D. seventeen years ago.

She thought about the isolated scientific community as she drove. They had lived there years ago, when they were first married, in a government-built apartment. Soon after Sara was born, Lee had persuaded Nick to move to nearby Santa Fe. The move had been a good one, as far as Lee was concerned. She loved the ancient city's sophisticated ambiance and colorful mixture of cultures. After working for several years as a free-lance writer, she had bought a half interest in the almost defunct **Santa Fe Today** magazine.

Nick never seemed to mind the commute to Los Alamos. He said the drive gave him time to focus his thoughts. And he was certainly focused, Lee thought irritably. On his work, that is.

She turned off the main highway and continued along a twisting, narrow road. In an effort to shake off her depressed mood, Lee popped a cassette into the tape player. Soon she was feeling better and singing along with Kenny Rogers:

"Why don't we go somewhere and love
It's been a long, long time.
Why don't we just go somewhere and love
And leave the whole world behind."

* * *

Lee began looking anxiously for some sign of civilization. Unless she'd taken a wrong turn somewhere, Cavado shouldn't be much farther. She'd been driving along isolated roads for over an hour and, except for a dilapidated pickup carrying a load of firewood, she hadn't seen another vehicle for ten miles.

The high desert landscape changed dramatically as the narrow road wound steadily higher, climbing past towering sandstone bluffs and rocky ravines into the forested foothills of the Sangre de Cristo mountain range. Rounding a curve, she was relieved to see a service station ahead on the right side of the road. Her gas gauge indicated almost half a tank, more than enough to get home. Still, she decided, better to play it safe. It wouldn't do to be stranded in this remote area. She pulled up beside the self-service pump and got out of the car.

Lee knew that she looked younger than her forty years. Slender and fit, she took pride in her good looks and usually appreciated the attention that they drew. But this was one of those times when she could have done without it.

Two attendants were leaning against the building watching her operate the gas pump. One of them, a tall, stoop-shouldered Anglo, said something out of the corner of his mouth that caused his Hispanic companion to laugh. Then he pushed his lanky frame away from the wall and sauntered toward her.

"Morning," he said, running his fingers through his disheveled hair in an unsuccessful attempt to tame it. "Need some help with that?"

"No thanks. I can manage."

"Good looking car," he said, patting the hood of her silver Subaru and moving closer. "Get good mileage?"

"Not bad." Lee stared at the flashing numbers on the gas pump gauge.

"Four-wheel drive?"

"Uh huh."

"That comes in handy in this neck of the woods." Crossing his arms across his chest, he leaned against the car. "You from around here?"

"Santa Fe." Lee shifted her weight, moving away from him.

"Great town. Or used to be, before all them rich folks and movie stars moved in." He shot her a look and grinned, revealing a badly chipped front tooth. "Say, now, you look a little familiar, come to think of it. You some kinda celebrity?"

"I'm afraid not."

"Well, you look like you could be." He took a toothpick out of his shirt pocket and stuck it in the corner of his mouth. "Where you headed?"

Lee tried to ignore the odors of gasoline and stale sweat drifting toward her. With relief she heard the click of the gas pump turning off. "I have an appointment," she said, hanging up the nozzle and securing the cap on the gas tank. "In Cavado." She got back inside her car and handed him her credit card through the open window.

The attendant took the card and studied her. "Cavado? That ain't much of a town to be having an appointment in." He chewed thoughtfully on the end of the toothpick. "Just a few old houses and a grocery store. And, of course, El Gallo. That's the name of the bar. Means the rooster." He chuckled. "But you don't want to go in there. Rough spot. No place for a lady like yourself." He narrowed his eyes. "It ain't none of my business, of course, but who you seeing in Cavado?"

She hesitated. As a writer, she had learned to gather all the information she could, even from unlikely sources. "Juan Mascareñas," she replied. "Do you know him?"

"Sure, I know Juan. Everybody around here knows everybody else. But I have to say, you don't look like the sort that would be visiting him."

"What do you mean?"

"Just that you don't look like someone who would be seeing a *curandero*."

"A what?"

"A *curandero*. You know, a healer." He bent his head near the open window. "Well, at least they claim to be healers. They chant some kind of mumbo-jumbo, and make medicines out of weeds. Most of the villages around here have their *curanderos*, and some folks swear by them. But me, I steer clear of that sort of thing. I ain't about to be treated by some witch doctor!" He laughed, blasting her with stale cigarette breath.

"I'm not going for any treatment. I'm interviewing him for an article I'm writing."

"A writer, huh? What kind of books do you write?"

"I write magazine articles. And I was told that Mr. Mascareñas would be able to fill me in on the history of this area."

"I guess so. After all, his people was here before God. Descended from them *conquistadors*, they say. They grabbed up most of the land around here long ago and held onto it. Fact is, old Juan owns damn near all of Cavado. Got more money than he knows what to do with. Guess that's why he acts so high and mighty."

"He sounded nice enough on the phone."

"Yeah, he has fancy manners. But I still say he's a little on the strange side. Be right back."

11

Lee watched him walk inside the station to write up the transaction. She reached for her note pad and wrote "Mascareñas— *curandero*?"

"Here you go," the attendant said, returning to the car. "Sign right here."

"How much farther is Cavado?"

"Couple miles. Just take that dirt road up ahead that cuts off to the right. You'll see a sign."

"Thanks." Lee started the engine and waited for him to move away from her car. Then she rolled up the window and drove away, following the winding dirt road.

Chapter 2

*T*he road snaked up a hill and crested to reveal a village nestled in the valley below. The entire community consisted of no more than a dozen adobe buildings, their corrugated tin roofs shaded by ancient cottonwood trees. In the center of the village stood a small adobe church. A weathered wooden cross on its steeple leaned precariously to one side, giving the building a forlorn, forgotten look.

I'll run a photo of that church with the article, Lee decided. It doesn't look like a thing has changed here for centuries. Not much action in Cavado.

A raven circling above the silent village caught Lee's eye. It flew toward her, then swooped down, landing on a branch of a *piñon* tree several car lengths ahead. She slowed to look at it, feeling a chill as the bird evoked memories of her dream the night before. That's a huge raven, she thought. I've never seen one anywhere near that size.

She pulled over to the side of the road and reached

into the back seat for her camera case. A photographer had been assigned to the story, but she might as well take a few shots of her own. A village untouched by time. That would be her story angle.

Camera in hand, she walked down the road toward the raven. It watched her approach with unblinking eyes. That's odd, she thought. That bird doesn't seem the least bit afraid of me. I wonder if it's tame? She removed the lens cover and focused her camera. An instant after she snapped the picture, the raven flapped its powerful wings and took flight. Soaring in a wide circle above her, it dropped toward the village and disappeared into the trees.

Lee continued walking. It was a beautiful spot. Maybe she could talk Nick into coming here some Sunday for a picnic. Just the two of them. It had been years since they had done anything like that.

As she snapped shots of the village, Lee was struck by how quiet it was. It was almost too quiet. Where is everyone? Isn't anybody home in Cavado? She detected no sound, no movement at all. Her uneasy feeling returned. I'd better locate Mr. Mascareñas, she thought, glancing at her watch. It's almost eleven o'clock. She hurried back to the car.

Lee drove on down the hill. On the outskirts of the village, she saw an orchard of gnarled apple trees lining the road to the right. Across the road stood a lifeless cottonwood tree, one side blackened as though scarred by a fierce fire. Behind the tree was a small, ancient-looking adobe house.

She stopped to consult her directions: Five miles on dirt road—just before entering village, first house on left. This must be the place. She parked beside a late model black pickup. Boy, talk about the middle of nowhere. And what happened to that tree? Lightning, maybe? It should be cut down before it falls over.

She got out of her car and took several quick pictures, finishing the roll of film. Then she gathered what she would need—notebook, tape recorder, a copy of the magazine—and walked up the dirt path to the house.

The front door was decorated with a string of garlic. To keep away werewolves, no doubt, Lee told herself as she knocked on the old unpainted wood. Or was it vampires? She glanced down at a bleached skull that seemed to grin at her from an empty clay pot beside the door. A dog skull? Probably a coyote. She took a deep breath and knocked.

The door was opened by a tall, well-built man dressed casually in Levi's, boots and a white Western shirt. His dark hair was long, covering his ears and curling over his shirt collar in the back. "*Señora* Lindsay," he said in the deep voice that Lee remembered from their telephone conversation the day before, "I'm Juan Mascareñas. Please, come in."

Lee stepped across the worn wooden threshold into a dimly lit room. She blinked, waiting for her eyes to adjust from the bright outdoors to the abrupt darkness. "I appreciate your taking the time to see me, Mr. Mascareñas," she said, extending her right hand.

He grasped her hand firmly in both of his. As her vision sharpened, Lee realized that he was older than his athletic appearance had first led her to assume. A network of lines creased his forehead and radiated from the outer corners of his eyes. He must be in his late forties, she noted. But he's obviously in good shape. Interesting face—handsome, actually, with those high cheekbones and piercing black eyes. A reddish, spider-shaped birthmark, slightly smaller than a quarter, lay just beneath his left cheekbone.

Lee felt her smile quiver. Feeling ill at ease, she withdrew her hand. "As I explained on the telephone, **Santa Fe Today** is featuring articles on several villages in this area," she said. "Mr. Archuleta at the Española Chamber of Commerce suggested that I talk to you. He said that you're an authority on local history."

"Ah, yes. It is a small passion of mine. I will try to be of assistance. Please, follow me."

Lee followed him into an even dimmer second room,

noticing that the window shades were tightly closed. The only light emanated from several flickering candles. She looked around in amazement. The room was filled with what appeared to be antique Spanish Colonial furniture. It was also cluttered with a startling collection of animal skulls, bones and various kinds of hides. Black wings with a three-foot wingspan were nailed to a wooden frame above a darkened window.

He helped her out of her jacket and hung it on a wooden peg on the wall in the corner of the room. "Sit there," he said, indicating a blanket-covered sofa. "Make yourself comfortable."

Lee sat down, arranged her notebook and tape recorder at her side, then looked up. She gasped and jerked back. Resting on a table, just inches from her arm, was a diamondback rattlesnake. She was already on her feet when Juan spoke. She could hear the amusement in his voice.

"*Descansa, señora*, have no fear. *El serpiente* can not harm you. He is no longer in his body."

Lee looked closer, squinting in the candlelight, and realized that it was just the skin of a rattlesnake, its dried head and long string of rattles still attached.

Embarrassed, heart still pounding, she sat back down—a bit farther from the table. "Former pet of yours?"

Juan smiled. "A pet? No, I wouldn't say that. Like all creatures, he was my brother." He seated himself across from her in a straight chair, stretching his long legs out in front of him.

"I see." Lee leaned over to recover her notepad from the floor where it had fallen, fighting a rapidly escalating apprehension. This was no time to be getting the jitters. Mascareñas might have strange decorating taste, but she needed his input for her story if she was going to meet her own deadline. And she had never missed a deadline. Besides, he must be on the level. He'd been recommended by the Chamber of Commerce.

"Are you familiar with **Santa Fe Today**?" She

handed him a copy of the latest issue. "It has a circulation of 15,000 and is distributed throughout New
Mexico, parts of Arizona and—"

"I have read the magazine," he interrupted, dropping
it without so much as a glance onto the floor beside his
chair. His eyes narrowed slightly as he studied her face.

"Oh. Well, that's good. Mr. Mascareñas—"

"Call me Juan. Please. And your first name?"

"Lee." She tried not to squirm under his steady gaze.
"First, I'd like a little background information on you,
Juan, if you don't mind," Lee said, trying to ease into
the interview. "I understand that you're a *curandero*."

He stiffened. "*Señora*," he said in a suddenly icy
voice, "I want no publicity about myself or my work. I
agreed only to discuss the history of my village." He
rose to his feet.

"Of course," she said quickly. "That's what I'm here
for—to talk about Cavado. Excuse me. I didn't mean to
pry. I was only making conversation."

Juan moved across the room to a small hot plate
where a teapot simmered. "*Bueno*, Lee," he said
smoothly. " No need to apologize. May I offer you
some tea?"

Relieved that the interview was not to be terminated,
Lee nodded. "Yes, thank you. That would be nice."
She swallowed hard. That was close. What a strange,
touchy man! And this place is straight out of a horror
movie. She took a deep breath. Relax, she scolded
herself. This is just another interview. Nothing I can't
handle.

Juan handed her a steaming stoneware cup. As he
leaned toward her, candlelight gleamed on an intricately
engraved silver pendant hanging from a chain around his
neck. About two inches wide, it was in the shape of
outspread wings. Two red stones were set in the center
like glowing almond-shaped eyes. Between the stones
was an elaborate spiral design. Intrigued, Lee stared at
the unusual necklace. Then her gaze moved up to the
spider-shaped birthmark on Juan's cheek. Something

stirred in the back of her mind.

"Drink this," Juan said. "It will be good for you." He sat down again, facing her, watching as she took her first sip of the tea.

She tried not to make a face at the unexpectedly bitter taste. Instantly, her mouth and tongue began to tingle. "I don't think I've had this particular brand before," she said. "What is it?"

"A special blend—from an old family recipe. It tastes better after the first few swallows."

"I see." Not wanting to appear rude, she forced another sip. The tea did, indeed, taste a little less bitter. In fact, it warmed her throat pleasantly. Reluctant to set the cup on the wooden arm of the antique sofa, she held it in her lap. "Do you mind if I tape our interview?" she asked. Seeing him stiffen again, Lee began to talk faster. "I find that it helps me to keep my facts straight. Also, it's a little dark in here, and it would be much easier than taking notes."

He leaned back in his chair. "*Bueno*. Use the recorder. Now, how may I help you?"

Lee punched the record button. "Well, for starters, how did the village get its name? What does Cavado mean?"

"*No sé*, I don't know," he said with a slight shrug of his shoulders. "It has been called Cavado for hundreds of years. The origin of the name has been lost. There is a legend that this area was sacred to the Ancient Ones, the Anasazi Indians. Perhaps the name comes from that forgotten time."

"That's interesting. So the name is a mystery?"

He nodded. "There are many mysteries in these mountains, *señora*. And many secrets that are best left undisturbed." A small smile played at the corners of his mouth. Then it was gone.

Lee was dismayed to find that her hand was shaking slightly as she again brought the tea to her lips. She took another quick drink, hoping he hadn't noticed. "Could you tell me a little about the village?" she asked.

"What's the population? I didn't see anyone on the streets down there when I drove in."

"About sixty, maybe sixty-five. Times have changed in Cavado. Like most of these small mountain villages, it is slowly dying as it loses its population. A man can no longer make a living by working a small plot of land. So while some commute to jobs in Taos or Española, many have moved away." He shook his head sadly. "This was a lively village when I was a boy. But most of the houses around the plaza are now deserted, crumbling with neglect. And the plaza itself is overgrown with weeds. Only ghosts meet there now, after sunset, to talk of the old days."

"Are you saying that Cavado is haunted?"

"All places are haunted by the events and personalities of the past."

She stared at him, puzzled. There was something about him, something vaguely familiar. At times he reminded her of someone. But she couldn't quite place who that might be.

"Of course our concept of time is just an illusion," he was saying. "Actually, the past, the present and the future all coexist in the spirit world."

She frowned. "What? I'm sorry, I'm afraid you lost me there."

"I was just saying that there are many simultaneous realities."

"That's an interesting theory." She drank more tea to give herself time to think. Her mind felt muddled. She cleared her throat, determined to get the interview back on track. "When did your family arrive here?"

"My forefathers came to this area from Spain in the mid-1600s, before the great Pueblo Revolt of 1680." He settled back in his chair, his eyes never leaving her face. "The local Indians were traditionally peaceful, but they tired of Spanish rule and of their forced conversion to Christianity. When the Indians finally rebelled, they killed about four hundred Spaniards. Most of the Mascareñases managed to escape the massacre by fleeing south, to what is now El Paso. They returned after the reconquest by Don Diego de Vargas some thirteen years later. We have been here, farming and ranching, since that time."

"So your family played an important role in the colonization of New Mexico."

He nodded. "The Mascareñas family roots are firmly attached to this rocky soil."

Lee leaned back against the sofa, feeling less tense. Although the setting was a little unnerving, the meeting was beginning to feel more like an interview. And Juan certainly knew his history. "It's difficult to imagine the hardship and isolation early settlers had to endure in order to settle this land," she said.

He shook his head. "You speak as though they succeeded in their efforts. That is an illusion, *señora*. This land will never be settled, and it will never be conquered. These hills will tolerate and sustain us only as long as we respect them. We are guests here, not conquerors."

Lee stared at him, intrigued by the passion in his voice. She glanced down to make certain that her tape recorder was running. That would be a great quote.

"But you are right," he continued. "There was much hardship in those days. Drought and disease were frequent visitors. The Spanish learned many survival skills from the Indians of nearby pueblos who brought gifts of food and medicinal herbs. And, because of the isolation, many old Spanish traditions and Native American beliefs have endured here in Cavado."

Lee felt herself continue to relax as Juan talked, elaborating on the history of the area and telling anec-dotes about his ancestors' lives. A feeling of peace and well-being settled over her and she listened, enthralled, as he went on to describe his strong attachment to the area. "You must understand that Cavado is a very special place," he said at one point. "It is a very spiri-tual place, a source of great power. It has been so for—"

He was interrupted by a knock at the door and politely excused himself to go into the front room. Lee turned off her tape recorder. She could hear a woman's voice and although her Spanish was minimal, she understood that the woman was ill. Lee strained to hear Juan's answer, but much of his rapid Spanish was incomprehensible to her. He reappeared and filled a small plastic bag with a brown powdered substance that was stored in a jar on a shelf near the door. Then he returned to the front room. Lee heard him tell the woman to go home and rest. He would see her again tomorrow morning. The woman thanked him, and their voices grew muffled as Juan escorted her out the front door and away from the house.

I guess he is some sort of healer, Lee thought, noticing bunches of herbs and plants hanging from the wooden vigas of the ceiling. I wonder how many people he treats? And for what ailments? She looked at her watch. Eleven-thirty! How could it be that late? She'd been talking to Juan for thirty minutes. Strange, it didn't seem like that much time had passed. She frowned, trying to remember if she'd asked all the necessary questions. Let's see, she thought, glancing through the carefully prepared questions in her notebook. We covered the early history...drought and Indians...the present-day population...

Heat radiated from a small wood-burning stove under the window. The dark room seemed to envelop Lee, making her feel drowsy. She yawned and leaned back against the sofa, closing her eyes.

She sat up with a start when she heard Juan return, shocked to realize that she had drifted off to sleep. "I...I was just...resting my eyes."

He paused by the sofa, looking down at her. Then, without a word, he retrieved her empty cup from the floor where she had put it and placed it on a table. He opened the drawer of an antique carved desk and withdrew a sheet of paper before returning to his chair. She turned her tape recorder back on, preparing to continue the interview.

"Turn the recorder off now," he said in a quiet voice. "And put away your notes." His dark eyes fastened on hers, willing her to obey.

"But I..." Her voice died in her throat and she found herself doing as he instructed.

"I want to read something to you," he said. "Something I have written. I hope it will help you to understand who I am."

Juan's voice was low and intimate, caressing the words as he read:

I am night in the sleeping desert
I am morning on the windswept bluff
I beat my wings and fly through the ages
I am yesterday and all tomorrows to come
Look beyond what you see and you will know me
You will hear the song of my heart
And answer my voice as it awakens
Sleeping memories in your soul.

He finished reading and looked up at her. His eyes seemed to burn into hers. "Do you understand what I'm saying?"

"That's beautiful."

"But do you understand?" His voice was urgent.

"I...I guess I do." She felt confused, unable to think. What exactly was she supposed to understand?

"I knew you would." He leaned toward her. "Look at me closely, Lee. Let me explain. I know many things about you. You are not simply who you appear to be. There is a part of you that is yearning to be set free, to soar through the air and reconnect with the energies of the earth."

Lee tried to think of an appropriate response. Her head felt weightless, as though it might detach from her body and float away. She watched the candlelight play across Juan's face—his prominent cheekbones, his finely molded nose, and his full sensuous lips.

He smiled and leaned forward in his chair. "I feel many things stirring in you," he said. "I feel your spirit struggling to be complete."

She managed to unlock her eyes from his and glanced at the tightly closed window, wanting to open it. The air in the room felt oppressively warm and heavy.

"Look at me," he commanded. "Don't look away. You are a special person, one who was given great gifts. When you free yourself of the burdens that hold you back, those gifts will blossom. It is time now. It is time for you to get in touch with who you really are and to experience the powers that exist within you. You've been feeling the need to explore your spirituality, haven't you?"

Lee felt only a muted surprise at the strange turn the interview had taken. "Well, yes," she admitted. "That's true. How did you know that?"

"As I said, I know many things about you. But please, elaborate for me. In what way does the metaphysical interest you?"

"Well, I've always believed that there was more to life than just the day-to-day world we get caught up in. But for years I've been so busy, publishing the magazine, raising my daughter and running a home. Lately, I've been thinking about setting aside some time just for me, to develop neglected aspects of myself. I guess you'd call them spiritual aspects."

"Yes," he said firmly. "Yes, it is time. You have wisdom and powers that you are not yet aware of." He leaned forward and took one of her hands in both of his. "I have a feeling that you have experienced other planes of reality," he continued. "Am I correct?"

Lee hesitated, flustered by the sudden intimacy that had developed between them. She started to remove her hand, but Juan squeezed it encouragingly—all the while staring into her eyes. She swallowed hard. "I...I'm sorry. What did you ask me?"

He smiled. "About your having experienced other planes of reality."

"Oh, yes. Well," she began, amazed by her willingness to confide in him, "this may sound crazy, and I haven't talked to many people about it, but when I was a child I had some strange experiences." She hesitated, then continued. "Sometimes I felt that I could separate from my body. I'd just sort of float away from it, especially when things were upsetting at home." She shook her head, remembering. "It really frightened me. I thought I was going crazy. I must have been seven or eight years old. I finally talked to a school counselor about it. She said that I had an over-active imagination and should just stop doing that if it frightened me. So I stopped, except for every now and then. And as I grew older I gradually lost the ability. Although sometimes I remember that feeling of detached freedom and I wonder if I could learn to do it again."

She laughed, a soft, nervous laugh. "I don't know why I'm telling you this. It sounds so bizarre." She looked down at his large brown hands holding her smaller pale one. She realized that she had no desire to pull her hand away.

"Lee, look at me. It doesn't sound bizarre. I am familiar with what you describe. Anglos call it astral projection. Indians call it soul travel. As children, we remember much that we later forget. We lose important knowledge as we grow older and more attached to our current lives."

"Our current lives?"

"We have all lived many lives," he said, "lives that influence who we are today. I think that your deep self knows that to be true."

She stared at him, fascinated.

"I sense that you've had other spiritual experiences," he continued. "Tell me about them."

Lee tensed as he began caressing her forearm. She hardly knew this man. Why was she letting him touch her like that? But before she could pull away, his eyes again captured hers, stilling the warning bell that was sounding somewhere in her head. "I...I don't know what's the matter with me," she stammered, " I keep losing my train of thought."

"You were describing your spiritual experiences."

"Oh, yes. Well, let's see. Something strange did happen to me about twelve years ago. Something I've never been able to forget." She found herself eager to share what she'd always considered to be a very private experience. "You see, it was a rather rocky period in my life, before I bought the magazine. My daughter was small, and my husband was gone most of the time. He's a scientist, and his work requires a lot of travel. I'm used to it now, but it was hard in those days. Anyway, Nick was out of the country, conducting an experiment somewhere—New Zealand, I think—when I got word that my parents had been killed in a car accident. I took it very hard."

"You were close to your parents?"

"I was very close to my mother. Dad had a lot of problems." She hesitated. "He was an alcoholic. In fact, that's what caused the accident. He'd had too much to drink at a Christmas party. Driving home, he tried to pass a truck on a curve. There was a head-on collision. Five people died instantly, including my mother. Dad died two days later."

Juan's expression was sympathetic. "You suffered much from that."

"I went through a really difficult time. I had insomnia and started taking sleeping pills pretty routinely." Lee's arm tingled where Juan was stroking it. She forced herself to concentrate on what she was saying. "The pills left me feeling groggy and even more depressed. I realized that I was on a dangerous downward spiral."

He nodded. "You listened to your inner wisdom. How did you change your path?"

"I enrolled in a yoga class. And that led me into a meditation class." She stopped, feeling a little embarrassed. "Do you really want to hear this?"

"Yes, very much." Juan slid his chair closer to her

and took her other hand in his.

She licked her bottom lip. Her mouth felt dry, and her throat was tight. "Well, the yoga and meditation classes really did help. I learned to relax myself to sleep at night and stopped relying on pills. I was very good at meditation. I practiced with a candle, staring at the flame and trying to block out all thoughts. Then I would close my eyes and hold the image of the flame in my mind." She stopped and cleared her throat. "I'm so thirsty. Could I have some water?"

"You need more tea." He refilled her cup with the steaming liquid and returned, pulling his chair so close that their knees were almost touching. Again, he looked hard into her eyes. "Now, please continue," he said.

Lee sipped the tea. It soothed her throat and warmed her chest as it went down. "Okay. But I have to warn you, I get emotional just thinking about this."

"There is nothing wrong with feeling emotions. When we cut off our emotions, we cut off our power."

His words touched something deep inside Lee, something that had been neglected for a long time. Shaken by what she was feeling, she looked away. After a moment, she took a deep breath and began to talk. "One night while I was meditating I had an unnerving experience," she said. "I've tried to tell myself that it was just a dream. But it was so vivid. It felt more like a memory than a dream."

She took another fortifying drink of tea before continuing. "I was small, just a child. And I was sitting on the bank of a shallow stream with a group of other children and several women. The sun felt warm on my face. I was kicking my feet in the water and laughing. One of the women with long black braids and a kind face, was kneeling beside me, filling a large clay pot with water. I remember that the pot was decorated with black rectangular designs.

This woman turned to smile at me, and I knew that she was my mother. I felt very happy..." Lee's voice broke. As she fought back tears, Juan gently squeezed her hand. "A moment later," Lee continued, "I heard a scream. My mother pushed me down in the tall grass and crouched beside me, looking toward the opposite bank of the stream. She motioned for me to stay where I was hidden. Then she crawled a few feet away. I lifted my head and saw men splashing across the stream, coming toward us. She got to her feet and started to run. I saw a man—he was almost naked and had long, filthy-looking hair—running after her. He tackled her and threw her to the ground. A moment later he made an angry, snarling sound and moved on. My mother didn't move.

I scrambled over to her. Her eyes were open and staring up at the sky. I shook her shoulder and her head rolled to one side. Then I saw the blood. It was all over the back of her head and on a sharp rock beneath it. I was old enough to know that she was dead. I threw myself across her body, crying. The grief that I felt was unbearable, so intense that I jerked myself awake. Only I didn't think that I'd been asleep.

The scene was so painful and realistic that it made me wonder if I hadn't been reliving some past-life traumatic experience. The thought frightened me. I stopped meditating after that, but the memory still haunts me. Lately I've been thinking about trying it again, to see if I could remember anything else."

Juan leaned back in his chair, studying her. When he spoke, he seemed to be choosing his words with care. "The veil between lifetimes is thin, Lee, and certain events can cause it to lift. The loss of your mother in this lifetime triggered the memory of a much older loss." He paused. "Some people have the ability to summon deep memories at will. I knew at once that you were one of those people."

"Really? What made you think so?"

"I could feel it. I have an ability to know things. In fact, you'd be surprised at how much I know about you."

"Like what?" Lee swallowed the last of the tea and placed the empty cup on the floor.

"Well, for example, I know that you have been through some health crisis recently. Am I correct?"

Lee blinked in surprise. She thought about a frightening appointment with her gynecologist last month. A lump in her breast had turned out to be a harmless cyst. "Why, yes. I did have a recent scare," she said. "But how could you know that?"

Juan smiled and reached once more for her hand. "I also know that you have a great connection to this land and a special communication with our animal brothers. Is that not true?"

"Yes, I do love this part of the country. And I've always been an animal lover. As a teenager, I spent weekends and summers working for a veterinarian. Doctor Harrison used to say that I had a real gift for comforting sick animals."

"Ah, yes. I would have expected that. You have always had many pets."

"You're right," Lee said, surprised. "I was continually bringing home stray cats and dogs. It drove my poor mother crazy. We lived on a farm in southern Colorado. From the time I was old enough to ride I had a horse. In fact, a beautiful little palomino named Moonbeam was my best friend until I went away to college."

"And now? What lucky animals share your life these days, Lee Lindsay?"

She returned his smile. "I'm down to just one cat. But he's a unique cat, and we're very close. In fact, my husband says that Mister and I read each other's minds."

"I wouldn't be surprised." His expression changed, becoming thoughtful. "There is no doubt. You are ready, ready to awaken the powers within you. Listen to your deep self. It is telling you that the time has come."

"Hmmm, maybe so. How would I do that? Awaken my powers, I mean."

"I will help you," he said. "I will guide you." He fixed her with a long, searching look. "But you must trust me, or you might lose the way. Do you trust me?"

Jann Arrington Wolcott

Lee nodded her head. Without understanding why, she felt complete confidence in this compelling man she had met less than an hour before. "What will you do? I mean, what are you going to guide me through?"

"Through an ancient ritual. A ritual almost as old as these mountains. Its true name cannot be spoken, but loosely translated it means 'the ceremony of awakening'." He paused, watching her closely. "The ritual consists of three parts, beginning with a sweating ceremony."

"Do you mean like Native American sweat lodges? I read an article about them in a recent **National Geographic**."

"This ceremony is very different from those you have read about. It is far older. And much more powerful. It involves anointing the body with a special oil and lying under a ceremonial sweat blanket. The blanket is then tightly rolled, preserving the sweat and evil spirits that have been cast off."

"Evil spirits?"

He shrugged. "Perhaps I should have used a more modern expression, like 'self-doubt' or 'negative mind set'. The meanings are the same."

Lee stared at him, thinking what a fascinating contradiction he seemed to be. One moment he was an archaic medicine man; the next instant he sounded quite contemporary.

"You look surprised," he said. "I should explain that I became familiar with such terms when I studied psychology at the University of New Mexico."

"You were a psychology major?"

"For two years. Until I realized that there is more wisdom in the old ways."

"I see." Lee leaned back against the sofa, wishing she could kick off her shoes and make herself more comfortable. Her eyelids felt heavy. "Tell me more about the awakening ceremony," she said. "What happens after the sweating part?"

"After the first ritual, on the night of the next full

29

moon, I will shake the blanket to the four directions, freeing you of all that you have cast off and preparing you for the spiritual awakening to come. That part of the ceremony will not require your attendance. In fact, I must conduct it alone." He hesitated. "Then there is a final ritual, a most powerful ceremony. But we will talk about that later. First, you must be made ready. You must be cleansed of the limitations you've imposed on yourself. Perhaps then you will be strong enough to commune with the spirits that reside here in Cavado."

Lee was filled with a wonderful feeling of relaxation. She raised her hand to her mouth, covering a yawn.

"The ceremonies will put you in touch with your true identity," Juan continued. "You will gain new strength and wisdom." He leaned forward in his chair, his necklace gleaming in the candlelight. Again, his eyes fastened on Lee's. "This is a strong time for the ceremony," he said. "The moon will soon be full. We should do it now."

Lee forced herself into a more upright position on the sofa, fighting the languor that had enveloped her. "You mean, right now?" She shook her head. "Oh, I'm afraid I can't today. I mean, I don't have time. I promised to meet my daughter and her friend for lunch at one-thirty in Santa Fe." She hesitated. "But I could make an appointment to come back and see you another time."

He looked at his watch. "It's just twelve o'clock. The ceremony only takes about half an hour. You could still be back in Santa Fe to meet your daughter. We have time to do it now." Although his voice was soft and coaxing, Lee detected determination in his eyes.

"I don't know—"

"Your deep self knows that this is something you need, Lee. Listen to your deep self."

"Well," she heard herself saying, "if you're sure it won't take long. I...I suppose I could."

Juan rose to his feet. "You must change into a ceremonial garment," he said, as he removed a rolled packet from under the table. He unwrapped a folded length of deerskin.

"Is that necessary? Can't I just wear my own clothes?"

"I'm afraid not. The ritual must be conducted in the sacred way."

Lee hesitated, feeling a flutter of fear. Did she really trust this man? Their eyes met again and Lee found her doubts dissolving. If it was the "sacred way," it must be all right. And the ceremony did sound intriguing. She'd recently read an article about a woman who traveled to the jungles of Peru to be treated for cancer by a native medicine man, reportedly with spectacular results. Too bad she'd promised she wouldn't write about Juan's work. This would make a fascinating story for the magazine. Well, if Juan wanted to help her—how did he put it—"awaken her spiritual powers," she might as well take him up on it. What harm could it do?

"Where can I change?" she asked, rising a little unsteadily to her feet. "Do you have a bathroom?"

"I have only a portable toilet in the back room. You are welcome to use it."

Lee followed him into a small room. He gestured toward a toilet in the corner. "It doesn't flush, but there is no need for embarrassment between us." He handed her the folded deerskin. "Remove all of your clothing," he instructed. "Everything."

"You mean even my underwear?"

"This is a ceremonial garment. To wear it with ordinary clothing would weaken its medicine." He turned and left her alone.

Lee leaned against the wall for a moment, feeling lightheaded. How did I get talked into this, she wondered. Oh, well, he said it wouldn't take long. Guess I'd better use his porta-potty after all that tea.

She looked around the makeshift bathroom. Stacks of old books filled one corner. A small refrigerator stood next to the door. On a shelf above it were a few folded blankets and a basket filled with dried weeds and flowers.

BRUJO

As she undressed, Lee again marveled at what she was doing. It was unbelievable. Certainly not your ordinary interview. She folded her wool pants and sweater and put them on a small table, along with her bra and pantyhose.

When she unfolded the soft buckskin, Lee discovered that the "ceremonial garment" consisted of two parts: a small leather halter top and a primitive sort of wrap-around skirt with a jagged hemline. She put them on and looked down at herself, dismayed. The halter, which tied at the neck and waist, barely covered her breasts and left most of her back bare. The skirt ended midway up her thighs.

I must look like Pocahontas, she thought, pulling at the sides of the halter in a futile attempt to stretch it. I really don't believe that I'm doing this. I could still change my mind. Put my clothes back on and get out of here. But then I would never know.... Without finishing the thought, she opened the door.

She stopped short, staring in disbelief. Clad only in a brief loincloth and the silver necklace, Juan was chanting and shaking a gourd rattle above a worn buffalo skin that lay on the wooden floor.

Chapter 3

*L*ee sidled past Juan and sat on the edge of the sofa, feeling as though she had stepped into an unknown world. He ignored her. Shifting his weight from foot to foot in a slow shuffling dance, he continued to chant— "Na Yah He, Na Yah He, Na Yah He"—and shake the rattle. She sat motionless, mesmerized.

After several minutes, he placed the rattle in the center of the buffalo skin rug and stood facing her. Candlelight played across his broad chest and cast shadows on his face. "You must remove your jewelry," he said.

Lee stood as if in a dream. She slowly raised her hands and removed her gold hoop earrings. They were her favorite piece of jewelry, an anniversary present from Nick. Then she unfastened the gold chain around her neck and opened the clasp on her watch. She held them in the palm of her hand and looked up at Juan.

He glanced at her left hand, "All of it." Reluctantly, she removed her wedding band.

He dropped the jewelry on a nearby table. Lee's eyes

fell on a sharp-fanged skull—a bobcat?—that also rested on the table. The jaws of the skull were open, as though frozen in perpetual laughter.

She glanced at Juan's exposed buttocks as he walked to the middle of the room and felt her cheeks flush. But her embarrassment turned to fascination as Juan began the ceremony.

He circled the buffalo skin three times, moving counterclockwise and shaking the rattle close to the floor. Then he stood tall, arms stretched overhead. "The sacred circle is cast," he announced. "The space between the worlds has been created."

"The space between the worlds...between the worlds...between the worlds..." The words seemed to echo in Lee's head, distantly familiar. She felt momentarily displaced in time.

Juan struck a match and lit a long-stemmed wooden pipe that was decorated with feathers and beads. The bowl of the pipe was carved in the shape of a flying bird. He inhaled deeply and blew a cloud of acrid smoke into Lee's face.

She drew back, closing her eyes and struggling to suppress a cough. What's in that pipe? she wondered. It sure didn't smell like tobacco.

He leaned over and blew a second mouthful of smoke across her suede-covered breasts. Then he knelt and blew smoke across her stomach, legs and feet. "You have been purified," he said, standing and taking her hand. "Now you may enter the sacred space." He guided her inside the invisible circle. "Kneel on Cibola, the sacred buffalo," he said. "Face toward the east, toward the window—while I invoke the guardian spirits of the four directions."

Eyes still burning from the evil-smelling smoke, Lee did as he instructed. Invoke the spirits? Was he serious?

Juan faced north and began speaking—harsh, unfamiliar words. Then he moved to face the west. More incomprehensible sounds. The performance was repeated facing south. Finally he stood behind her, facing east. What language was he speaking? She wished she was getting it on tape.

For a moment there was silence. Lee fought an impulse to look over her shoulder. Was he through invoking spirits? What next?

"Turn and face me," he said.

She started to get to her feet, then felt his restraining hand on her shoulder. "No, remain kneeling, just turn toward me." Lee moved around on her knees. Juan knelt in front of her. He dipped his finger in a bowl of oil and applied it to her face—three slashes across her forehead and on each cheek. "This is to make you a strong warrior," he said.

Lee thought of Nick and stifled a smile, picturing his surprise were she to confront him dressed in war paint and wielding a tomahawk.

Juan rose, rattling the gourd above her head. Her eyes were level with his loincloth, which flapped up and down as he resumed his dance. She noticed that his uncircumcised penis was soft. At least she was in no immediate danger of being raped. An erection would be hard to hide in that outfit.

Juan began to chant—his deep voice resonating in the small dark room. Lee stared at the huge wings hanging above the window. They blurred as she tried to focus on them; then they appeared to flap slightly, keeping time to the chanting. She closed her eyes. Soon she was rocked by warm waves of relaxation and felt herself swaying in her kneeling position. She could hear Juan chanting and could feel vibrations through the wooden floor as he danced, but the scene had acquired a distant, unreal quality.

"Drink," Juan said. His voice startled her out of her dream-like state. "It is water from the sacred stream." Once again, he was kneeling across from her, his knees touching hers. He handed her a small pottery bowl containing water and several small twigs. She did as instructed, and then watched as he refilled the bowl from

a leather canteen and drank the contents. "Now we eat
of the powder of life. Open your mouth." He placed a
pinch of something gritty, the consistency of cornmeal,
on her tongue. Lee rolled it around the inside of her
mouth. In spite of the water she had just drunk, her
throat was too dry to swallow.

"Lie down," he said. "On your stomach." She
hesitated, then lay flat on the dusty rug, her face turned
toward the window. "First, the cleansing oil," he
whispered in her ear. Starting at her shoulders, he
rubbed oil down her body to her feet. She stiffened
when his hands slid under her skirt and over her buttocks.

"Trust me," he said. "Release your fear."

Her muscles went limp under his strong hands, and
she lay placidly, the buffalo fur against her face.

"Now turn over."

Lee rolled onto her back and closed her eyes. She
felt his hands kneading the muscles in her neck, then
gently gripping her naked shoulders. When his hands
slid over her breasts, she jerked to awareness. Opening
her eyes, she saw that the halter had been untied at the
neck. Her breasts were naked and glistening with oil.

"No!" she said. "Just a minute—"

"*Descansa*," he said softly. "Relax. This is a
necessary part of the ceremony. There is no cause for
alarm. Trust me."

Another wave of relaxation rolled over Lee, numbing
her anxiety. She lay completely still as he worked the
oil into her thighs, knees and calves. When he reached
her feet, he gently rubbed oil between each toe.

Lee felt herself being covered with a heavy warm
blanket. Juan's voice came from somewhere above her.
"You are relaxed now," he said, "and feeling very safe.
You have no cares or concerns. Your body feels heavy
and is sinking deeper and deeper into the buffalo fur."

Lee floated in and out of a timeless state while the
chanting and rattling continued above her. When Juan
accidently stepped on her hand during his rhythmic

dance, she tried to rouse herself. I should open my eyes, she thought. I should watch what he's doing. But her eyes wouldn't stay open, and she surrendered once more to the darkness.

Lee was only vaguely aware of Juan removing the blanket. Again she was rubbed, neck to toes, this time with a strong-smelling oil that reminded her of rotting fruit and some kind of flower she couldn't place. "This is the sweating oil," Juan said. His voice was a whisper in her ear. "Now roll over, so I can rub it on your back."

Lee obeyed, then felt the blanket cover her again. Suddenly she realized that Juan was lying under it, beside her. She opened her eyes, jerked back, and sat up. The halter, tied only at the waist, hung down into her lap. She yanked it up to cover her breasts.

"Rub the oil on me now," he ordered. "Do it quickly." She fumbled to retie the halter straps around her neck. "Quickly," he repeated.

She hesitated, then took the small clay pot containing the oil. Pouring some of the golden oil into her palm, Lee was again aware of the pungent odor. She felt a fresh flash of alarm. Why was she doing this? She shouldn't be.... Then, reality retreated and she found herself sliding her oiled hands over his arms, back, naked buttocks and legs.

"You have strong hands," Juan whispered, as he rolled over onto his back. "I knew that they would be strong. Now my front, quickly."

Lee's face felt hot with embarrassment. Without looking at his face, she did as she was told, spreading oil across his chest and arms and down his flat, hard stomach. Carefully avoiding his loin cloth, she oiled the front of his legs and his feet. Juan continued to chant softly.

"Lie back down," Juan's voice was soft but commanding. He pulled the heavy blanket over both of their bodies. "Put your arms around me and hold on tight," he instructed. "You must squeeze me hard." His arms went around her, pulling her against his chest. "Now release all your tension and fear," he coached as he massaged her rigid back. Lee was aware of the soft fur beneath one cheek and the hard bones of Juan's cheek against the other side of her face. The smell of the sweating oil grew stronger. Juan continued to chant in harsh exhalations—"Huh Ya! Huh Ya! Huh Ya!"—and to coax Lee to "squeeze tighter, tighter."

"The tighter you hold onto me, the more doubt and fear you release into me," he whispered against her cheek. "I will take it from you. Release, release the tension. *Bueno*. That's good. That's very good."

Lee tried to shift her lower body away from his, but he pulled her closer. His right leg slid over hers, capturing her in a tight embrace. Only a vague awareness of her vulnerable position passed through Lee's head. I couldn't run out of here.... I don't remember where I put my clothes.... Anyway, I wouldn't be able to get away from him if I wanted to. He's too strong.

She felt the muscles in Juan's stomach contract and relax as he began to chant again. The rhythmic sound seemed to fill her entire body, to become part of her. She soon lost all thought and concern, content to float on the buffalo skin rug in Juan's slippery embrace.

"What are you feeling?" Juan's whisper in her ear brought Lee back from her reverie.

"Peaceful," she said. "So peaceful." Images of her husband and daughter flashed through her mind, disrupting her tranquility. What would they say if they could see her lying half naked under a blanket with this strange man? They wouldn't believe their eyes. Lee didn't really believe it herself. "I feel like I must be dreaming," she whispered.

She heard Juan laugh softly. His hand ran up and down her wet back. "You're starting to sweat now," he said. "That's good. Squeeze harder, harder." His hand rubbed the back of her neck. "*Bueno*. The oil is working well."

Lee felt an uncomfortable numbness in her legs. The weight of Juan's leg was cutting off the blood circulation. How long have I been here? she wondered. Then his low, hypnotic chanting filled her head, and she began to drift away again. Time lost all meaning. She was unable to hold a thought for more than a few seconds.

The chanting stopped, pulling Lee back to awareness. Juan released her and helped her up into a kneeling position. He positioned himself close behind her and drew the sweat blanket around both of them. Feeling dizzy and disoriented, she closed her eyes, as they both sat back on their heels, facing the window. Juan fanned the blanket open and closed like giant wings as he continued to pray and chant.

"Open your eyes and look toward the light," he whispered in her ear. His voice had a strange urgency about it.

"Which light?"

"Look at the candle!"

Lee tried to think. What was happening? Why was he so agitated? She stared at the flickering candle under the window.

"It is through the light that you will see your door opening. The door that leads into the void that is the spirit world. You must concentrate. Which direction is the door facing?"

"I don't know," Lee said fretfully. "I can't tell." She didn't see a door. And she sure as hell didn't want to go into any void.

"We must try again," he said, and resumed his chanting. After a moment he repeated the question. "Which direction is your door facing?"

The answer came to Lee suddenly. "The south," she whispered. "It's toward the south."

"*Bueno*," Juan said. Lee heard the triumph in his voice. "Your deep self is awakening. The south corresponds to fire and strong emotions, as well as to innocence and trust. That's the door we will go through during the next ceremony."

He continued to chant, fanning the blanket open and closed over their bodies. Lee shut her eyes and leaned back against him. It felt like they were flying. She felt his arms tighten around her, across her breasts. The chanting was interspersed with what sounded like an invocation. She tried to pay attention, to remember some of the strange words, but Juan's voice seemed to fade in and out.

Juan shifted his weight and stood up, startling her out of a half-formed dream. She rolled off her knees onto her left hip, trying to think. Had she been asleep? She closed her eyes, fighting dizziness.

"Drink," Juan ordered, touching a cool bowl to her lips. Lee took a small swallow, noticing again the twigs in the bottom of the bowl. Sacred stream water, wasn't that what he'd called it? She hoped he wasn't going to insist that she eat the twigs too. At that point, nothing would have surprised her.

Juan dipped his fingers into the remaining water and sprinkled it across Lee's chest. Only then did she realize that her halter top was again untied at the neck. With dazed eyes, she watched the iridescent drops cling to her nipples, then roll onto her deerskin skirt. She made no effort to retie the straps.

"Now, kneel at the other end of the sweat blanket," he instructed. "And roll it tightly toward me."

Lee rolled the blanket toward him on her hands and knees. When she had finished, she looked up at him. Juan's face seemed to shimmer in the candlelight. The silver necklace gleamed around his neck.

He stood, and once again began moving counter-clockwise, addressing the four directions in a mysterious language. After what seemed like a long time, he took her arm and helped her to her feet. "The circle is open," he said.

Taking a cloth from a nearby table, he gently blotted the oil from her face, neck and breasts. Then he helped her to her feet, and they stood facing each other.

He placed his hands on each side of her face and looked deeply into her eyes. Finally, he spoke. "It is done," he said. "You may dress now."

He led her into the back room and left, closing the door behind him. Lee dressed in a daze. Then she returned to the candle-lit room where Juan sat quietly, wearing only his Levis.

"That was a powerful ceremony," he said, breaking the silence. "The strongest I have experienced in a very long time. Do you want me to tell you why?"

Lee nodded, not trusting herself to speak.

"We have performed that ceremony before," he said. "In a previous lifetime. I recognized you. I knew that we had been together before, as soon as you walked through the door. I realized that was why you had come."

"But that's not true! I came to interview you. I had no idea—"

"I know you didn't," he said, taking both of her hands in his, "at least not on a conscious level. But that's of no concern now. Tell me, how are you feeling?"

"I really don't know how I feel," she answered. "This has been such a confusing experience. I've never done anything like this before."

"You don't think you have," he said. "But perhaps the ceremony will unlock memories." He squeezed her hands and then released them. "Drink this before you go," he said, handing her a glass of what looked like milk. "It will clear your head from the effects of the ceremony."

"What is it? Another old family recipe?"

He smiled. "As a matter of fact, it is."

Lee took a swallow, realizing that it was, indeed, milk. It tasted unusually good, as though it had been sweetened with something. She drained the glass.

"Come back a week from today," Juan said. "There is much to be done, much you must understand, before we continue."

"You said that there's another part to this ceremony?"

"That's right. I must conduct it alone, on the night of

41

the next full moon. After that, you and I must prepare for the final ritual."

"What happens during this 'final ritual'?"

"We go through your door together, the door into the spirit world. There your eyes will be opened, and you will reclaim your power." He stood, walked to the desk and handed her a four-inch tall, wooden figure. "This is Ye-na-lo-he, an ancient Indian spirit. She offers great protection. You will carry her on our spiritual journey."

Lee held the small carved fetish. Dressed in red fabric, it had the body of a woman and the face of a sharp-billed bird. Tiny black feathers covered the arms and head.

"I will take this, my totem," Juan said, unwrapping a small black statue of a bird. "There are those who believe the raven is evil. But they are mistaken. Raven is beyond limited concepts of good and evil. He is a messenger between the earth plane and the spirit world—a bringer of magic and healing energy." He pointed to the dark wings above the window. "His wings protect those who acknowledge him."

"I was wondering about your necklace," Lee said, her eyes drawn once more to the red stones set between silver wings. "It's very...unusual."

"My amulet is certainly that."

"I don't understand. What exactly is an amulet?"

"An amulet is strong medicine. It shields the wearer from danger. This one is very old and powerful. It belonged to my mother."

"What are the stones? They seem to glow. I've never seen anything like them."

"It's a rare crystal. Found only in the mountains of northern Mexico."

Lee looked away, feeling at a loss for words. "I don't know what to say...or think...about any of this," she said.

Juan gently touched her cheek. "It will all become clear to you—in time. You are feeling well enough to drive?"

"I'm okay, I think."

"Come next week," he said, helping her into her jacket. "Next Tuesday." He collected her purse, tape recorder and notebook and handed them to her. They walked into the next room and Juan opened the front door.

She turned to go, feeling like someone awakening from a dream. The outside world looked a little unfamiliar. Dazzled by the bright sunlight, she shaded her eyes.

"Wait. You're forgetting something." Juan left the front room and returned with her jewelry. He pulled her against him in a quick embrace. "*Hasta luego*," he said in a husky voice. "Until we meet again."

Lee felt as though she were floating down the pathway to her car. She slid inside and relaxed against the headrest. After a moment she remembered the jewelry in her hand and slowly put it on. It seemed to take a long time to locate the car keys in her purse and start the engine. She stared at the clock on the dashboard in amazement as the concept of time snapped back into her mind. Sara and Wendy! She would be at least twenty minutes late meeting the girls in Santa Fe.

She put the car in reverse and backed past the dead tree with its bare, ravaged branches. The sound of Juan's chants were echoing in her head as she shifted into forward to drive over the wooden bridge and up the hill.

Chapter 4

Lee sat in her parked car near the Santa Fe plaza. She had absolutely no memory of the drive back from Cavado. Bizarre. But then the whole morning had been bizarre. She'd have to sort it out later; Sara would be getting worried. She locked the car and hurried down San Francisco Street, waving to Sara and Wendy when she spotted them at their designated meeting place on the plaza. The girls, dressed in their usual costumes of skin-tight Levi's and denim jackets, were sitting on a white wrought iron bench, feeding popcorn to a flock of pigeons.

"Oh, Mom, there you are. Finally!" Sara tossed out the last of her popcorn and sprang to her feet. "Quick, before we go to lunch, I want to show you something."

Lee followed the girls across the brick paving of Palace Avenue to the Palace of the Governors. As usual, the full-length portal of the historic adobe building was crowded with tourists buying souvenirs from the Indians.

Sara squatted in front of a jewelry display tended by

44

an Indian man wearing long braids, a black Stetson, and an expression of serene indifference. "Aren't these great?" she asked, pushing her hair back and holding dangling beaded earrings to her ears. "Can I get them, please? Please? I'll save my allowance for two weeks to pay you back. Wendy thinks they make me look at least eighteen."

Lee shook her head. "Sorry. I want you to continue to look fifteen for a while longer. Now, come on. Let's go have lunch at The Shed. Where's Wendy?"

Sara sighed, returned the earrings reluctantly to the Indian, and motioned to Wendy who was several displays away examining a turquoise bracelet. "So," Sara said as they continued up the street. "How was your morning?"

* * *

The lunch crowd had thinned out, leaving the restaurant almost empty. Lee felt relaxed and oddly detached as she sat across the table from the girls.

Sara and Wendy chatted and giggled, ogling the busboy who filled their water glasses. Lee swallowed the last of her water and reached for her iced tea.

"I couldn't believe it when Lisa shaved the sides of her head," Sara said. "It looks totally gross. My parents would kill me if I did that. Right, Mom?"

Lee stared off into space, holding her half-empty iced tea glass.

"Wouldn't you? Mom?"

She blinked and focused on her daughter. "What?"

"Wouldn't you kill me?"

"Kill you?"

"If I shaved the sides of my head. Like Lisa."

"I certainly wouldn't kill you, sweetheart. I'd just lock you in your room until it grew back. Oh good, here comes our lunch."

The waiter presented the two girls with hamburgers and Lee with a cheese enchilada. "This looks delicious," Lee said, suddenly feeling hungry.

"Lisa's planning to get a tattoo next," Sara continued.

"When she visits her father in Los Angeles. What about that, Mom?"

"Hmmm?" Lee put her napkin in her lap, wishing she had asked for more iced tea. She didn't know when she'd been so thirsty.

"What if I get a tattoo? Maybe a rose. Or a snake winding around my ankle."

"A snake winding—? What on earth are you talking about, Sara?"

"I was just teasing." Sara frowned at her. "Are you okay, Mom? You act like you're somewhere in outer space."

"I'm sorry, honey. I was just thinking about my interview." She took a bite of her enchilada, trying to bring herself back to the present. "Well, are you girls all shopped out?"

"No way," said Sara, carefully removing the onions from her burger. "Do you think you could drop us off at the Mall after we eat? I need to find something totally devastating to wear to the Halloween dance."

"Totally devastating?" Lee felt a rush of affection for her daughter. "Well, I had planned to go back to the office this afternoon. But, what the heck, I haven't had an afternoon off in a long time. I think I'll play hooky and go with you."

"No kidding? Great!" Sara studied her mother approvingly. "You're sure in a mellow mood."

"I wonder if he's got a girl friend?" Wendy whispered, watching the busboy clear the next table. "Maybe I should call him over and ask him."

"You wouldn't," Sara said. "I dare you."

Wendy motioned to the busboy. When he returned to their table, she turned crimson. "Could, uh, could I have more water, please?"

Sara hid her face in her napkin. "Wendy," she said, giggling, "You are just too much. Isn't she, Mom?"

Lee smiled vaguely and smoothed the slightly oily curls on the nape of her neck.

* * *

Lee's mood of calm detachment lasted throughout the afternoon. She accompanied the girls to several stores in the shopping mall, until she finally announced that she'd had enough and herded them, loaded with packages, out to the car. When she passed The Camera Shop on her way back through town she remembered the pictures she'd taken in Cavado and pulled over to the curb.

"Do me a favor," she said to Sara. "Run this roll of film in and tell them I need to have the prints as soon as possible."

* * *

It was almost six o'clock by the time Lee and Sara had taken Wendy home and pulled into the driveway of their own two-story adobe house. Lee hit the controls of the automatic garage door opener. The door rolled upward, revealing Nick's late model Volvo.

"Dad's home early," Lee said, suddenly feeling tired and a little edgy. She needed some time alone to think about what had happened in Cavado that morning and to decide how much she should tell Nick about it. One thing was clear. Her husband would not approve of her encounter with Juan. She wasn't sure how she felt about it herself. Her knees felt weak as she walked into the house.

Nick was standing behind the bar opening a bottle of Jack Daniels when Lee and Sara entered the large family room. He greeted them over his shoulder. "Well, I don't have to ask what you two have been up to. Did you buy out the stores?"

"Hi, Dad. Wait till you see the really killer outfits I got!" Sara hurried up the stairs with her packages.

"Killer outfits?" Nick shook his head. "Whatever happened to nice little school dresses?"

"You're hopelessly out of date, dear," Lee said. "Why don't you fix me one of those."

Nick raised an eyebrow. "I haven't seen you drink anything but an occasional glass of wine for ages. Rough day?"

47

"It certainly was an unusual one." She slipped off her shoes and sat on the sofa, staring out of the window at the nearby Sangre de Cristo Mountains. The aspens had begun to change color several weeks before, decorating the high green slopes with brilliant splashes of gold. It was a beautiful view, especially in the early evenings when the setting sun turned the mountains the deep rose color that had given them their name. But this evening the spectacular light did little to calm Lee's growing anxiety.

A gray cat with white markings came running down the hall, his feet making soft thumping sounds on the polished bricks. He jumped into Lee's lap, purring loudly. "Hello, Mister," she whispered, stroking his silky fur. "How's my sweet old kitty?" Mister closed his eyes and pressed his head against her stomach, his front paws busily kneading her thigh.

Lee sipped the whiskey and water that Nick handed her, taking care not to disturb the blissful cat. She made a slight face as the liquid burned its way down her throat. "This is going to knock me on my ear," she said.

"Well, now," Nick said, joining her on the sofa. "Tell me about your day. I think you mentioned that you had an interview. Where was it?"

"Cavado. It's in the mountains north of Chimayo."

"Oh. Well, how did it go?"

Lee shook her head. "The strangest thing happened to me there," she said. As she described her experience in Cavado, Lee found herself omitting certain details. She couldn't bring herself to admit that Juan had untied her halter top—or that he had joined her under the sweating blanket. She absentmindedly stroked Mister as she talked.

"And then I rolled the blanket up and got dressed. Juan said he would shake it to the four directions when the moon is full. That's supposed to dispose of all my fears and self-doubt." She took another sip of her drink. When she looked up at Nick, his horrified expression told her that she had been wise in giving him an edited version of the morning's events.

He stared at her. "I can't believe my ears. Christ, Lee! How could you have put yourself in such a dangerous position?"

"Well, I don't know. It just happened. I—"

"What do you mean, 'It just happened'?" Nick stood up and stalked to the bar. He splashed more whiskey into his drink and stood staring at her. "I'm absolutely dumbfounded. You could have been raped! Murdered!"

"I guess it does sound pretty crazy. But I didn't expect you to be this upset."

"You didn't expect me to be upset? You sit here calmly telling me that you interviewed some Indian medicine man in the middle of nowhere and then changed into a little costume and let him give you a massage! Don't you think that's taking your writer's curiosity a bit far?"

Lee drained her glass. She could feel a headache coming on. "Okay, okay," she said, rubbing her forehead. "I can see now that it wasn't a very bright thing to do. I really don't know why I did it. It just didn't seem dangerous at the time."

"This is just so unlike you! I mean, you're usually so level-headed. Why were you even talking to this jerk? I thought you were working on an article about the history of—what is it?—Cavado?"

"I am. A man at the Española Chamber of Commerce suggested that I talk to Juan. He's considered to be something of a local historian. I had no idea that he was a *curandero*."

"A what?"

"*Curandero*—a folk healer. I guess they're a fairly common fixture in those little villages."

Nick walked back to the sofa and stood looking down at her. His face was flushed, the space between his eyes creased into deep frown lines. Then his face softened, and he sat close beside her. "I'm just glad you didn't get hurt, honey," he said, putting his arm around her. "You certainly could have been."

Lee leaned against his shoulder and closed her eyes. Her head was really throbbing. "By the way, Juan isn't an Indian," she said. "He's from an old Spanish family."

"I don't give a damn about his family! Civilized people don't dance around in loincloths during interviews! I don't understand why you didn't run out of there when he first suggested his little—what was it?— 'awakening ceremony'."

"I don't understand it either." Lee pulled away from Nick and brought her fingertips to her temples, rubbing in small circles. "It seems crazy now, I agree. But at the time—"

"How old is this character anyway?"

"I don't know. Late forties, I guess. Why?"

"I just wondered. What does he look like?"

"Well, he's Hispanic—dark hair and eyes. Could use a haircut. And he's about your height."

"Good looking?"

Lee shrugged. "I guess so, in a brooding sort of way."

Nick shook his head. "The world is full of nuts. You know that. And, my God, you're a beautiful woman. You shouldn't even be driving around those isolated little villages by yourself." He stopped and studied her face, frowning. "Your eyes look a little glassy to me," he said, feeling her forehead. "And you feel very warm. Are you getting sick?"

"I just have a headache." She scooted Mister out of her lap and stood up. "I'm going to stick a frozen casserole in the oven and get some aspirin."

As she walked into the kitchen, Lee felt faint. She held onto the countertop waiting for the feeling to pass.

Nick came into the kitchen behind her. "Honey? What's wrong?"

"I don't know," she said. "All of a sudden I feel really sick." The dizziness passed, only to be followed by a wave of nausea.

"Forget dinner. Let's get you to bed," Nick said,

taking her arm and leading her out of the kitchen.

Lee insisted on taking a shower, in spite of Nick's objections. She washed her hair twice and soaped herself all over several times, leaning against the shower wall while hot water cascaded over her body. Then she quickly dried off, towel-dried her hair, and pulled a flannel nightgown over her head. Shivering, she fell into bed.

* * *

Lee found herself in a long dark tunnel. She saw a dim light far ahead and began to struggle toward it. The air was dense, weighing her down and making it hard to move. Someone called her name, and the sound echoed around her. She stopped, confused. That wasn't her name. And yet, somehow, she knew that it was. She turned in a slow, dream-like motion.

Juan materialized out of the darkness, his powerful body illuminated by an eerie light. As he drew closer, she saw that he was naked, except for the silver amulet gleaming around his neck.

"Trust me," he said. "Don't be afraid. It's time for you to awaken to who you really are. It's time for you to regain your power." Then his arms were around her. His hands began to move on her body, and she pressed herself closer, aroused by his touch.

But something was wrong. With a shock she realized that his arms and shoulders were covered with feathers. "Remember," he whispered. "Let yourself remember."

Suddenly there was a strong wind in her face, pushing her back several steps. Juan's face blurred. Round yellow eyes shone in the darkness. A long sharp beak opened and closed. Horrified, she watched Juan transform into a huge black bird. The sound of beating wings filled the tunnel.

"No! Get away!" She tried to run through the suffocating darkness, but her movements were slow and uncoordinated. He caught her, wrapping her in his wings.

* * *

"Lee?" Nick was gently shaking her shoulder. "It's

all right, honey. You're just having another bad dream."
He felt her forehead. "You're trembling. And you're
definitely feverish. You must have the flu. I'm going to
get you some aspirin," he said, getting out of bed. "If
you're not a lot better in the morning, I want you to call
Doctor Zimmerman."

* * *

By morning her temperature was almost back to
normal. "I'm feeling better," she said. "But I think I'll
stay in bed for awhile. I'll probably go into work this
afternoon. Would you hand me my appointment book?
It's there on the desk."

"You're pale as a ghost," Nick said, handing her the
thick book. "Why don't you spend the whole day in
bed?"

"I've got too much to do. I took yesterday afternoon
off."

"Annabel can cover for you. You've got to learn to
take care of yourself, honey."

"You're a fine one to talk. Did Sara get off to
school?"

"Mr. Wonderful just picked her up in his vintage hot
rod," Nick said, arranging papers in his briefcase.
"What's his name? The pretty one with the long, blond
hair."

"Kevin," murmured Lee. "He's a nice boy."

"Well, I think he removed most of the gravel from
the driveway when he took off. I'm going to talk to that
kid about his driving." He bent to kiss her cheek.
"Take care of yourself. Do you want me to put Mister
out?"

"No, leave him in here with me." She stroked the
sleeping cat. "He's a great bed partner."

"Well, each to his own taste. See you tonight."

Lee picked up the phone on her nightstand table and
dialed Annabel's home number. "Hi, Annie. Listen, I
guess I've caught a bug. It seems to be going away, but
I still feel pretty weak. Do you think you could cover
for me this morning?" She opened her appointment

book. "Let's see. I'm scheduled to interview a free-lance writer at nine-thirty. Richard Perry. He just moved here from Denver. Also, we need to follow up on that article about the Fine Arts Museum. Kirt Conners has that assignment, and it was due two days ago. There are several stories on my desk to be edited, if you can get to them... Okay... thanks. I may be in this afternoon. Call if you need me. Bye."

She pulled the thick down comforter over her shoulders and closed her eyes. Seconds later, she was sound asleep with Mister nestled against her stomach.

* * *

Lee swam slowly up out of a deep, dream-filled sleep. She moved her leg, waking Mister. He stood and arched into a graceful, feline stretch. Lee peered at the clock on her nightstand. Twelve-thirty. She groaned and rolled onto her back. Mister responded with a soft purr and walked across her chest. He put his nose down to hers, his whiskers tickling her cheek.

"We've been asleep all morning, Mister. Poor kitty. You must be starving." Lee sat up, which caused a soft throbbing in her temples. Mister jumped off the bed and walked to the bedroom door. Then he stopped and turned, waiting for her to follow. "Okay, okay, I'm coming." She stood up and walked into the bathroom on rubbery legs.

After feeding Mister, Lee carried a steaming cup of tea back to the bedroom and set it on her nightstand. There's no way I can go into work, she thought. I'm completely wiped out. She climbed back into bed, fluffed two pillows behind her head and closed her eyes. A short time later, something pulled her out of another half-formed dream. A strong, familiar odor drifted through the room. Almost sickeningly sweet, like rotten apples. Mixed with...something else. Her eyes flew open, and she sat upright in bed.

What is that smell? she wondered. Then the realization hit her. The oil. Oh, my God, I smell Juan's sweating oil! But that's not possible. I took a shower last night. I washed it all off. It's my imagination, she told herself, lying back and sliding under the covers. I'm just sick, that's all. This bug has distorted my sense of smell. She took a deep breath, trying to relax.

Lee heard soft, padding, cat footsteps enter the darkened bedroom. She opened her eyes. Mister had stopped several feet inside the doorway, his body rigid. The fur stood up along his back and tail. He took a step toward the bed, then turned his head sharply toward the sliding patio door. His ears flattened against his head as he hissed at the closed draperies.

"Mister? What...?" Lee watched as the cat hissed once more. Then, with his eyes fixed on the door, he backed out of the room. She slid from the bed and opened the draperies to stare at the empty balcony beyond the glass door. "There's nothing there. What scared you, Mister?" As she checked the double lock on the door, she was hit once more by the odor of sweating oil. A wave of dizziness washed over her, and she stumbled back to bed.

There must be a dog outside, she told herself. One of the neighbor's afghan hounds probably got loose again. Moments later, just as she was dropping off to sleep, Lee heard another hiss followed by Mister's low, threatening growl.

Chapter 5

"Mom?" Sara peeked around the bedroom door. "Uh oh, did I wake you?"

Lee opened her eyes. Her head was throbbing and her throat felt dry and scratchy. "That's okay. I've been sleeping most of the day."

"Gosh, you're really sick, aren't you? I'll bet it's the flu. Everyone at school has it." She sat down on the edge of the bed and tossed her hair over one shoulder.

Lee frowned at her daughter. Sara was dressed in tight Levi's and a faded T-shirt with the word "SUPERBITCH" stretched across her small breasts. "Please tell me you didn't wear that shirt to school today," she groaned.

"Oh, Mom, don't get uptight. I wore my Levi jacket over it so only 'SUPERB' showed." She giggled.

"You're a real character," Lee said, managing a small smile.

"Thanks." Sara stood up. "I'm gonna fix a snack. Can I get you anything?"

"Some ice water would be nice. Thanks, baby."

Sara started out the door. "What's wrong with Mister?"

"What do you mean?"

"He's hiding under the dining room table and won't come out. Acting really weird. Well, I'll be right back."

Lee rolled onto her side and closed her eyes. The next thing she knew, the room was dark, and Nick was shaking her shoulder. "Babe? I hated to wake you, but I was getting worried. How do you feel?" He placed a cool hand on her forehead.

"Oh, Nick. You're home already? What time is it?"

"Almost eight o'clock. I think you're still running a slight fever. Here, take these," he said, shaking two aspirins out of the bottle. "I meant to call to check on you today, but I got tied up in meetings."

"That's okay." She sat up and swallowed the tablets. "I've been zonked most of the day. Must be the flu."

"Well, if you aren't much better in the morning, I want you to call the doctor. We have to get you well." He hesitated. "Remember, I'm flying to Fairbanks day after tomorrow. I would hate to go if you were still sick."

"I'll be fine. I'm sure the worst is over now." She got out of bed and walked into the bathroom, surprised at how weak she felt. She splashed cold water on her face and peered into the mirror. Her face looked puffy and pale. She ran a comb through her tangled hair and brushed her teeth.

When she returned to the bedroom, Nick was sitting at his desk, sorting through papers. "Can I get you something to eat?" he asked without looking up. "Some soup? Sara and I finished off the casserole."

"No, thanks. I'm just thirsty," she said. She got back into bed and drained her water glass. "I feel completely wiped out."

"Well, you certainly had a rough night last night, with all those nightmares," Nick said, glancing up from his paperwork.

"Nightmares?"

"Don't you remember? You woke me several times, whimpering and thrashing around."

Lee stared at the ceiling as fragments of the dream came back to her. Juan was in it, wearing just his silver necklace. And there was something about a huge black bird. Lee shivered and snuggled under the covers. Then she remembered the sweating-oil smell she had noticed in the early afternoon. "Nick?"

"Hmm?" He was adding figures on his pocket calculator.

"Did you notice a strange odor in the house when you came home?"

"Odor?" He glanced up at her. "What kind of odor?"

"I don't know, kind of sweet. And really strong. It's hard to describe."

"I didn't notice anything." He went back to his columns of numbers.

"Just my imagination, I guess." Lee closed her eyes, determined to put it out of her mind. Sometime later she felt Nick getting into his side of the bed. The lights were out, and the house was quiet.

* * *

Lee slept soundly through the night, not waking until the alarm went off at six-thirty the next morning. Her fever and headache were gone, but she stayed in bed, not wanting to get up. She dozed until Nick and Sara yelled their respective good-byes and left. Then she got up and put on her robe. I'll go into work a little later this morning, she decided, going downstairs to fix herself a cup of herbal tea. She carried the tea back upstairs to her study.

She stared at her notebook and tape recorder laying on the desk. Nick was right. It was stupid and reckless to take part in that ceremony. Anything could have happened. She rewound the tape and sat back in her chair to listen to the interview with Juan Mascareñas.

His deep voice hit her with a shock. Lee's hand jerked, spilling tea in her lap. She brushed at it, barely feeling the hot sting, and sat for thirty minutes as the tape played through. Her tea cooled, forgotten, on the table beside her.

She turned the tape recorder off and stared out her study window. *Piñon*-covered hills gently rolled beyond the house to the west. Across a sandy arroyo, several hundred yards away, rose the light brown adobe home of her nearest neighbor. Santa Fe sprawled to the south, one of the oldest continually inhabited cities in the United States, now a center for art and culture. In spite of its international popularity, Santa Fe managed to preserve an intimate southwestern charm. Lee loved living on its outskirts and had always relished the location of her home. It offered privacy, views of the mountains and city, and yet was only a short drive from the downtown plaza. But now she suddenly felt uncomfortably isolated.

She picked up her notes on Cavado and studied them for a moment before putting them into her briefcase. Better get going. Things were undoubtedly piling up at the office. She walked wearily into her bedroom to dress.

* * *

"Hey! You doing okay?" Annabel's voice in the doorway jolted Lee out of her reverie.

"What? Oh, I'm all right. Just a little spacey, I guess."

"I'll say. Each time I've gone by this office today you've been staring at the wall. If I didn't know you so well, I'd say you were in love."

"Of course I am. With my husband."

"Right. But that's not the kind of love I mean." She peered at Lee over the top of purple-rimmed half glasses perched on the end of her nose. "Seriously, Lee. If you aren't feeling well, go on home. Things are pretty much under control here."

"No, I'm okay. Just running in low gear today." She picked up her pen and glanced down at the papers in front of her, hoping Annabel would get the hint and be on her way.

"Well, if you're sure. How do those color separations for the museum story look?"

"Oh, God. I forgot to pick them up. Damn. They're due at the printer's in the morning."

"Relax. I'll send Julie out to get them. Take it easy, kiddo. I'm worried about you. You're obviously not over that bug."

"I'm fine, Annie. Don't fuss over me. Just let me get back to work."

Annabel was right. Lee's mind hadn't been on her work all day. Her thoughts kept returning to Cavado and Juan Mascareñas. She felt increasingly agitated as the afternoon wore on. What on earth had possessed her, to agree to that strange ceremony, to wear that revealing little costume? How could she have been so unprofessional? When she left the magazine office a little after five o'clock, Lee couldn't remember when she'd had a less productive day.

* * *

"For God's sake, Lee, let it go," Nick said, after Sara had left the dinner table. "It was a foolish thing to do, but you were lucky. Nothing terrible happened. Just let it be a lesson. You can't rush into an interview without knowing what kind of situation you're getting into."

"That's a little easier said than done," she retorted. "People aren't that easy to predict. They don't fall into neat mathematical formulas. The point is that I've always shown good judgment in the past. I just don't understand how I let that happen."

"Well, I'd stop dwelling on it if I were you." Nick pushed back from the table. "What's done is done. Now, if you'll excuse me, I have to get ready for tomorrow's trip. I'll need to pack my woolies. Wouldn't want to freeze my buns off," he said with a wink. Then he patted Lee on the cheek and left her sitting alone at the dining room table.

* * *

The next morning was bright and cloudless, a preview of the perfect Indian summer weather predicted for the weekend. Nick put his suitcase down in the sunny foyer and kissed Lee good-bye. "I'll be home before you know it. You know how fast two weeks go by. I'll call you in a day or two."

She followed him outside to his car. "Take care of yourself, babe," he shouted and drove away, gravel crunching beneath his tires.

Lee got into her car and headed for work. It would be a lonely weekend. Sara was spending the night with a girlfriend and would be gone most of tomorrow. Even when she was at home these days, Sara was too caught up in her teenage world to be much of a companion. Lee remembered the Buchanans' party and sighed. Oh, well. It would give her something to do over the weekend.

* * *

I have to get this damned story written, Lee thought, staring at the blank screen of her computer. She flipped through her notes, then typed "Cavado: A Glimpse of the Past." She stopped and stared out of the window, remembering Juan's two-room adobe house. He didn't live there, she felt sure. He must live somewhere else in Cavado. She closed her eyes, remembering the service station attendant's words: "Mascareñases was here before God...old Juan damn near owns Cavado...he's one of them *curanderos*."

She stood up and crossed the room to the bookshelf. Finding her Spanish-English dictionary, she looked under "C" until she found: "*Curandero*: healer(not a doctor); quack; medicine man (among Indians)."

So she'd been treated by a medicine man. A "quack" who wore a strange necklace. But he had referred to it as an "amulet," and said it had belonged to his mother. She looked up that word in her Webster's New World Dictionary and spent a moment considering the definition. "Amulet: something worn on the body because of its supposed magic power to protect against injury or evil: a charm."

Magic power? Did Juan actually believe that his 'amulet' had some sort of magic power? Come to think of it, he did say something about it protecting him from harm. But that's just superstitious nonsense. Surely he wasn't serious. After all, he's an educated man. He's been to college. But then, on the other hand, that ceremony of his was pure pagan—all that business about the sacred circle and invoking the spirits of different directions.

She sat back down and tried to concentrate on outlining the story, but details of the awakening ceremony kept flashing through her mind. She remembered the feeling of his hands sliding down her back and over her buttocks, spreading the pungent sweating oil. The strength of his arms as she lay in his warm embrace on the buffalo skin rug. His command, "Hold me tighter, tighter," as he clasped her sweaty body against his.

Lee felt flushed and uncomfortably warm. Taking a deep breath, she closed her eyes and leaned back in her chair. Then her eyes flew open. What...? She half rose to her feet. Oh, my God, she thought, as a sickeningly sweet odor filled the room. No, it can't be! I smell sweating oil! I really do smell it this time. But that's impossible. What's happening to me?

Her heart was pounding as she fumbled through the phone book, then dialed a number. "Is Doctor Mallory in?" Her voice shook. "This is Lee Lindsay. Please, this is urgent. I have to see him as soon as possible."

Chapter 6

*T*he carved wooden sign above the door read "James E. Mallory, M.D." Lee stepped into an empty waiting room that was decorated in soothing tones of beige and brown. She sat in a chair near the door and nervously checked her watch. Five-thirty. The secretary had gone home, leaving her desk neat and cleared for the next day's work.

A side door opened and Jim Mallory stuck his head into the waiting room. His nearly bald crown shone in the overhead light. A few long strands of brown hair were carefully combed up from the sides and over the top of his head. "Hi, stranger," he said. "Come on in."

Lee clasped the psychiatrist's extended hand and smiled down at him. She had forgotten again how short he actually was. His aura of quiet confidence distracted from his diminutive size. "I appreciate your seeing me on such short notice," she said. "Especially after hours."

"Well, it's good to connect with you again. It's been awhile. Almost two years, as a matter of fact. My secretary said that you sounded upset on the phone." He gestured toward the sofa. "Have a seat."

Lee sat on the sofa with a feeling of *deja vu*. She had once spent many hours in this room, talking to this soft-spoken man with warm brown eyes. She had first come to see him seven years ago, after the death of her parents. In addition to the grief and rage she had felt about the accident, she was disillusioned with her marriage. Mallory had gently guided her through that bleak period in her life, encouraging her to develop more emotional independence. He had been a life saver. Without his support, she probably wouldn't have dared to invest her small inheritance in the magazine. She had seen him occasionally since then for what she thought of as emotional "tune-ups." He had always given her sound advice and a fresh perspective. She hoped he hadn't lost his touch.

Mallory picked up a yellow legal pad and a pencil from his desk before settling himself in the chair facing her. "Catch me up," he said. "How's Nick? And Sara?"

"They're both fine. Sara's growing up much too fast. She's in high school and almost as tall as I am." She paused. "Nick's still on the go a lot. As a matter of fact, he left this morning for Alaska. To accelerate electrons into the aurora borealis, no less."

"How are you handling his traveling?"

She shrugged. "Okay. I'm too busy myself to let it get me down."

"How's the magazine business?"

"It's hard work, but I love it. We made a nice profit last year."

"I'm delighted to hear that. Congratulations." He reached into a large glass bowl filled with hard candy. "Would you like a mint?"

Lee shook her head. "No, thanks."

"I've become addicted to them since I gave up the evil weed last year. Just substituted one addiction for another, I'm afraid. But I decided I'd better stop smoking—before it stunts my growth." He grinned and unwrapped a mint. Popping it into his mouth, he leaned back in his chair, studying her. "It sounds like things are going smoothly for you, Lee. Why are you here?"

She took a deep breath. "I need to talk about something that happened during an interview three days ago. Something very strange."

For the next thirty minutes, Lee presented an uncensored version of her experience in Cavado. Mallory listened, occasionally interrupting with a question and taking notes. By the time she had finished describing the mysterious recurring odor, her hands were tingling. She nervously rubbed them together while Mallory sat quietly, watching her.

"That's quite a story," he said, after a long moment. He uncrossed his legs and leaned forward in his chair. "Okay. A few things seem obvious to me. For starters, I'm almost certain that you were drugged during the interview. In addition, I suspect that you were hypnotized."

Lee stared at him, speechless.

"Let's talk about the drug first. There are some locally grown drugs, including strains of marijuana, that are incredibly smooth, potent and long-lasting. I think Mascareñas slipped you some in your tea."

"My God, that never even occurred to me. I've smoked marijuana a few times—years ago, in college—but I always hated the feeling and couldn't wait for it to wear off. It frightened me to feel that I wasn't in complete control of myself. I certainly didn't feel any of that panic in Cavado. In fact, I felt relaxed and very peaceful."

"Of course. You had no reason to suspect that you were drugged, so you didn't worry about it. You didn't spend time analyzing your actions and reactions, like you did when you knew that you were stoned. Besides, when marijuana is ingested, the effect is far more subtle and gradual than when it's smoked. And as I said, I think your 'medicine man' gave you a dose of some very smooth, first-class 'medicine'."

"But why? What did he hope to gain by drugging me?"

"He got you under the blanket." Mallory grinned. "That was undoubtedly the highlight of his day. I'm sorry, Lee. I didn't mean to sound flip. But you are a very attractive woman. He probably just saw an opportunity and decided to take advantage of it."

"You obviously don't believe that Juan was on the level with his 'awakening ceremony' and story about our past-life connection."

"No, I don't," he said. "Let me backtrack a bit, and I'll explain why. I've done considerable research on *curanderismo*, or Hispanic folk healing. The words '*curanderismo*' and '*curandero*' come from the Spanish verb '*curar*' which means 'to heal'. *Curanderos* are generally very religious, and they believe that their healing powers come directly from God. They've played an important role, both medically and socially, for centuries in both Mexico and the American Southwest. After all, native medicinal wisdom is the source of much of our pharmacological knowledge. We didn't exactly invent medicine in the twentieth century, much as we'd like to take the credit. My personal experience with local *curanderos* has convinced me that there's still a lot they could teach us. In fact, on occasion, I've referred Hispanic patients who don't trust modern Anglo psychology to a *curandero* who lives in Pojoaque. With excellent results, I might add."

He smiled at her surprise. "Old Manuel comes from a long line of healers. People used to travel up from Albuquerque to be treated by his father when he was alive. Anyway, Manuel's an ethical man, and he knows his herbs. From what I can tell, he uses standard *curanderismo* methods, which, by the way, assume supernatural sources of illness."

"Supernatural sources?"

"That's right. *Curanderos* attribute many illnesses to magic and witchcraft, which they have traditional methods of combating. Let me give you an example. A *curandero* might pass an egg, which is believed to have cleansing qualities, back and forth over a patient's body three times to remove the curse of the '*mal de ojo*' or 'evil eye' that he believes is causing depression or illness. Then he would break the egg into a bowl of water and place it behind the patient's head, instructing him to rest until the spell is removed. After a refreshing snooze, the patient would be served some soothing chamomile tea and—more often than not—they would experience a remarkable recovery." He shrugged. "It works because they believe in it. And if it works, who can knock it?"

"Do you know of any *curanderos* here in Santa Fe?"

"As a matter of fact, a *curandera* called Tia Delfina lives on Salazar Street, just off Agua Fria. I haven't met her. But I understand she's a delightful old lady, who cheerfully dispenses herbs, massage, and a little benevolent magic." He paused, his smile fading. "But I've also encountered a few unethical and even dangerous *curanderos*. In fact, I did a psychological evaluation on one several years ago that made my hair stand on end."

"Really?" Lee tried not to smile at the mental image of Mallory's few long strands of hair spiking out from his temples.

"It was during the trial of Leroy Martinez, who was convicted of poisoning his uncle in Pecos. Does that ring a bell?"

"No, I don't think so."

"Well, it got a lot of publicity at the time. Leroy admitted to poisoning his uncle. Used rat poison, in fact. But he maintained that he did it against his will. He claimed he was bewitched into doing it by a local *brujo* who hated his uncle."

"*Brujo*?"

"A *brujo* is a sorcerer, a practitioner of the so-called black arts. I'll let you in on a well-kept secret. Witchcraft is alive and well here in the Southwest."

Lee stared at him in amazement. "Of course, I've

heard folk tales. But I assumed that's all they were."

"Most Anglos are unaware of the old Spanish and Indian traditions that still flourish around here, especially in the rural villages and pueblos. Those people are understandably reluctant to discuss their supernatural beliefs and experiences with outsiders." He leaned back in his chair. "Examples of the belief in witchcraft are all around us in New Mexico, although most people these days don't take them seriously. For instance, there's the ancient tradition of painting doors and window frames blue. Do you know how that originated?"

"I've read that it's supposed to ward off evil influences. But isn't that just colorful Santa Fe lore?"

"There's more to it than that. For centuries the Spanish have used blue, the color traditionally associated with the Virgin Mary, to protect their homes from witches. Many still do. And the Indians use turquoise, the color of the sky, for the same purpose." He stood up and walked to a coffee pot sitting on a table by the door. "How about some coffee? It's strong enough to melt bullets by now."

"No, thanks." Lee said. "I'm trying to cut down on caffeine."

He chuckled as he poured himself a cup full of the dark brown liquid. "Oh, that's right. You prefer the local tea."

Lee smiled. "I have to say, it feels good to be able to joke about it."

Mallory sat down in his chair and took a cautious sip of the steaming coffee. "Now, let's see, where was I? Oh yes, I started to tell you about Leroy Martinez and the *brujo*. Well, Leroy swore that this *brujo*—Pedro Armijo was his name—had put a spell on him, causing him to murder his uncle. He maintained that Armijo had caused the deaths, in one way or another, of five or six Pecos residents throughout the past decade or so. Most of the villagers came forward to support Leroy's story and to insist that Armijo, rather than Leroy, be brought to justice."

"Are you serious?"

"I'm afraid so. There was such an uproar that the court ordered a psychological evaluation of Armijo." Mallory shook his head, remembering. "I have never encountered a more cold-blooded bastard in all my years of practice. He tested out as a textbook sociopath. Absolutely no conscience. Naturally, he denied having had anything to do with the murder. He admitted to being a *curandero*, but denied any connection with black magic. However, he expressed absolute glee over the uncle's death. Said the entire Lopez family deserved to die. It was obvious during the trial that Leroy and his family were terrified of Armijo. They wouldn't even look at him."

"What happened?"

"Leroy was convicted of first degree murder. Nothing could be proven against Armijo. He left the courtroom smiling ear to ear." Mallory grimaced. "As far as I know, he's still living in Pecos, terrorizing the community."

"You don't really believe that he was a...*brujo*?" Lee asked incredulously.

"I believe that he thought he was. And he'd certainly managed to convince the Pecos residents of his supernatural powers."

"Just a minute. You aren't saying that you think Juan Mascareñas could be some kind of sorcerer?"

"I don't believe in the supernatural," Mallory explained, "but from what you've told me, I don't believe Mascareñas is a simple, well-meaning *curandero* either. In the first place, reputable *curanderos* don't drug journalists and talk them into taking off their clothes. They don't need to drum up business. You would have to request treatment. And since you are a '*gringa*', an Anglo, a typical *curandero* would probably refuse."

Mallory reached into the candy bowl. "Also, most *curanderos* carefully avoid anything that smacks of the occult, in order to protect their reputations." He put another mint into his mouth. "You mentioned that he referred to the raven as having some special significance to him."

"That's right. He said it was a 'powerful spirit', or something like that."

"Well, the raven is almost universally associated with black magic. Legends about them certainly abound in this part of the country. A prevalent belief is that witches can assume the form of an animal. When they're up to mischief, they often turn themselves into an owl, a crow or a raven."

"People in this day and age actually believe that sort of thing?"

"You'd be surprised. A friend of mine, who happens to be a brilliant and successful lawyer, grew up in one of those isolated little mountain villages. He once told me that, as a child, he had trapped a *bruja*."

"Trapped her? How?"

"By placing a pair of scissors, opened to form the shape of a cross, under her chair. He swears that the woman was unable to stand up until someone removed the scissors."

Lee shook her head, smiling.

"He was very serious. Apparently lived for years in terror of her retaliation. To this day, he suffers from a phobic fear of birds."

In spite of herself, Lee started to laugh.

"I know, it's hard to believe. But my point is that a deep-seated, cultural belief in witchcraft still exists, even among many educated, professional people. Now, let's get back to your experience in Cavado. Based on all that you've said, especially Juan's reference to the raven, my guess is that he aspires to be more *brujo* than *curandero*."

"There was something else. He was wearing a very strange silver necklace. He referred to it as an 'amulet'."

"What did it look like?"

"Well, it was two outstretched wings and in the center were reddish stones that looked like eyes. There was a spiral design running between the two stones. The tips of the wings were attached to a heavy silver chain."

"Interesting."

"There were also black wings nailed to the wall in his little house. And he talked about taking a raven fetish with him when we do the second ceremony!"

"I certainly don't like the sound of that," Mallory said. "I hope you don't plan to see him again. I think you would be asking for serious trouble if you participated in his next ceremony."

"What do you mean?"

"I expect it would involve an hallucinatory drug, probably peyote or datura. And I'd be willing to bet that this time the ceremony would include having sex with the medicine man."

Lee felt her face flush. "How do you explain the odor of sweating oil? I smelled it twice, the day after the ceremony and this afternoon when I was in my office."

"I said I also suspected that you were hypnotized. I think the smell is an aftereffect of the hypnotic experience. It's surprisingly easy to hypnotize most people, and it doesn't require swinging a watch back and forth in front of their eyes. A soothing tone of voice in a darkened room will usually do the trick. A low, repetitive chant is also very effective."

"But would I be able to remember the experience if I'd been hypnotized?"

"Sure you would, if you weren't under very far. Hypnosis is simply an altered state of consciousness, similar to a meditational trance. And there are many different levels. It's only deep hypnotic trances that produce amnesia or hallucination. A mild hypnotic state would just make you feel very relaxed and would slowly wear off. But combined with your marijuana toddy, it would leave you open to suggestion, to say the least. And you could certainly experience trance aftereffects for several days. Like smelling the sweating oil."

"The first time I noticed the smell, I thought it was

just because I was sick."

"You were sick? When?"

"It hit me the night after the interview." She frowned, remembering. "I felt fine before I went to Cavado. And I felt okay all afternoon after the ceremony. I met Sara and one of her friends downtown afterwards and took them to lunch. Then I took the afternoon off, and we went shopping. I remember thinking that I felt unusually relaxed." She paused. "Come to think of it, I bought Sara several outfits that I normally would have vetoed. I must have been drugged!"

"When did you start feeling sick?"

"Early that evening, when I was describing the experience to Nick. I gave him a rather edited version, omitting the fact that Juan untied my halter top and joined me under the blanket. It's a good thing I did, too. Nick had a fit as it was, going on about what a stupid and dangerous thing I had done. That was before dinner. As a matter of fact, I skipped dinner. My head started pounding and I felt dizzy. I just showered and went right to bed."

"How long did the symptoms last?"

"I slept most of the next day. I had a headache and felt very weak. I assumed it was the flu."

"Did you feel dehydrated? Thirsty?"

"Why, yes, I did. But I attributed that to the fever I was running."

"And the next day you felt okay. Let's see, that was yesterday, right?"

"That's right. I still felt a little weak and very nervous. I couldn't stop thinking about what had happened. I felt like a gullible fool. Then when the smell returned, I panicked."

"I don't think you had the flu. I think you just reacted to whatever was in the tea and possibly the water you drank during the ceremony. And didn't you say you ate some kind of powder?"

"I thought it was corn meal."

"Maybe. But maybe not. Mind-altering drugs, even in mild doses, usually have a dehydrating aftereffect. Sometimes severe enough to cause serious illness. And we really don't know what he gave you."

"I almost forgot—I also drank some milk. Very sweet-tasting milk. Juan said it would clear my head from the effects of the ceremony."

"One for the road, huh?" Mallory shook his head. "Heaven only knows what combination of drugs you ingested. I think that explains all your symptoms since Tuesday night, including the sweating oil smell. Also, dramatic events sometimes leave a recurring reaction. For example, people who survive auto accidents sometimes report smelling gasoline or burning rubber weeks later. They're just re-experiencing vivid memories of the accident. It could be something like that. Anyway, it's nothing to worry about. It probably won't happen again."

He glanced at the clock on the wall behind her. "We're going to have to stop now, Lee. Avoid this Juan character in the future. I think he's bad news. And try not to feel bad about what happened." He smiled at her. "Look at it this way. You were given a peek into a world that is closed to most Anglos, a cultural phenomenon and a fascinating experience. It'll make a great magazine article."

Lee grimaced. "Someone else can write it. I feel like such a fool. Talk about losing control of an interview! My God. I go in there with my notepad and tape recorder, and half an hour later I'm on a moth-eaten buffalo rug—allowing an almost naked man to rub me down with snake oil! I'd be laughed out of town." She stood up. "Doctor Mallory, thank you. I feel sane again."

"I'm glad I could help. Call me again if you need to talk more about it." He hesitated. "You know, it might be interesting to talk to Socorro Tafoya-Hall about your experience. Do you know her?"

"Only professionally. Her gallery advertises in the

magazine."

"That's right. Socorro and her husband, Howard, own Galería de Canyon Road. Howard's from Dallas and a real character, usually wears a big Stetson with a turquoise-studded headband. Nice guy. Socorro and my wife are close friends. As you may know, Socorro's a Native American. She's a fascinating woman—very bright, with a master's degree in art history. She might be able to shed some light on your 'awakening ceremony'. At any rate, it would be interesting to get her reaction. She grew up with that sort of thing."

"You don't think she'd mind talking to me about it? I know that Native Americans are sometimes reluctant to talk to outsiders about their ceremonies."

"Tell her that I suggested it. You can usually reach her at the gallery. And just so you'll be prepared, Socorro also claims to be a psychic."

"An Indian psychic with a master's in art history. Sounds like a typical Santa Fean."

"She's anything but typical. Incidentally, 'Socorro' means 'help' in Spanish. Let's see if she lives up to her name. Let me know what happens. And call if you have any more problems with this experience."

"I will," Lee said, moving toward the door. "Thanks again. Good-bye."

The small side street where Lee had parked her car was deserted and gloomy in the early evening darkness. She hurried along, glancing over her shoulder and fumbling through her purse for car keys. There's no reason to be so nervous, she chided herself, as she located the keys and unlocked the car door. As Mallory said, it was an interesting experience, but now it's behind me. No real harm done. She locked herself inside and took a deep breath before starting the engine. Then she drove carefully through the narrow winding streets of downtown Santa Fe, eager to get home.

Chapter 7

*T*he house was dark when Lee drove into the driveway, and she felt a stab of alarm before remembering that Sara was spending the night with Wendy. She turned off the engine and waited until the garage door closed safely behind her before getting out of the car.

Mister came running down the hall to meet her in the kitchen. "Hi, sweet kitty," she said, bending down to rub him under his chin. "Could I interest you in a little dinner?" He wound himself around her legs, purring happily.

She filled his bowl with dry cat food. "It's just you and me tonight, old buddy," she said, giving his head an affectionate pat. "Good thing we enjoy each other's company." Although she rarely drank alone, she poured herself a glass of wine before going upstairs to undress. After slipping into a warm flannel robe, she carried her wine through the sliding patio door and onto the second-floor balcony off the master bedroom.

It was her favorite part of the house. She relished quiet moments spent there, unwinding and thinking private thoughts. Leaning against the balcony wall, Lee gazed out across peaceful moonlit hills at the lights of Santa Fe glittering below. The crisp evening air was perfumed by the aroma of *piñon* wood burning in some neighbor's fireplace. What a beautiful night, she thought, looking up at a black velvet sky crowded with stars. She took a deep breath and, ignoring a wave of loneliness, sank into a redwood deck chair. Pulling her robe tighter around her, she began to review her session with Dr. Mallory. His words replayed in her mind. "You were drugged...hypnotized...he sounds like a *brujo* to me...a *brujo*."

A furry body leaped out of the darkness and into Lee's lap, spilling her wine. "Mister!" she exclaimed. "You scared me!" She put her glass on the table beside her and stroked the cat. Suddenly, the quiet night seemed ominous and the lights of Santa Fe much too far away. "Let's go inside," she said, scooping the cat up in her arms. As she got to her feet, she heard the phone ring in the bedroom.

Hurrying inside, she dropped Mister onto the bed and lifted the receiver. "Hello?"

"Lee?" The deep, familiar voice hit her like a slap. "Is this Lee Lindsay?"

She stood frozen with the phone to her ear. When she finally found her voice, it was little more than a whisper. "Juan?"

"You recognize my voice," he said approvingly. "I'm flattered."

"How did you find me? I mean, how did you get my home phone number? It's unlisted."

"I called your magazine office this afternoon. I explained to your receptionist that you had interviewed me. I told her that we had unfinished business." He paused. "She was most cooperative."

"She was?" Lee frowned. Julie usually showed better judgment. She was certainly going to hear about this!

"You are alone," Juan said. It was a statement and

not a question.

"How do you know that?" she demanded. "How do you know that I'm alone?"

"I told you. I know many things about you."

Lee sat on the edge of the bed, speechless, but unable to hang up the phone.

"I had to speak with you," he continued. "You have been—how shall I say it?—you have been strong in my mind the past few days. How are you feeling?"

"Better now. But I've been ill."

"Yes. That was from the ceremony. The body is sometimes shocked by an awakening process. The weakness will soon pass, and your strength will return. You will be stronger than ever." Another pause. "It was a very powerful ceremony."

"You should have warned me that it would make me sick." Her voice shook. "I haven't known what to think about our...ceremony. It left me confused and frightened."

"I must be honest with you. In some ways it frightened me too."

"What?"

"The power of our ceremony. It moved me very much. More than anything has in a long, long time."

"What did you do to me? Did you drug me?"

"Drug you?" He laughed softly. "No, I didn't drug you. Why do you ask that?"

"Because it's so unlike me to—"

"Listen to me," he broke in. His voice suddenly had a hard, impatient edge to it. "You must open to your real self, to your power. As I told you, you are much more than the person you appear to be. The time has come to cast aside the illusions of this life and get in touch with who you *really* are." His voice softened. "But we must be patient. The understanding will come."

"What understanding? I don't know what you're talking about."

"You ask too many questions. Just listen. And trust me. In two nights the moon will be full, and I will go into the hills to perform the second ceremony. I will shake your sweat blanket to the four directions and scatter your fears. You will feel your strength return soon after that. And you will return to Cavado on Tuesday morning."

"Oh, no! I...I can't. I'm really busy."

"We must meet again. You know that, don't you? You and I really do have unfinished business." His voice, intimate and coaxing, held her—somehow scattering her thoughts and dissolving her fear. It would be so easy to agree....

"No!" she said, struggling to maintain her resolve. "I can't do the next ceremony. I mean, I don't want to."

"I won't rush you. The final ritual can wait. It can be postponed until you are ready. But I must see you. Soon."

"I don't think—"

"Tuesday morning. I will be waiting. Now you are tired. Very tired. It is time for you to sleep. Go to bed, Lee, and sleep. Put all your fears to rest. Sleep. *Buenas noches.*"

The line went dead. Lee sat motionless, staring into space, then slowly replaced the receiver. She felt weak and disoriented. I need to sleep, she thought numbly. And put my fears to rest. She untied her robe and let it fall to the floor before climbing naked into bed. Almost immediately, a black wave of sleep carried her away.

Chapter 8

*L*ee sat up in bed the next morning, surprised to discover that she was nude. She always slept in a nightgown, even on the warmest summer nights. For a moment she felt utterly confused, as though she'd just returned from a long journey. What day of the week was it? She stared at the clock on the nightstand until she got her bearings. Six-twenty. Saturday. Her mind returned to the mystery of her missing nightgown. There was some sort of gap in her memory. She couldn't remember going to bed the night before. She'd been out on the patio.... Her breath caught in her throat as memories of Juan's phone call returned. She slid back under the protection of the warm covers, trying to reconstruct the strange conversation of the night before.

It was spooky. He seemed to know that she was alone. But that's impossible. He couldn't have known that. He had insisted that she come to see him again next Tuesday morning and he'd hung up before she could refuse. He just wouldn't listen. He was so damned insistent. "Oh, God," she groaned aloud, "why didn't I just tell him to get lost?"

At the sound of her voice, Mister raised his head from the comforter at the foot of the bed. He rolled onto his back, exposing a fat gray and white striped stomach. After a long stretch, he rolled upright and walked to the head of the bed. His cool nose touched Lee's and he began a deep-throated, rumbling purr. "Good morning, you sweet old thing," she said, scratching his head. Mister's amber eyes closed in contentment.

Lee rose and went into the bathroom. Moments later she put on the robe that was lying on the floor by the bed and walked to the sliding glass door. It was unlocked. She hadn't even closed the draperies. I must have really been wiped out last night, she thought. I guess I was still weak from my Cavado illness—whatever that was. Come to think of it, I didn't have any dinner either, just a glass of wine. Well, skipping an occasional meal won't hurt me. It'll help ward off middle-aged spread.

She opened the door and walked out onto the balcony. The sky to the east was rosy gold, with shafts of sunlight lancing between purple clouds covering the tops of the Sangre de Cristo Mountains. Savoring the cool morning air, she took a deep breath and stretched her arms out wide. I feel fine today, she realized, completely recovered. But I must have spent the whole night in one position. I'm as stiff as a board. Better do some yoga.

She walked back into the bedroom and untied her robe, letting it slip from her shoulders. She stood naked in front of the tall mirror in her dressing room, critically evaluating her body. Her small breasts weren't quite as firm as they once were. Or as high. But they still looked pretty good, for a middle-aged broad. She ran her hand over a reasonably flat stomach that was laced with faint stretch marks from her pregnancy and a thin scar from the surgery performed after her miscarriage thirteen years ago. She turned a little, frowning. Something was definitely happening to the back of her thighs. Cellulite. That does it, she decided, sitting down on the carpeted floor. Time to get on a serious exercise program. Long walks, maybe an aerobics class. Daily yoga. She closed her eyes and did some deep breathing exercises. For the next half hour, she concentrated on a routine of slow stretching exercises. Afterwards she dressed quickly in a sweat shirt and pants before following an impatient and loudly complaining Mister down the stairs and into the kitchen.

While Mister ate his breakfast, Lee fixed herself a cup of tea. She ate half a grapefruit and a bowl of yogurt while she read the morning paper. Then she cleaned the Mexican tiles decorating the kitchen countertops and shook out the Navajo rugs that covered the hall and foyer floors. Finally, she climbed the stairs and went into her study. She'd put it off long enough. It was time to get started on the Cavado article.

Bracing herself, she sat down and listened again to the tape she'd made in Juan's office. She sat quietly for a moment after it was over. Then she partially rewound the tape. She hit the play button again, feeling an odd thrill as Juan's deep voice filled the room.

"There was much hardship to be endured in those days. Drought and disease were frequent visitors. The Spanish—" Lee hit the fast-forward button. "...many old Spanish traditions and Native American beliefs have endured here in Cavado," Juan's voice concluded.

"Yes, yes, hmmm...I see." Lee frowned at the sound of her own voice, struck by how strange she sounded. Rather detached. And sleepy. She replayed the last ten minutes of the tape, leaning forward in her chair.

"Cavado is a very special place," Juan's voice continued. "It is a very spiritual place, a source of great power. It has been so for—" There was a faint knocking. "Will you please excuse me for a moment?"

"Ummmm...yes...of course." A quick click as the recorder was turned off. Another click. Then Juan's voice. "Turn the recorder off now. And put away your notes." Click.

Lee sat staring at the recorder as the tape continued

to run soundlessly. "Well, I'll be damned," she said
aloud. "I do sound stoned. Mallory, you were right."

She glanced at the clock on the wall and made a
quick decision. It would be interesting to talk to someone else about this. Who knows, it might even be
helpful. She reached for the telephone book and found
the number.

"Galería de Canyon Road. May I help you?" The
voice was soft and slightly husky.

"Hello. May I speak to Socorro Tafoya-Hall,
please?"

"Speaking."

"Socorro, this is Lee Lindsay. From **Santa Fe Today**
magazine. Jim Mallory suggested that I call you.
There's something I really need to talk to you about. I
know this is short notice, but would you have any free
time today?"

Socorro suggested that they meet for lunch at eleven
forty-five at the Guadalupe Cafe. Lee hung up the
phone and turned off her computer. The story would
have to wait. She hurried to shower and dress.

* * *

The restaurant on Guadalupe Street was filled with
people, some of whom looked familiar to Lee as she sat
alone at a small table. She recognized the handsome
face of a former soap opera actor sitting several tables
away. And the woman at the next table also looked
familiar. An actress maybe? You never knew whom
you might see in Santa Fe these days. It had become a
popular hideaway for the rich and famous.

Lee studied the collection of framed posters com-
memorating The Santa Fe Opera, Indian Market, and
Rodeo de Santa Fe that hung on the whitewashed adobe
wall. She glanced at her watch. Socorro was already
fifteen minutes late. Sipping a glass of mineral water,
she watched the door.

A dark complexioned, attractive woman dressed in
red suede pants and matching tunic top paused in the
doorway, her eyes searching the tables. She wore a

massive turquoise and silver concho belt around her slender waist. Large silver hoops hung from her ears and silver bangle bracelets decorated both forearms. Her black hair cascaded from a middle part and flowed across her shoulders. Lee estimated the woman's age at somewhere around thirty-five, although she had the type of exotic good looks that made age hard to pinpoint.

"Socorro!" A man with his hair pulled back in a pony tail waved from a crowded table by the window.

The woman waved back. "Hello, David. Why aren't you in your studio working? Your clay baskets sell as fast as I get them in."

"I'll be back at work, right after lunch," the man retorted. "Even artists have to eat occasionally." Quick laughter rose from the table. She joined in the laughter and blew him a kiss. Then she spotted Lee, sitting alone in a corner. Lee raised her hand in greeting, and watched the woman glide through the tables toward her.

"Hi," she said, pulling her chair out and sitting down. "Sorry I'm late. It's been a frantic morning at the gallery. But don't get me wrong; I'm not complaining. I hope the tourists keep flooding into town."

"So do I. They keep all of us in business." Lee hesitated. "I really appreciate your meeting me today," she said. "As I told you on the phone, Jim Mallory said that you might be able to help me with something."

"I'll sure try." Socorro smiled. "Jim and Edie are two of my favorite people. I met Edie about ten years ago, when we were both enrolled in a photography course at the College of Santa Fe. We've been good friends ever since."

"I've never met Edie. But I've known Doctor Mallory for several years. I think he's terrific. He's helped me through some pretty rough spots."

"You're going through a rough time right now, aren't you?" Socorro's large, dark eyes studied Lee's face.

"Why, yes. I guess so. Does it show?"

"Your aura is cloudy. You're confused—possibly even frightened."

Lee stared at Socorro across the table. "Doctor Mallory said you're a psychic."

"Did he? I can't believe that's the reason he wanted you to see me." She smiled and leaned forward, her elbows on the table. "The good doctor has made it very clear that he doesn't believe in that sort of thing."

"Well, actually, he thought you might be able to help because of your background. You might be able to shed some light on something that happened to me in Cavado last week."

The smile froze on Socorro's face. "Cavado?"

"Yes, I was there to gather historical background for an article I'm writing. I interviewed a man named Juan Mascareñas. Do you know him?"

"No, I don't think so. But Mascareñas is an old and distinguished name around here. They were among the first Spanish settlers in northern New Mexico." Socorro hesitated. "I can tell you, however, that Cavado is a strong vortex of psychic energy, much of it evil. I've only been there twice, and both times I was very uncomfortable. The last time, I actually felt sick. It's a real power spot, psychically speaking." She motioned to the waitress. "Let's order lunch. Then I want to hear exactly what happened to you in Cavado."

Over a steaming bowl of green chile stew, Lee described her strange experience in the isolated village. Socorro picked at a spinach salad, listening intently. Lee saw her eyes narrow at the mention of the amulet Juan wore. And she noted an unmistakable expression of alarm cross Socorro's face when she reported Juan's references to the raven after the awakening ceremony.

"During this ceremony, did he use a drum?"

"No. Just a rattle, some sort of a gourd rattle, while he was chanting."

"That explains why you felt so out of it. A shaman, a good one that is, can easily induce an altered state by using a rattle, a drum, or just by chanting."

"That's what Doctor Mallory said. He feels certain that I was hypnotized."

"I'm glad that Jim and I agree." She grinned. "It's encouraging to see medical science making such strides."

"He also thinks that I was drugged by Juan's tea."

"I wouldn't be surprised. How long did your illness last?"

"A couple of days. Let's see, I got sick Tuesday night, after the ceremony. And I still felt—"

"Tuesday?" Socorro interrupted. "You went to Cavado on Tuesday?"

"That's right."

"Tuesdays and Fridays are known by my people as 'witches days'. Any magic worked on those days is especially potent. How did you feel on Friday?"

"Let's see. Yesterday was Friday. I didn't really feel sick by then, just a little weak. But I certainly felt off balance. In fact, something happened yesterday that sent me running to Doctor Mallory."

Lee told Socorro about the distinctive odor that had filled her office Friday morning. "It smelled like the sweating oil Juan rubbed on me. A strong, rotting fruit smell, mixed with something else. Some kind of flower or weed. It happened twice. Just came out of nowhere. The first time it happened was Wednesday afternoon, just before I fell asleep. I thought it was my fevered imagination. But then, when I smelled it again, it really scared me."

"It should have." Socorro studied Lee for a moment, then put her palms up on the table. "Give me your hands," she said.

Lee hesitated, then put her hands in Socorro's. Socorro's hands felt dry and cool. Lee looked at her expectantly.

"Now, I want you to close your eyes and think of Juan. Fix him in your mind. Visualize his face, recall his voice."

Lee resisted the temptation to glance around the room. She did as Socorro instructed, hoping no one was watching. She had no trouble remembering Juan's face

or his deep, intimate voice. A long moment passed
before Lee hesitantly opened her eyes. She stared across
the table, fascinated.

Socorro was sitting erect and motionless with her
eyes tightly shut. Although the restaurant was cool, her
forehead was shiny with perspiration. Lee watched her
frown, shake her head slightly, then frown again. Beads
of perspiration appeared on her upper lip. Lee was
uncomfortably aware of her hands in Socorro's firm
grip. They were feeling very warm, almost hot. She
forced herself to sit still.

Finally, Socorro opened her eyes. She blinked
several times and took a deep breath. Her hands tightened on Lee's. "I felt a great psychic force," she said,
her voice shaking slightly. "Something dark and fierce."

"What do you mean? What is it?"

Socorro released Lee's sweating hands and looked
into Lee's eyes. "I fear for you, Lee," she said in a
hushed voice. "You encountered a *brujo*. A very
powerful one. I will do what I can to help you."

Lee found herself at a loss for words. Was this
woman on the level? Socorro certainly didn't look like
she was joking. In fact, she looked genuinely shaken.
Before Lee could think of how to respond, Socorro
glanced at the check and reached for her purse, obviously eager to leave the restaurant.

"No, please," Lee said. "You're my guest."

"Thank you. Now I must go. I need time alone to
meditate, to confer with my spirit guides, before I go
back to the gallery."

"Spirit guides?"

"Yes. They help me to see beyond the distractions of
the physical world," she explained matter-of-factly.

"Wait a minute. Are you saying that you actually
talk to spirits?"

"Yes, I do. My guides have been with me since I was
a child."

"No kidding? Who do you think they are? And how
do they—?" Lee stopped, embarrassed. "I'm sorry. I

don't mean to pry. I'm just curious."

"I understand. And I don't mind talking about them, not to people who are genuinely interested. Perhaps I'll tell you more about my guides someday when we have more time." With a quick graceful movement, Socorro was on her feet. "I'll do some checking around, find out what I can about Juan Mascareñas and get back to you."

"Great." Lee opened her purse and took out a business card. She wrote her home number on it and handed it to Socorro. "You can reach me at home or at the office."

Socorro took the card and gave Lee's hand a quick squeeze. "Try not to worry. But don't ever go back to Cavado. Don't even talk to Juan again. Hang up if he calls you." She started to go, then turned back to Lee. "I would advise you to light a candle or two in your bedroom at night at least an hour before you go to sleep," she said. "In fact, light one during the day too, at work. Candlelight has a purifying effect. It will weaken any negative influences that might be affecting you." She brushed long black strands of hair away from her face. "I'll talk to you soon."

Lee sat alone at the table, staring into space. Doctor Mallory had been right. Socorro did add to her information about Cavado. But now the experience seemed more mysterious than ever. Spirit guides. *Brujos.* The whole thing was incredible. Absolutely ridiculous.

She paid the bill and left the restaurant. On the way home, she stopped at the grocery store.

Pushing her cart past the produce section, Lee stopped in alarm. Several feet away, standing with his back to her, was a tall, well-built man with dark hair curling past his ears. Her entire body went cold. When the man turned and walked past her, Lee felt weak with relief. It wasn't Juan. He didn't even look that much like Juan.

She turned her cart around and hurried to the check-out counter, forgetting the other items she had planned to buy. Her hands were shaking so hard that she had trouble writing the check. Grabbing her sack of groceries, she almost ran to her car. I've got to get a grip on myself, she thought. Somehow I have to put this craziness out of my mind. She forced herself to take several deep, calming breaths before driving home.

Chapter 9

Rock music blared from upstairs as Lee walked into the kitchen. She put the groceries away, then climbed the stairs and knocked on Sara's door. "Hello in there," she yelled over the music.

Sara opened the door wearing a lavender bra and matching bikini underpants. Her hair was pulled back with a rubber band, and her face was plastered in a partially dried oatmeal masque. "Hi, Mom," she murmured, trying not to move her mouth. "I can't talk."

"Oh, my God." Lee pulled back in mock horror. "An alien! What have you done with my little girl?"

"Don't make me laugh," said Sara, trying to keep her face still.

"I wouldn't dream of it." She grabbed Sara around her slender waist, tickling her ribs.

Sara pressed her lips together, squealing. Lee was struck by how frail Sara felt in her arms. She was still so young, so vulnerable. And trying to grow up too fast. Lee hugged her daughter hard for a moment, blinking back tears. "Did you have a good time at Wendy's last night?" She tried to make her voice light.

Sara nodded, her hand over her mouth.

"Great. Tell me about it later. I'm going into the study to write for awhile. Oh, honey, I have to go out for a couple of hours tonight. One of my advertisers is having a party to show off his new house. Didn't you say you have a date with Kevin?"

Sara nodded again.

"Okay. Don't forget, it's your turn to vacuum and dust the downstairs." Lee walked into her bedroom and kicked off her shoes. She exchanged her silk blouse and slacks for comfortable jeans and a sweat shirt. Then she closed herself in her study. She knew she'd feel better if she could get some work done. Finishing the article about Cavado would make her feel more in control.

The rest of the afternoon passed quickly as she wrote. She was only vaguely aware of the whir of the vacuum cleaner and of Sara's phone ringing from time to time. Finally, she leaned back in her chair and looked at the clock. Five-thirty. She reread what she had written with satisfaction, stretched her arms over her head and yawned. That came together easily enough. Stoned or not, she managed to get enough information for a damned good article. Some final polishing and she could get it to the typesetter on Monday, four days ahead of deadline.

* * *

Lee was in her bathrobe, debating what to wear to the party when Sara walked into her bedroom an hour later. She was wearing black stretch pants and an oversized hot pink sweater. Iridescent pink eye shadow gleamed under her eyebrows and across her eyelids. "Kevin will be here any minute," she said. "How do I look?"

"Beautiful. Except for that eye shadow."

"It's called Amorous Amethyst. Wendy and I found it last week at the drug store. Isn't it wild?"

"Wild. Rub at least half of it off." Lee decided on a long-sleeved black jersey dress. Nice but understated. "Will you zip me up, sweetie? Where are you and

Kevin going?"

"For a pizza, then to a movie. Will you be out late?"

"No. I just have to put in an appearance. Business politics." She slipped her feet in black suede boots and tied a silk scarf around her neck.

Sara followed Lee into the bathroom. She moved Mister off the dressing table stool and sat down, staring at herself in the mirror. "Mom? Did you know right away that you were in love with Dad?"

"Hmmm? Well, let me think. I liked him right away. But it took quite a few dates to get to the 'in love' stage. Why?"

"I was just wondering. About being in love, I mean. How do you know for sure when you are?"

"Oh, honey. That's a tough question. People have been trying to figure that one out for a long time. There are many different kinds of love. And at your age—"

The doorbell rang and Sara jumped to her feet. "He's here!"

"Sara, that eye shadow!"

"Mom, please. I'll fix it in the car." She gave Lee a quick kiss on the cheek. "Bye!"

"Have fun and be home by eleven-thirty."

Sara ran down the stairs. Lee walked to the window, watching the battered red Mustang spray gravel out of the driveway and turn right on the dirt road toward town. Oh, Sara, she thought. Don't be in such a hurry to fall in love. It's rarely all that it's cracked up to be. She quickly touched up her makeup, told Mister good-bye and left the house.

* * *

Bill and Samantha Buchanan's new house was impressive. Perched on top of a hill west of town, the sprawling hacienda-style structure commanded 360-degree views of the surrounding mountains and high desert terrain. The inside was filled with southwestern antiques and art.

"This place looks like a museum," whispered Annabel, who had come to join Lee in a corner of the massive living room. "The Cowboy Hall of Fame or something."

Lee grinned. "It's something all right. How many square feet do you suppose?"

"Judy Katz is their decorator. She told me there's close to 8,000, and that doesn't count the guest house and servants' quarters. But I guess Bill and Sam need that much space in order to live under one roof. I've heard that they fight like cats and dogs."

"You should be writing a gossip column, Annie. 'The Santa Fe Scoop' or something."

Annabel snorted. "You'd better be glad I'm not. I'd have to write about George Jennings, your tireless admirer. Brace yourself, kiddo. Here he comes."

Lee groaned. "God, I'm not up for old George tonight. Where are the Buchanans? I'm going to make my excuses and turn into a pumpkin." As she turned to go, she felt an arm slide around her waist.

"Lee, you gorgeous creature. I was hoping you'd be here."

"Hello, George." She turned her head so that his kiss landed near her ear.

"Your glass is empty. Let me get you more cham-pagne. Where's Nick? Out of town I hope."

Lee ignored his question. "Thanks anyway, but I was just leaving. Another engagement. See you Monday, Annie. Good-bye, George." She pulled out of his embrace and moved through the crowd.

* * *

Lee walked into the house and sighed. It had been along day. Mister came running down the hall to greet her. "Hi, old buddy," she said, bending to pick him up. "Did you miss me?" Mister purred loudly, pressing his nose to her cheek. "I can always count on you to be here for me, can't I?" She buried her face in his fur for a long moment, then carried the cat up the stairs.

Lee put on the faded flannel nightgown she usually wore when Nick was out of town and climbed into bed with a book. Engrossed in the novel, she jumped when the phone beside her rang an hour later. Hesitantly she picked up the receiver.

"Lee? How are things there?" Nick's voice sounded very far away.

"Oh, hi. Everything's fine. I went to the Buchanan bash for a little while tonight."

"Oh, yeah. How was it?"

"Very posh. A mob of people. I escaped as soon as I could. I'm in bed now, with Mister and a book."

"Sara's out with Mr. Wonderful?"

"That's right. Pizza and a movie. How's Alaska?"

"Cold. I've been setting up the experiment all day. Just got back to my room."

"What did you have for dinner?"

"I feel guilty telling you," he said. "A mountain of king crab."

"Sounds like rough duty."

"Well, someone's got to do it."

Lee knew her laugh sounded strained. "Is everything still on schedule?"

"So far. The first rocket shot is scheduled for early Tuesday morning. Of course that could change if we get bad weather."

"Well, good luck. Don't freeze or overdose on crab."

"I'll be careful on both counts." There was a short pause. "Everything's okay there? You're feeling all right?"

"I'm fine."

"You haven't had more interactions with demented medicine men, have you?" he asked in a teasing voice.

"None worth mentioning," she forced herself to joke back. She hesitated, then decided not to say anything about her visit to Dr. Mallory, or her lunch with Socorro. "Everything's under control here," she said, striving to keep her voice casual.

"That's my girl. Well, hold down the fort."

"Okay. Stay safe." She hesitated. "Nick?"

"Yes?"

"I miss you."

"Miss you, too, babe. Talk to you soon."

Lee hung up the phone, feeling alone and depressed. She bent down to the foot of the bed to pick up a sleeping Mister. Then she laid back, staring at the wall and cradling the purring cat against her chest.

* * *

At eleven thirty-five, Lee heard the front door open and close. Sara walked up the stairs into her mother's room, rubbing at her eye shadow. "Hi, I'm home."

"Hi, yourself. Did you lock the front door?"

Sara nodded. "We saw the coolest movie—"

"Did you remember the dead-bolt?"

"Yeah." Sara shot her mother a concerned look. "You okay? You've been acting a little uptight lately."

Lee closed her book, a romantic thriller that wasn't holding her interest despite its gratuitous sex, and put it on the nightstand. "I'm fine, honey. Just tired and a little on edge. I guess I'm not completely over that bug I had last week. Tell me about the movie."

"It was really neat. Kinda violent though. You would've hated it."

"No doubt. I can't handle blood and gore. Oh, your Dad called."

"Yeah? Where is he this time? I can't keep track."

"Alaska. Studying the atmosphere and eating king crab."

"I could go for the crab part." She bent to kiss Lee's cheek. "Night, Mom."

"Sleep tight, honey." Lee turned out her light. After forty-five minutes, she was still wide awake. Finally, she sat up, remembering Socorro's suggestion about lighting a candle. What did she say? Candlelight chases away evil spirits, or something like that. She shrugged and got out of bed. Well, why not, she thought, picking up one of the candles on the bathroom shelf. It can't hurt.

She lit it, placed it on the nightstand and stood in the darkness, watching the flickering light. Maybe I ought to try some meditation, she decided. See if I can still do it. It might help me to relax. She hiked up her night-gown and sat cross-legged on the carpet, staring at the candle and concentrating on relaxing every muscle in her body. The flame seemed to grow larger and brighter, slowly filling her mind as her eyes began to close.

* * *

Her legs felt stiff from sitting too long in a cross-legged position. The only light came from a small fire burning before her. The air was thick with the smell of smoke and perspiration. Where was she? Some kind of cave? As her eyes grew accustomed to the darkness, she could make out the shapes of ten or twelve people, sitting with her in a circle around the fire. They were swaying to the throbbing sound of a drum. And someone was chanting. From behind her came a deep, rhythmic, "Hi-yuh-yuh-yuh! Hi-yuh-yuh-yuh!"

Adjusting her leg position, she noticed that she was sitting on a pelt of thick dark fur. She looked down at the short skirt covering her stomach and upper thighs. Except for a necklace of multicolored beads, she was naked from the waist up. Her skin felt sticky, covered with a rancid-smelling oil that made her heavy bare breasts glisten in the firelight. She stared down at her large dark nipples. Long black hair tickled her shoulders and back when she moved her head. A drop of perspiration ran between her breasts and onto her skirt. She brushed it away, touching soft leather.

Smoothly, the drum beat and the chanting built to an intense climax and stopped. Her heart raced with excitement. The time had come. She stood, her feet bare on the fur rug, and slowly raised her arms above her head as a howling animalistic song burst from her lips. An answering chant rose from the shadowy group seated around her. She began to sway to the new chant, shifting her weight from foot to foot.

A tall figure stepped forward, wearing a shoulder-wide headdress of deer antlers. His only other garment was a length of leather, tied around his waist and reaching halfway down his muscular thighs. His broad forehead was painted with white zigzagged lines, and his straight black hair hung down his bare chest almost to his waist. The strand of beads around his neck was identical to the one she was wearing. As she stared up at him, her eyes fastened on a ruddy, spider-shaped birthmark that lay across his lower left cheek.

His black eyes relayed a silent message of encouragement. She allowed her fingers to linger on his as she took a small stone bowl from his hands. Then she poured some of the sand-like mixture from the bowl into her palm and tossed it into the fire.

The flames flared brighter. She tossed her hair out of her eyes and began to dance in a widening circle, as the drum beat and chanting grew steadily louder.

* * *

Lee jerked backwards, catching herself on one elbow. She looked wildly around the room. The candle had burned halfway down; wax was overflowing the candle holder and puddling on the nightstand. She scrambled to her feet and flipped on the light.

Mister stared at her from the bed. She ran her hand through her wet hair and looked down at her sweat-soaked nightgown. "What on earth?" she mumbled to herself. "Did I fall asleep? I must have been dreaming." She shivered, suddenly chilled, then struggled out of her nightgown and stumbled into the bathroom.

Her face, flushed and damp, stared back at her in the mirror. Trembling with exhaustion, she stood for a moment staring at her small naked breasts. Then she slipped on a fresh nightgown and hurried to bed, leaning to blow out the candle before tumbling into a deep, dreamless sleep.

Chapter 10

*B*y seven-thirty the next morning Lee was up, dressed in a warm-up suit and running shoes. She grabbed a lightweight ski jacket and left the house, determined to begin her day with some exercise.

Swinging her arms, she walked down the driveway and cut across the arroyo toward Camino Encantado. She quickened her pace on the deserted road, listening to the cheerful chatter of sparrows in the *piñon* trees and taking deep breaths of the invigorating morning air. An elderly woman in a white bathrobe waved and bent to pick up her Sunday edition of **The Santa Fe New Mexican**. A tiny brown poodle ran to the edge of the driveway, yipping furiously. "Macho, stop that!" the woman called. "Bad boy! You come back here!"

Lee smiled and waved. She was already feeling better. The disquieting dream of the night before seemed less threatening in the clear morning sunshine. Of course, it had been a dream, she assured herself. But she had to admit that it hadn't felt like one. At least, not like an ordinary dream. It was more like the other

candle-meditation dream she had related to Juan—
complete with smells and physical sensations. Could
they possibly be past-life memories?

Nick's reaction to her interest in reincarnation was
amusement and absolute skepticism. In fact, he viewed
the entire concept as nonsense. She knew he would
laugh at her if he were here this morning. "Float back
down to earth, babe," he would say. "You're letting
your romantic imagination run away with you."

And he would probably be right. She had been a
basket case ever since encountering Juan Mascareñas.
No doubt about that. It was certainly time to put that
experience behind her. On the other hand, she had
stumbled upon a fascinating story. Witchcraft in New
Mexico. It would make an interesting magazine article.
It deserves some research, she concluded, but not all this
emotional turmoil.

Her leg muscles were tingling with pleasant fatigue
when she walked into the house an hour later. She
found Sara sitting at the snack bar in a faded cotton
nightshirt, eating English muffins and reading the
Sunday comics.

"Wow, it's Mom, the superjock," she said sarcasti-
cally. "How many miles did you log?"

"Close to three."

"I'm impressed. What are you in training for?"

"You never know, sweetie." Lee poured herself a
glass of orange juice. "You just never know."

* * *

Lee spent the afternoon in the public library,
researching witchcraft. She was surprised to find
several books dealing with witchcraft in the American
Southwest. She sat at a table in the back of the room,
reading and scribbling occasional notes. Although she
found scattered references to various occult ceremonies,
she was disappointed that none of them described the
ceremony that Juan had performed with her. She opened
another book and read:

Hispano-Indian Witchcraft is a combination of European beliefs (brought to New Mexico by l6th century Spanish explorers) and ancient Native American practices. American Indian witchcraft dates back to prehistoric times. Witchcraft (brujería) and sorcery (hechicería) remain integral parts of Mexican folk culture and continue to be practiced, especially in rural villages.

Witches are called "brujas" or "brujos," depending on sex. They are believed to possess supernatural powers capable of causing illness, injury, even death. They are also believed capable of curing illness and injuries.

Food or drink offered by a brujo may be contaminated and is often suspected to be the source of supernatural illness or affliction.

Lee thought of the tea that Juan had given her during the interview. The source of a supernatural affliction? She certainly preferred Mallory's theory that it had been laced with marijuana. Frowning, she continued to read:

According to ancient belief, brujos can transform themselves into birds and animals, as well as cast magical spells. Pueblo Indians in northern New Mexico still associate crows, ravens and owls with witchery.

Brujos have been accused of preparing love potions and seducing unsuspecting victims. An ancient legend refers to a sacred plant that was boiled into a tea for the purpose of seduction...

Lee made a few more notes and leaned back in her chair to relieve the ache between her shoulder blades. She glanced at her watch. Almost five o'clock! How did it get to be so late?

She checked out one of the books and hurried outside, glancing up at the darkening sky as she buttoned her jacket. A chilly breeze was sweeping down from the mountains, pushing dead leaves along the quiet street. She hurried to her car in the almost deserted parking lot.

* * *

The house was quiet as Lee opened the garage door and walked into the kitchen. "Sara? I'm home," she called.

No answer. She dropped her notebook and book on the snack bar. There was a note from Sara stuck on the refrigerator door. "Mom—Kevin invited me to his house for spaghetti. I couldn't wait for you to get back. Home by 9:00. Hugs and kisses, S."

Lee sighed, then bent to stroke Mister who wound around her legs. "Well, at least I have you for company, old buddy," she said. Still wearing her jacket, she wandered out onto the patio. Mister followed closely behind and jumped up on the wooden railing, looking out into the arroyo. A brilliant tangerine and gold-colored sunset lit up the sky as the sun dropped behind the hills. Lee filled a large plastic watering can and began to water the dwarf evergreens that grew in clay pots on the patio. The mild weather couldn't last much longer. Last year it had snowed on Halloween. She'd had a real battle convincing Sara to wear a ski parka over her Gypsy Halloween costume.

She refilled the watering can and started toward the potted shrubs at the east end of the patio. A full yellow moon was rising over the mountain peaks. Lee stopped, her breath caught in her throat. As she stared at the moon, she suddenly saw Juan in her mind's eye—standing on the top of a lonely hill. He was holding her sweat blanket high above his head. The cool night breeze ruffled his dark hair and plastered his shirt against his muscular chest. Chanting mysterious words, he began shaking the blanket to the four directions.

Lee shivered as the vivid image slowly faded from her mind. She put down the watering can and hurried into the house, locking the sliding door behind her. Feeling unnerved, she poured herself a glass of wine. She carried it into the living room where she sat, staring out the window at the moon as it cleared the dark outline of the mountains and floated across a deep lavender sky.

* * *

Sometime later, Lee realized that her glass was empty. How long had she been sitting there? She closed the wooden shades and walked into the kitchen. Pausing in front of the refrigerator, she debated whether or not to have more wine. Why not? Maybe it would help her relax.

The phone on the kitchen wall rang, causing her to jump. She quickly poured herself another glass of wine and picked up the receiver.

"Lee? It's Socorro. How are you doing?"

"Oh, hi. I'm okay, I guess. A little spooked."

"That's understandable. Listen, I called a few of my psychic friends here in town. None of them know Juan Mascareñas. But one of them—you may know her— Clarity Light?"

"No, I don't think so."

"Well, anyway, Clarity agreed that Cavado is a very negative place. She said that she stopped for a picnic there one day last month on her way to Taos, but got such a headache she had to leave. The psychic vibrations were just too strong."

"Really?" Lee tried to hide a slight impatience. She wanted facts, not psychic mumbo-jumbo.

"I'm going to visit my grandmother at Santa Clara Pueblo tomorrow. I'll ask around there and see what I can find out. If Juan's a *brujo*, Grandma will probably know about him. She's eighty-six and knows everything that has ever happened with a two-hundred-mile radius of the pueblo."

"Thanks. I'd appreciate any information you can uncover. I feel absolutely obsessed by this thing. I can't seem to think about anything else."

"I was afraid of that. Lee, did you leave anything in Cavado? Clothing or any personal object?"

"No. I almost left my jewelry, but Juan gave it to me as I was leaving. Why?"

"He returned your jewelry? That surprises me. *Brujos* need something belonging to a person in order to cast a spell on them. Of course, he does have your perspiration on the sweat blanket. If he's as powerful as I think he is, that might be enough."

"How about urine?"

"What?"

"I used Juan's portable toilet before the ceremony. It doesn't flush."

There was a long silence. "That explains it," Socorro said in a strained voice. "He didn't need the jewelry. With your urine he could cast a very strong spell."

"You don't really believe that he put a spell on me, do you?"

"It's certainly possible. I'm getting very disturbing readings. And you just admitted to feeling obsessed."

"Well, sure, I'm preoccupied with all this. Who wouldn't be?" Lee's voice was shaking. "I mean, I can accept being drugged and maybe even hypnotized, but a *spell*? That's just too damned freaky!"

"I'm sorry. I didn't mean to upset you. Try not to worry. I'll see what I can find out tomorrow."

Lee took a deep breath. "All right. Thanks, Socorro. I really do appreciate what you're doing. This whole thing has me very strung out."

"I don't blame you. Take care, and remember to keep candles burning in your house. It would also be a good idea to take frequent baths or showers. Water drains off negative psychic forces that might be affecting you. I'll call you soon."

Lee hung the receiver and finished her glass of wine. Although she wasn't really hungry, she forced herself to eat a bowl of soup. She hoped she hadn't been rude on the phone. Socorro had some pretty strange ideas, but she was sincerely trying to help.

* * *

Lee really felt on edge. The wine had done little to calm her nerves. As she walked through the large house checking the locks on doors and windows, she found herself wishing for an alarm system. Nick had talked about having one installed after a neighbor's house had been burglarized several months ago, but they'd never gotten around to doing it. She made a mental note to call the alarm company. Better safe than sorry. The crime rate was up everywhere, even in Santa Fe.

She remembered the .32-caliber handgun that Nick kept loaded and hidden on the top shelf of the closet, behind his ski boots. She knew how to use it. Nick had insisted she accompany him to the target range for practice sessions several years ago. He'd maintained that the gun would give her a feeling of security when he was gone. But Lee tried not to think about it. Just knowing the weapon was there in the closet gave her the creeps.

Feeling a need to keep busy, she hurried up the stairs into her study. After doing some final editing on her Cavado story, she went back downstairs. Doctor Mallory would call this compulsive behavior, she realized, as she rechecked all the locks. I'm acting neurotic as hell. Mister followed her from room to room, nervously twitching his tail.

Finally, Lee settled herself in bed with two pillows at her back and reached for the book on her nightstand, **Indian Witchcraft: Sorcery and Spells**. She opened the book and began to read:

Sorcery is essentially an enchantment by spell. The sorcerer need not encounter his victim personally. All that is required is an item of the victim's clothing or, better still, something from the victim's body, such as hair, fingernail clippings, feces or urine...

Urine and sweat. Lee fought rising wave of anxiety. The author forgot to mention sweat. She took a deep breath and continued reading:

...which the sorcerer will then bury under a light-ning-struck tree...

A lightning-struck tree! She felt goose-bumps rise along her arms as she remembered the half-charred cottonwood in front of Juan's house. Okay, okay, calm down, she ordered herself. That's just a coincidence. Lightning strikes trees all the time. It doesn't mean that Juan uses that tree to.... Knock it off, Lindsay. You're letting your imagination run away with you again! She slid further under the covers before continuing:

The sorcerer will then cast a spell, causing the victim to be under his control and sometimes to sicken and/or die.

Lee skimmed the next page until her eyes fell on the following words:

...Sorcerers are said to sometimes cast spells while stepping over the unsuspecting body of a victim.

An image of Juan stepping back and forth over her body as she lay under the sweat blanket flashed into Lee's mind. And he was murmuring, chanting to himself the whole time! She made herself continue:

Some chants may be used to bewitch. Chants are instruments of great power which are usually intended for good. But an evil medicine man may use the power of chants for his own malevolent purposes.

Lee closed the book. Okay, that's enough. This is not the best time for witchcraft research. Not at night. Not when I'm all alone. She returned the book to her nightstand and reached for the television remote control. *Murder She Wrote* was half over. For a moment, Lee watched Angela Lansbury stalk a suspect through a dark, deserted building. Then she switched through the channels until she found a lighthearted sitcom.

* * *

An hour later, after Sara was safely home and in bed, Lee was still wide awake. She got out of bed and walked over to the large bedroom window, parting the draperies to look outside. The full moon flooded the silent hills with a ghostly radiance. Lee felt a chill. Was Juan really out there somewhere chanting to his ancient gods? Hugging herself, she turned away from the window. She climbed back into bed and curled close to Mister, grateful for his purring warmth and companionship.

* * *

Mondays were always busy at **Santa Fe Today**. When Lee arrived at eight-fifteen, all three telephone lines were ringing. She waited by Julie's desk until the receptionist had handled the calls. "I need to talk to you about something," she said.

"Just a sec," Julie said as she scribbled a short note to herself. Then she looked up, smiling.

"Julie, I'm going to tell you again—please do not give my home number to people who call here. Nick gets very annoyed when work-related calls start coming in at night. That's why I have an unlisted number. Just take a message, and tell them I'll get back to them."

Julie looked puzzled. "That's what I always do. I've never given your number out."

"You didn't give it to a man who called on Friday? A man who said that I'd interviewed him earlier?"

"I wouldn't do that."

"Could anyone else have talked to him?"

"I was the only one answering the phones. Bruce was on vacation. Pat was sick. Marcia and Al were out on assignment most of the day."

"But he said—"

"Who?"

"Never mind. It's not important." She hurried into her office.

* * *

Lee hardly looked up from her desk all day long. By throwing herself into her work, she was able to bury—at least for the moment—the disturbing thoughts that haunted her. On her way home late that afternoon, she made a quick stop at The Camera Shop. Her Cavado prints had been ready for several days.

That's strange, she thought, shuffling through the pictures a second time. I know I took a picture of that huge raven, just before it flew away. It was right before I took these shots of the cows. I wonder why it didn't turn out? She shrugged, then turned her attention to the shots looking down into the village. Not bad, she congratulated herself. Should have used the telephoto lens, though. She put the prints in her purse and drove home.

* * *

After Sara had gone to bed that night, Lee decided to do some yoga exercises. Slow stretches were relaxing. Maybe they would help her get to sleep. She stripped to her panties and sat on the carpet in front of the floor-to-ceiling mirror in her bedroom.

Raising both hands over her head, she pressed her palms together and turned slowly to the right and then to the left. Next, she bent toward the floor, her arms out straight behind her. Taking a long breath, she sat up, relaxed her arms, and dropped her head to her chest to begin neck rolls. Suddenly she stopped, staring down at her small breasts and pink nipples.

Her mind slipped into a mental image of dark brown nipples seen from the same angle. Heavy, brown breasts, shining with oil and perspiration. Her scalp began to tingle. She hadn't allowed herself to think about her candle meditation dream since her walk yesterday morning. Had it been just a dream? Even though her body had been unfamiliar, it was she herself that she had dreamed about. She felt certain of that. Vivid memories flooded her mind—smoke burning her eyes and nose, the rancid odor of her skin, the weight of her breasts as she swayed and danced.

Juan's voice echoed suddenly in her ears, "*It's time to get in touch with who you really are. The memory*

*and the understanding will come. You and I have
performed that ceremony before, in a different lifetime.*"

In a different lifetime! She frowned, recalling long
black hair sticking to her perspiring shoulders. She'd
been topless in the 'dream' wearing only a short leather
skirt similar to the one that Juan had given her for the
awakening ceremony.

She closed her eyes, trying to remember the face of
the painted, antler-bedecked man who had handed her a
small stone bowl. He'd looked like an Indian, his dark
forehead decorated with white paint. She had a fleeting
memory of straight black hair and piercing black eyes.
And on his cheek had been a strange red mark. Her eyes
flew open. He'd had a spider-shaped birthmark, exactly
like Juan's!

Lee stood up and put on her robe. She paced around
the bedroom, her mind racing. Were those memories
from a past life? Or was she just going off the deep
end?

She thought of the dream, or flashback, she'd
experienced ten years ago—the violent death of a
woman with long black braids. She'd been practicing
candle-meditation when that had happened, too.

When she'd described that experience to Juan, he
didn't seem at all skeptical. In fact, he'd said something
about her having the ability to summon "deep memories." And he said several times that she'd be amazed at
how much he knew about her. What was he hinting at?
Could he possibly have information about her past
lifetimes? Somehow, the thought that he might didn't
seem quite so incredible.

A decision was already forming in Lee's mind,
overriding her fear and better judgment. It was almost
as though the decision was being made for her. They'll
have to get along without me at the office tomorrow, she
thought. I'm going back to Cavado. I have to go
back—despite Socorro's warnings. And Doctor
Mallory's. There's something going on here, something
that won't let me rest. And I have to get to the bottom

of it. It'll be all right. I'll be very careful this time. I won't eat or drink anything, and I certainly won't participate in any more ceremonies.

Lee saw Juan's face in her mind—his sensuous smile and dark compelling eyes—and felt a thrill of excitement. It can't hurt to just talk to him again, she convinced herself. I wouldn't be in any danger. Surely. He's just a village *curandero*. This *brujo* business is nonsense. Superstitious nonsense. Besides, I don't really have any choice. I want answers and there's only one way to get them. I have to see Juan again, for my own peace of mind. But I'll sure as hell keep my clothes on this time!

Chapter 11

*L*ee fought with herself as she drove toward Cavado the next morning. I don't believe I'm doing this! What if Juan really is dangerous? She remembered the alarm on Socorro's face after her trance—or whatever it was—in the Guadalupe Cafe. "I fear for you, Lee," she had said. "You encountered a *brujo*."

Socorro had also said something about Tuesdays and Fridays being "witches days," days when any magic being worked was especially potent. Today was Tuesday.

For a moment Lee reconsidered. There was still time to change her mind, to just turn the car around. And yet she knew she couldn't do that. The compulsion to see Juan again was too strong. If she didn't follow through with this, she'd never know the truth about their past-life connection. And she'd always wonder.

Again, she saw Juan's face, his penetrating eyes, and the graceful movements of his muscular body as he danced around the buffalo skin rug. Something deep within her—something wild and dangerous—stirred in response to the memory. In spite of the cool day, Lee suddenly felt flushed. She cracked the car window to get some air.

This is insane, she thought wildly. Every instinct I have is telling me to stay away from Cavado. And yet, I can't seem to do that. Damn, I'm almost there! What should I do? I need to talk to someone who knows Juan. Someone who could shed a little light on who—or what—he really is. When she came to the gas station, she pulled in beside the full-service pump.

The tall, thin attendant who had talked to her before sauntered over. "Thought it was you," he said with a grin. "Recognized the car soon as you came around the bend."

"I need to ask you a few questions. And I might as well get some gas, too."

"Sure thing. Fill 'er up?" She nodded. He filled the gas tank and walked around the car, wiping his hands on a dirty rag. He rested an elbow against the car window and bent down level with Lee's face. "Now then. What can I tell a city gal like yourself that you don't already know?"

Lee pulled back slightly, but forced a pleasant expression. "Well, as I told you last week, I'm writing about this area. I thought you might be able to provide some local background."

"I'd be happy to provide you with anything you might need, pretty lady. You can count on that."

She ignored both the suggestive comment and accompanying leer. "Last week you said that Juan Mascareñas was a *curandero*. What else can you tell me about him?"

"Not a whole lot more. He drops by to gas up that black pickup of his is all. Don't say much. Kinda keeps to hisself. Now, Pablo—he's from Cavado—could tell you more about him. He's around back, working on that low rider rattletrap of his. Hold on. I'll get him."

Pablo was small and brown, with close-set, darting eyes. He reminded Lee of a fox. Obviously reluctant to talk to Lee, he approached cautiously and stopped several feet from her car, arms crossed in front of his chest.

Lee opened the car door and got out. "Hi. I won't take much of your time," she said. "I just wondered what you could tell me about Juan Mascareñas, the *curandero* in Cavado."

"Why do you want to know about him?" Pablo's eyes were suspicious slits.

"I'm writing a magazine story about Cavado. And he seems to be an important person there."

No response.

"Isn't Juan the village *curandero*?"

He nodded, mouth tight and grim.

"Do you know him well?"

"No, *señora*."

"Has he ever treated you?"

"No."

Lee sighed. This was like pulling teeth. Pablo wasn't going to volunteer a thing.

"But he saved my little sister's life."

Lee blinked in surprise. "He did? How?"

"She fell from a tree. Hit her head, very bad. Blood came from her ears and nose. There was no time to drive to the hospital in Española. My mother took her to Juan, and he saved her."

"How? How did he save her?"

Pablo shrugged. "He has ways. Treated her for two days. On the third day she was climbing trees again." He smiled a tentative smile, showing discolored front teeth.

Lee smiled back, feeling reassured. "I'm glad to hear that. That information is very helpful. Thank you."

"*De nada.*" Pablo turned and walked away.

Lee paid for the gas and got back in the car. The Anglo waved good-bye. "You come back real soon now, doll," he hollered. "You hear?"

Don't hold your breath, buster, Lee thought. She pulled out of the station and turned down the dirt road that led to Cavado.

* * *

Juan's pickup was parked beside the tiny adobe house with its drawn window shades. Lee parked her car beside the dead tree and turned off the engine. As before, she was acutely aware of the silence. Except for a bony, black dog trotting down the dusty road, she could detect no signs of life in the village down the hill.

She sat in the car for a moment, trying to calm her racing heart. There's nothing to be afraid of, she told herself. He's a healer. Pablo just confirmed that. I've come this far, I may as well go in and talk to him. Just talk. No more ceremonies. A memory of Juan blotting sweat from her naked breasts made her mouth go dry. This is crazy, she thought, I can't just sit here all day. She took a deep breath, forcing herself to open the car door.

She walked slowly up the dirt path. Standing beside the front door, she experienced a moment of near panic—accompanied by a strong impulse to turn and run. Then the door opened and it was too late.

"I've been waiting for you." Juan's arm went around her waist, pulling her into the warm, candle-lit room. He closed the door behind her.

She blinked, momentarily blinded. As her eyes began to adjust to the darkness, she raised them to Juan's face. Words stuck in her throat as she stared up at him. The silver amulet gleamed in the hollow of his neck.

"I knew you would come," he said, pulling her close. His dark eyes locked on hers as he ran one hand up the back of her neck, cradling her head.

She tried to pull away. "No! Don't. I...I need to talk to you."

"Later, *mi vida*," he whispered, holding her fast. "This is not a time for words." His warm, moist lips fastened on hers.

Lee felt something like an electric shock run through her body. Her knees felt weak. Frantically, she jerked

111

her head to one side. "Let me go! What do you think you're doing?"

He clasped her chin, forcing her to look at him. His eyes held her, awakening feelings too deep and powerful for her to identify. Once again, his lips met hers. She struggled for only an instant before all strength and reason deserted her. As if she had fallen into a dream, Lee closed her eyes and leaned against him. She was only dimly aware that her sweater and purse had dropped to the wooden floor.

He kissed her gently, unhurriedly, his lips moving softly as his tongue explored her mouth. Lee felt a tidal wave of desire surge through her, drowning all rational thoughts. The outside world slipped away, leaving only Juan's searching lips. All at once, she was aware of his hands unfastening the buttons on the back of her blouse.

"No! Juan, no..." His lips stopped her words and her blouse fell open in back. He pulled away far enough to slide the blouse off her shoulders and toss it to one side. Her eyes followed its fall, and she noticed that his feet were bare.

"Wait a minute! Don't—"

Ignoring her words, he drew her to him once more, pressing warm kisses down her neck as he unbuttoned her skirt. An instant later, she heard the zipper sliding down and felt the skirt being tugged gently over her hips. She twisted in his embrace. "No! Stop! I can't..."

As her skirt fell to the floor, Juan bent and slipped one arm under her knees, lifting her effortlessly. "Don't fight it, *querida*," he said in a soft voice, as he carried her into the back room. "You don't want to fight it."

He lowered her gently onto the buffalo skin rug and reached to remove her low-heeled pumps. Kneeling beside her, he unbuttoned his shirt and tossed it aside. Then he deftly unfastened the front hook of her bra. His hair shone blue-black in the candlelight as he bent toward her breasts. Slowly, his tongue teased each nipple before sucking it into his mouth. Lee shut her eyes as pleasure shuddered down the length of her body.

"Lift your hips," he said. "Quickly." The next thing she knew, he had pulled her pantyhose down past her hips and slid them off her legs. She felt his lips brush back and forth across her quivering stomach. Then, in a swift movement, he rose to his feet and removed his Levi's. He wore no underwear.

Lee looked up at him in disbelief. Candlelight flickered across his erect penis. Is this really happening? she wondered. My God, am I really doing this?

Then he was lying beside her. She made one last attempt to break away, to fight her way through the mindless passion that engulfed her. But he held her, pressing her back into the bearskin rug, his eyes locked on hers. Nothing made sense to Lee at that moment. She felt disconnected from the self she'd always known. And when he began to kiss her again, nothing mattered but surrendering to a fierce and altogether alien passion. She ran her hands across his smooth wide shoulders and up his neck, burying her fingers deep in his hair.

"At last, at last," he murmured, between passionate kisses. "You are mine again, at last." His words barely registered as she pressed against him, her mouth searching for his.

"I can wait no longer," he panted. "Open to me." She was vaguely aware of her own sobbing breath as she spread her legs and locked her feet across his back. She felt his hands slide under her hips and grasp her buttocks. She gasped as he thrust into her. The room beyond his shoulders became a shadowed blur as her body began to move to his rhythm.

Her eyes fastened on the dark wings nailed to the wall above the window. They seemed to move as the candlelight cast flickering shadows on the wall. Juan's body suddenly tensed and jerked convulsively. He buried his face in her hair and cried out something she couldn't understand. Then her own climax exploded, taking her breath away.

* * *

Afterwards they lay side by side on the buffalo skin rug. Lee felt stunned, unable to deal with what had happened. Juan propped himself up on one elbow, looking down into her face. The amulet dangled—its crystal eyes glowing—against his naked chest.

She turned away from him. "Oh, God," she groaned. "I can't believe..." Tears rolled down her cheeks.

He gently turned her face back toward his and brushed her tears away with his finger. "Yes, you can, *mi vida*," he whispered. "You can believe what is true."

"Juan," she whispered, searching his dark eyes. "What have you done to me?"

He pulled her against his chest. "Some things are meant to happen," he said. "They cannot be controlled any more than the wind can be commanded not to blow."

She drew back, looking at him. "But I had no idea when I came here this morning that we would...that any of this would happen." She lay back, her head on his upper arm. "I'm so confused. I came here today to ask you questions, to try to find answers."

"And did you not succeed?" His voice sounded faintly amused.

"What do you mean?"

"Doesn't the passion that we shared answer your questions about me? About us?"

"No," she said, shaking her head. "I feel more bewildered than ever. I can't believe what just happened between us."

He grasped her chin and turned her head toward him. "You must not feel regret, *querida*," he said. "We have no time for regret." He kissed her, gently at first, then with rising passion.

Lee felt her body respond to his caresses. "You must be a *brujo*," she whispered, "to be able to do this again—so soon."

"I am a man who has waited for a long time," he said. "A very long time."

I can't believe this is happening...can't believe how

much I want it to happen, she thought, as they began making love again.

* * *

They lay exhausted in each other's arms. After a few moments, Juan pulled away and rose to his hands and knees, reaching for a blanket that was rolled against the wall. He shook it open and lay back down, drawing it over their sweaty bodies.

"Juan?" Lee turned her head toward him. His profile was sharply outlined in the light of the single candle still burning on the table by the sofa. His spider-shaped birthmark seemed to cling to the hollow of his cheek. An image of deer antlers above another shadowed face flashed in her mind, and she closed her eyes. When she opened them a few seconds later, he was studying her.

"Talk to me," she said. "Tell me about yourself. Are you married?" She shook her head in amazement. "This is so unreal. We've made love twice this morning, and I don't even know if you're married."

"I have no wife." He was silent for a moment and when he spoke again, his voice was husky. "This lifetime has been a solitary one for me." He turned toward her and brushed her hair back from her forehead. "Sometimes it is necessary to be lonely. There is an old Spanish saying, '*Lo que no sé puede remediar, hay que aguantar*' it means 'What cannot be remedied must be endured'."

"Where do you live? You don't live in this building, do you?"

"No. This is just where I work. My home is not far from here, on the other side of the village." He pulled the blanket up over her shoulders. "I live in a *hacienda* built by my grandfather, Don Antonio Mascareñas. It has been added onto from time to time over the years. Now it is quite large."

"And you live there all alone?"

A shadow seemed to pass across his face. "My mother lived there, too, until she passed from the flesh many years ago."

"You have no other family? No brothers or sisters?"

"I was an only child. My father died before I was born. But enough about me." He raised himself on one elbow, looking down at her. "Tell me about yourself. Do you come from a large family?"

Lee shook her head. "I have an older sister. And a few relatives in Arizona. But I've been out of touch with them since my parents died."

"You will be reunited with your parents someday. In a new relationship, a new lifetime."

"Do you really believe that?"

"I know it to be true. And soon you will, too." He abruptly changed the subject. "Your sister, are you close to her?"

"Not really. She moved to Boston when I was still in high school. We've never really had a chance to know each other as adults."

"So you have only your husband and a daughter." He smiled slowly, then bent to kiss her neck, brushing his lips down and across her collar bone.

Lee was struck by the strange, thoughtful tone in his voice. "Tell me about your work," she said. "What exactly does a *curandero* do?"

"People come to me to be helped, to be healed. I do what must be done for them." He gently ran a finger up and down the side of her neck. "I accept no money for what I do. When money is exchanged, it weakens the medicine."

"Do they call here for an appointment?" She realized that she hadn't noticed a telephone in either of the small dark rooms.

"Not here. I allow no electronic interruptions while I am working. The number you have is for my telephone at home."

"What kind of illnesses do you treat?"

"Colds, aches and pains. Sometimes the *mal de ojo*."

"*Mal de ojo*? Evil eye?" She watched him closely.

"That's right," he said.

"Are you talking about removing some kind of

116

spell?"

"You might call it a spell. It is a sickness certain people can cause by their jealousy."

"How did you learn these things?"

"From my mother. She was an exceptional woman. A woman of great power." He saw her shiver. "I'm going to get you another blanket," he said, getting up. "You must not catch a cold." Then he smiled down at her. "Of course, if you do, I will be happy to treat you."

She managed a small smile in return, and watched Juan walk naked into the tiny back room where she had used the portable toilet during her previous visit. He came back, carrying a soft woolen blanket that he draped carefully around her shoulders. "Would you like some tea?" he asked.

"No! No tea." She looked away.

He laughed. "Oh, yes, I forgot. You think I put something in your tea when you were here last week. You think I drugged you. Lee," he said, kneeling beside her. "My beautiful Lee. You must trust me." He caressed her cheek. "I would never hurt you."

She stared at him. Was that the truth? What kind of man was he, really? She searched his face for answers.

"How about a beer instead?" he asked. "I have some in the refrigerator. I'll be right back."

Lee recalled seeing a small refrigerator in the back room. So, she thought, medicine men drink beer.

When he returned, they sat quietly, drinking from frosty bottles. "This is delicious," she said. "I haven't had a beer in years."

"No?"

"I usually drink white wine. Beer's too fattening."

"You worry about that? That you will be fat?" He looked amused. "You are *muy flaca*, my love. Very skinny."

"I guess I can thank my metabolism for that," she said, taking a sip. "I've always been slender."

"No, not always," he said, watching her.

"What do you mean?"

117

"When we were together before, long ago, you were not skinny," he said in a soft, matter-of-fact voice. "Your body was much fuller then."

She lowered her beer, staring at him.

"Have you begun to remember? Are the memories coming back?" He moved closer to her, putting his arm around her shoulders.

Lee's stomach twisted into a hard knot, threatening to bring up her last swallow of beer. She had a sudden bitter taste in her mouth. "Juan," she said, "you scare the hell out of me."

She lay back in his arms and described what had happened late Saturday night as she meditated. When she finished, she turned to look at him. "I tried to convince myself that it was just a dream, that I had fallen asleep." She watched him shake his head. "You don't think so, though, do you?" she asked.

Juan was silent for a moment. When he spoke, his voice trembled slightly. "You were beautiful then as you are now," he said. "But you had a different kind of beauty. Your name...it meant She Who Talks to Animals. You were very gifted, a most powerful medicine woman."

"I was an Indian?"

"We were both Indians, living on a mesa beneath what we now call the Jémez Mountains."

"You mean Los Alamos?" She sat up and turned to stare at him.

"Near there. Even the ruins are gone now. It was very long ago." He caressed her partially exposed shoulder. "But I have said enough. It is better that you remember for yourself."

She pulled away from him. "That's it? That's all you're going to tell me?"

"*Descansa*, Lee. Just relax."

"Relax? How can I relax?" She pulled away from him, her voice rising. "This is too damned creepy. I mean, I can't even believe I came back here. Much less that I've been screwing my brains out with someone I hardly know—"

"Is that what you think? That I am someone you hardly know? You try my patience, woman! Stop hiding from yourself."

Lee yanked the blanket up, trying to cover her naked shoulders. Her mind raced. *This is insanity! I've got to get out of here.* She tried to get to her feet, but her legs were tangled in the blanket, and her vision was blurred by sudden tears.

The weight of Juan's hand on her shoulder stopped her struggle. "*Lo siento*," he said. "I'm sorry. I spoke too harshly. Sit back down, please."

Engulfed by shame and confusion, Lee wept, hiding her face in the blanket. She felt herself drawn once more into Juan's strong embrace.

"Trust me, *querida*," he whispered in her ear. "Let me take your unhappiness from you. This is not a time for tears. It's a time for rejoicing. We are together again. And you are growing stronger, more in touch with who you really are."

He placed a hand on each side of her face and looked into her eyes. "Your sweat blanket was heavy with the demons of self-doubt and fear. They clung to the blanket as I shook it. But when the ceremony was complete, I felt your strength began to grow." He paused. "It will soon be time for the final ceremony— time for me to take you through the door."

"No. I told you, I don't want to do that. I'm afraid—"

"You will not be afraid when the time comes. But do not let that concern you now. There is no rush."

"I mean it, Juan. I'm not—"

He bent to kiss her shoulder. "We have time. And I have much to teach you."

"Teach me?"

"I will help you to get back in touch with the earth, to regain the hidden wisdom that you have forgotten. You will remember how the plants feel and how to communicate with animals." Juan's eyes glistened with a strange passion. "I will teach you to talk to the birds again. I will return your medicine power to you. Together, we will be as we were before."

"What do you mean? I don't understand."

"I will take you to my mother's people in the mountains of northwestern Mexico. I lived with them for two years after I left the University of New Mexico. They have powers that will amaze you, powers they will impart to you."

Something cold fluttered in Lee's stomach. "Mexico? Your mother came from Mexico? I thought your family had lived in Cavado for generations."

"My mother was a Yaqui Indian. My father met her on a trip to Chihuahua."

"That explains your connections to Native American traditions."

"My knowledge comes from all my people, both Hispanic and Indian," Juan continued. "But you will soon understand this. This and much more. I will make special ceremonial skins for you before we leave."

"Leave?" The impact of what he was saying struck her. "Wait a minute. What are you talking about? I can't go to Mexico with you. That's impossible. I have a family, a husband and a daughter. Not to mention the magazine..." Her voice trailed off as she stared at his frozen face.

"Listen to me," he said in an sharp voice. "Our souls were bound together long ago. We made a sacred pledge. You belong with me!" His tone softened. "But never mind. You will come to understand that."

Lee felt as though she couldn't breathe. She had to escape. Where were her clothes? "I have to go now," she said. "I...I have an appointment in Santa Fe. I can't be late."

Juan's face was expressionless. "If you must go, I will get your things," he said, helping her to her feet. "Most of them are in the front room."

Lee dressed quickly, managing to button only a few of the buttons on the back of her blouse. "Good-bye," she murmured, moving past him to the door.

He caught her arm. "You will return soon, *mi vida*," he said. He held her face in both his hands, forcing her to look at him. "And I will be waiting." Then, pulling her against his naked body, he kissed her cold lips.

She broke away, grabbed her sweater and purse and opened the door, shading her eyes from the glare of bright noon as she ran to her car. In seconds she was safely inside, speeding down the dusty road, away from Cavado.

Chapter 12

Lee drove back to Santa Fe in a state of shock. She still found it hard to believe what had happened. The passion she had experienced in Juan's arms had been overpowering. She wouldn't have believed it possible to be swept away like that. It had almost felt as though her body belonged to someone else.

At last she was home. She parked the car in the garage and glanced at the clock on the dashboard. One-thirty. The drive had taken an hour. She had spent three hours with Juan. Three incredible hours.

Lee went up the stairs to her bedroom. She kicked off her shoes and collapsed, fully clothed, on the bed. Pulling the comforter up over her shoulders, she closed her eyes. Images of Juan's face and of his naked body circled through her mind as she sank gratefully into dark oblivion.

* * *

She was hurrying uphill, following a narrow path worn deeply into cream-colored sandstone and etched into the side of the mesa thrusting high above. It wasn't much farther. She was almost home. A thin trail of white smoke rose into the air from a cooking fire above.

She paused on the edge of a flat stone ledge and adjusted the shoulder strap of her back sling. It had been a successful day, producing a good harvest of roots, herbs and berries. As she gazed across the rocky canyon stretching far below, a gust of wind blew long black hair across her face. She brushed it out of her eyes and inhaled the good rain smell. It was coming. The long dry season was ending. It would be a powerful storm.

The sky darkened as massive purple thunderheads obscured the sun. There was no time to waste. She felt the first drops of rain strike her bare arms as she scrambled up the path, using familiar toe and finger holds worn into the rock. Carefully balancing her weight, she reached for the thick exposed root that ran across a rock overhead. Then she wedged her yucca sandal into a small space between two tall boulders and pulled herself up.

With a loud snap, the root broke in her hand. She gasped, digging her fingernails into the hard sandstone surface, frantically searching for a hold. For a long moment she clung to smooth bare rock. Then, with her fingers sliding and scratching, she began to fall backward. She screamed as she felt her right ankle twist and snap. Sharp pain flooded her senses, followed by a bright red flash as she smashed against the ground.

She lay still, unable to open her eyes, but aware of throbbing pain in her ankle and head. From far away came a ringing sound. She allowed herself to drift once more into a cloud of darkness. But gradually a cold, wet sensation nagged her to awareness. Rain. It was raining hard. Pain stabbed her scalp as she jerked her head to one side. Her hair was caught on something. Squinting through wet eyelashes, she stared at sharp branches close to her face. She was cold. Somehow she must get to her feet and continue the journey up the trail. Warmth and safety waited above.

BRUJO

A crow landed within inches of her face, flapping its ebony wings against the rain. "Bright Eyes," she whispered, "help me." She focused through her pain and reached into the bird's mind. Go at once, she ordered. Fly to your master. Tell Kamulko that I am injured. Make haste, Bright Eyes, make haste. The crow's yellow eyes locked on hers. Then it flew toward the village on the mesa above.

She lifted her arm to shield her eyes from the rain. The irritating ringing sound was growing louder. She frowned, trying to identify it. The high-pitched call came from no creature that she could identify. But it seemed to be coming from nearby, growing louder. She cried out as she tried to move her ankle. Thick blackness engulfed her, blotting out the pain and the wetness. She felt herself leaving her body, slowly floating upward. Ring...ring...ring.

* * *

Lee sat up, gasping, her head pounding, and stared at the phone. She ran her hand through her short hair and frowned. My hair. What happened to my long, black hair? She shook her head. It had seemed... "Oh God," she whispered to the empty room. "What's happening? Am I going crazy?" Another ring. She lifted the receiver.

"Lee? Is that you?"

"What? I...Yes?"

"Hi, it's Socorro. Are you all right?"

"I...I don't know. I was asleep. Dreaming, I guess. I heard the phone, but I couldn't seem to wake up." Lee reached under the covers to rub a dull ache in her right ankle.

"Oh, I'm sorry. Shall I call back later?"

"No. It's okay." She glanced at the bedside clock and saw that it was almost three o'clock. Sara would be home from school soon. She threw the covers back and stared at her ankle as she rotated her foot in a slow circle.

"You sound strange," Socorro said. "And I'm getting

124

some bad vibrations. Are you sure you're all right?"

"I'm just a little groggy." She stretched her leg out straight and took a deep breath. There, her ankle seemed all right now. The throbbing was gone. It must have been some sort of cramp.

"Well, if you're sure," Socorro said in a concerned voice. "Listen, I need to talk to you. As soon as possible. I have some information about Juan Mascareñas."

Lee hesitated. She wasn't sure she wanted to hear what Socorro had to report.

"It's important," Socorro said urgently.

The tone of Socorro's voice caused Lee's stomach to lurch. "I'm going to be home in the morning," she heard herself say. "Can you come by?"

"Is eight-thirty too early?"

"That'd be fine." By the time she'd given directions to her house, Lee was feeling queasy. There was a terrible pounding in her temples. "I've got to go. See you tomorrow." She hung up the phone and lay back on the pillow, her forearm over her eyes. She felt physically ill. Aching and bruised—as though her body actually had experienced a terrible fall.

* * *

She was still in bed with a cold washcloth across her forehead when Sara opened the front door. "Mom? I'm home," she called down the hall.

"In here, honey," Lee said. Her head and body still ached, but her nausea was gone. She tried not to think about her morning with Juan or Socorro's phone call, but images from her dream continued to dance through her head. Stark bluffs. The storm. And a crow with shining golden eyes. "Bright Eyes?" She shivered under the warm covers.

Sara burst into the room, carrying Mister. "Look who I found waiting outside the front door," she said. She stopped when she saw Lee. "You sick again, Mom?" she asked, her smile fading.

"Just a headache. How was school?"

"Okay. The usual grind. I lived through the algebra exam. Just barely." She dropped Mister onto the bed. "I think I passed it, though."

"Good for you," Lee dropped the damp washcloth to the floor beside the bed and sat up. She held out her arms to her daughter. "Come here, baby," she said. "I need a hug."

* * *

Lee awoke the next morning feeling groggy and depressed. But her aches and pains seemed to have disappeared. It was almost eight o'clock. Sara had left for school without waking her. She rolled over on her back, staring up at the ceiling. Oh my God, she thought as memories of the previous day returned. It really happened. Juan and I made love. No, not 'made love'. We had sex. Twice. She pulled the covers up under her chin.

The thought of Nick entered her mind for the first time in almost twenty-four hours. She caught her breath. I've cheated on my husband, she thought in amazement. After all these years of being a faithful wife. And with someone who may be a witch, for all I know. She buried her face in the pillow. What's the matter with me? I don't believe in witchcraft. Juan's a *curandero*, a healer. It's crazy to believe that he's anything else. After all, he healed that station guy's little sister. And that woman came to him with a stomach ache during the interview.

She rolled over and stared at the ceiling. It was time to get out of bed and pull herself together. Socorro would be arriving soon—Socorro, with her spirit guides and vortices of evil energy. I know she means well, Lee thought, and I can't help but like her. But, let's face it, the woman is a little nutty. "Meta-fizzled," as Nick would say. Lee frowned, wondering what urgent news Socorro was bringing. She certainly didn't want to talk about Juan to anyone just now. Not after yesterday morning in Cavado.

Almost against her will, Lee's thoughts returned to

Juan's lovemaking. It was incredible, unlike anything she'd ever experienced. Sex with Nick, infrequent as it was these days, was something she usually enjoyed. But the raw passion that she'd felt with Juan was a completely new emotion. And she wasn't sure that she even liked the man. She certainly didn't trust him. But when he touched her—dear God, the way he made her feel! She closed her eyes, remembering.

He was strong and demanding, yet gentle with her. It was as though he had read her mind and knew her sexual fantasies. Her hand slipped under her nightgown, and she began to caress herself. The memory of those secret hours with Juan left her aching with desire. She clenched her hand into a fist as guilt washed over her. Nick would never believe this. His wife fucking some backwoods *brujo* simply would not compute. And he'd be right. She could hardly believe it herself.

She sat up and noticed Mister w. ;hing her thoughtfully from the foot of the bed. "Oh, Mister," she said to the cat. "You're worried about me, aren't you? Well, that makes two of us. Poor kitty, I'll bet Sara didn't feed you before she left. Come on," she said, swinging her legs out of bed. "Let's go rustle up some tea and cat food."

* * *

Wearing a fringed leather shirt and masses of silver Indian jewelry, Socorro rang the doorbell promptly at eight-thirty. She was a knockout, Lee had to admit, even at that early hour. Her black jeans were tucked into tall snakeskin cowboy boots, and her hair hung in a thick dark braid over one shoulder. She was carrying a small drum and a large canvas tote bag.

"Hi. Come in," Lee said, trying to sound more cheerful than she felt. She looked at the drum and tote bag. "What's all this?"

"I'll explain in a few minutes," Socorro said, stepping into the foyer. "First things first."

"Let's sit in the kitchen," Lee suggested. "Can I get you something to drink? Coffee? Orange juice?"

"Juice would be great."

Socorro sat at the kitchen table, watching Lee pour the juice. "You're not doing very well this morning, are you?" she asked.

Lee grimaced. "So much for my acting abilities. Is it that obvious?"

"It is to me. Your aura—or spirit body, as I prefer to call it—is muddy, almost grey."

"I'm just tired," Lee said, feeling uncomfortable under Socorro's searching gaze. "I had a hard time getting to sleep last night." She carried the glasses to the kitchen table and sat down.

Socorro raised an eyebrow. "Are you burning a candle in your bedroom, as I suggested?"

"No. Actually, I did try it...one night. But I'm afraid I'll fall asleep and burn the house down."

"Well, I think I have a remedy for that," Socorro said, reaching into her bag and handing Lee a small, gaily wrapped box.

"What's this?" Lee asked.

"Open it."

"A present? What's the occasion?"

"I don't need an occasion to give a gift to someone I like. It's just something I picked up for you at the Wicked Wick."

Lee unwrapped the box and looked inside. "A vase? It's beautiful."

"No, it's not a vase. It's a pottery candle."

Lee took the candle out of the box and put it on the table between them. It was dark blue, with a small white lizard painted on one side.

"Animals—all creature beings—are our teachers," Socorro explained, her fingernail tracing the reptilian tail that curved up the bowl of the candle. "We need only to pay attention and be willing to learn. My people honor the spirit of the lizard because she's a survivor. If she loses her tail escaping a foe, she wastes no time regretting it. She simply grows another one. We could all learn a lesson from the lizard."

She sipped her juice and smiled at the thoughtful expression on Lee's face. "The candle's easy to use. Just fill the base with lamp oil and pull the wick part-way up through the hole in that little ball so that you can light it. It'll burn for several days, until you need to replace the wick or refill it with oil. There are extra wicks in the box." She patted Lee's hand. "Now you don't need to worry about candle wax dripping while you sleep. And perhaps the spirit of the lizard will give you courage."

Lee's eyes filled with tears. "Oh, Socorro," she said in a choked voice, "thank you. I really do appreciate your concern."

"You're very welcome. I had it blessed by Dream Singer, a Cheyenne-Arapahoe medicine man. It should provide some protection."

"Protection?"

"Let's just say that you shouldn't sleep in total darkness for awhile." She paused. "I drove to the pueblo Monday morning and talked to my grandmother about Juan Mascareñas."

Lee felt her body tense.

"I'm afraid I was right about Juan being more than a *curandero*," Socorro continued. "He's the son of Sinopa Mascareñas, a powerful Mexican *bruja*. She's dead now, but the older people at the pueblo still cross themselves when they speak of her. They remember the old rumors."

"What rumors?"

"Well, there are those who believe that she killed her husband, Juan's father, when he discovered that she was practicing black magic and tried to put a stop to it. And there was another story about a Cavado woman who died mysteriously after accusing Sinopa of bewitching her husband. There were no formal charges in either case. The Mascareñas name and wealth protected her."

Lee sat frozen in her chair.

Socorro laid her hand on Lee's arm. "Now listen. *Brujeria*, or sorcery, is usually passed from one generation to another. It's almost certain that Sinopa passed her powers on to Juan before she died. I have to tell you that I'm worried. My spirit guides agree that you are in great danger. You must never," she paused for emphasis, "never go back to Cavado."

Lee took a deep breath. "This is all so hard to believe," she whispered.

Socorro's eyes filled with compassion. "I know it is," she said. "You've entered a world you don't understand. But please believe that Juan is not a man to be taken lightly. Chances are that he's up to no good."

"But why? What would he want from me?"

"I don't know the answer to that. I'm getting conflicting readings. At first I thought he might be a spirit-sucker. But now I'm not so sure."

"A what?" Lee almost laughed.

"I know," Socorro said with a slight smile. "It does sound obscene." Her eyes narrowed. "And believe me, it is. A spirit-sucker is a sorcerer—or *brujo*—with the ability to steal another person's spirit. The spirit-sucker then has control over that person."

"Are you serious?"

"Very serious. Victims have no choice but to do whatever the spirit-sucker wishes. They are *embrujáda,* bewitched. Only the death of the spirit-sucker can free them. And those who have encountered one will tell you that a spirit-sucker doesn't die easily."

"That sounds like something out of a horror story."

"Let me explain about magic," Socorro said, "and about different kinds of so-called 'witches'. Magic most certainly exists. Simply put, it's the ability to influence events through extraordinary means such as ceremony and focused will. It's been around for a long time. In fact, methods of moving into and utilizing a hidden reality are probably twenty or thirty thousand years old. But the concept is terribly misunderstood in the present-day Anglo culture.

"You see, the power of magic is in itself neither good nor evil. It's a neutral force, like electricity. We use electricity to enhance our lives. But it can be a deadly force if proper precautions aren't taken. You wouldn't condemn lightning as evil for striking someone standing under a tree in a rainstorm, would you? And it's the individual operating the electric chair that makes it an instrument for destruction, not the current itself. Like electricity, magic can be used for good or for evil, depending upon the intent of the person using it. And any form of magic which manipulates or harms another person is black magic—a misuse of the Power."

"You're talking about 'white' versus 'black' witch-craft?"

"That's right. Unfortunately, we've been conditioned to think of all 'witchcraft' as evil. In truth, the Power can be—and most often is—used to promote good. To bring about healing or good fortune. Ethical as well as unethical 'witches' have been part of all societies since prehistoric times. The ethical 'white witches' have been the healers, the midwives and the psychics."

"Psychics?"

"Sure. Psychics are just people who are born with an unusual sensitivity to what goes on in other people's minds, plus a talent for tapping into the Universal Intelligence. There are many people who would con-sider me a witch because of my psychic abilities. The point is that those practicing white magic are careful not to cause harm. In fact, most witches believe that whatever kind of magic they work will come back to them, if not in this lifetime, then in another. That belief prevents a lot of black magic."

"I'll bet."

"But there's a completely different magical tradi-tion," Socorro continued, "an ancient Indian tradition of the evil sorcerer—or spirit-sucker—that far predates the European 'witch' traditions brought to New Mexico by the Spaniards. I'm afraid a spirit-sucker isn't inhibited by fear of karmic reprisal. He doesn't hesitate to work magic for his own selfish ends."

"Okay, assuming that such a thing is possible, that

Juan is some sort of spirit-sucking *brujo*, how would he go about it?"

"That's one thing that's confusing me as far as Juan is concerned. *Brujos* usually use sex to steal a woman's spirit. But you said that Juan didn't try to have sex with you after your interview."

Lee shifted in her chair, unable to meet Socorro's eyes.

"So, I just don't know," Socorro continued, lost in her own thoughts. "And there are other inconsistencies. I can't seem to get a clear reading on Juan. My intuition tells me that his motives are complicated." She glanced at her watch. "Okay, it's time to get down to business. We have serious work to do. But first, drink that. You need to keep up your strength."

"What do you mean, we have work to do?" Lee forced herself to finish her juice.

Socorro began unloading the contents of her bag onto the kitchen table: an eagle feather, a beaded leather pouch, a cigar-shaped bundle of what looked like dried weeds, held together with a red string and resting in a large abalone shell, and, finally, four grapefruit-sized rocks painted with strange symbols.

She smiled at the puzzled look on Lee's face. "I'm very worried about you, my friend. You are, as the saying goes, in deep shit. I think I can help. Anyway, I'm going to give it my best shot. First, I'll draw a protective circle around this house. Enclose it, actually, within a medicine wheel. That will create a sacred space and provide some psychic protection."

"How? What exactly is a 'medicine wheel'?"

"As a circle, it's probably the most ancient and universal religious symbol on earth. Because it has neither beginning nor end, the circle has represented life and the Creative Force in many cultures for thousands of years. To Native Americans it is still a powerful protective and healing symbol. I'll place these rocks at proper points on the circle."

"What's painted on them?"

"Ancient symbols, representing the four cardinal directions. Briefly, the east is represented by this yellow morning star symbol, the south by the red sun symbol, and the west by the black half moon. The north is depicted by a white spiral, which symbolizes the continuing cycles of life and death."

"Socorro, do you believe in reincarnation?"

"Absolutely. It's the only thing that makes any sense to me. You can't graduate from college by taking just one class. Besides, my spirit guides warn me that I'm doomed to keep on doing it until I finally get it right." She stood up. "Now, let's get started. While I'm doing my thing outside, I want you to take a long shower."

"But I just took a shower. Look, my hair's still wet."

"Well, I'm asking you to take another one. And this time close your eyes and visualize the water as a healing spray of golden light. See it cleansing you, inside and out, from head to toe. Ask the light to go to all of those places within you that need healing—releasing emotional pain, anxiety and fear. Picture your entire body filling with that warm golden light. Hold that image, and stay in the shower until I come and get you out. Where's your bathroom?"

"Upstairs. But is this really necessary?"

"Humor me, dear. I won't be long."

Lee watched from the window as Socorro began walking around the outside of the house, drawing a circle with a sharp stick as she went. Her lips were moving as though in prayer.

Dear God, Lee thought, as she climbed the stairs to her bathroom. What's happened to my nice, sane life? Now I'm living inside a medicine wheel and showering in golden light. She stripped off her clothes and turned on the water.

* * *

After what seemed like a long time, Socorro was knocking on the shower door. "You can come out now," she shouted over the noise of the water.

Lee turned off the water and stepped from the shower stall, reaching for a towel.

"Wait, let me look at you," Socorro said, squinting her eyes and staring intently at Lee's naked body.

Flustered, Lee froze.

Socorro smiled and nodded. "That helped. Your spirit body looks much brighter."

"Well, that's nice," Lee retorted, grabbing the towel, "but my regular body is freezing." She turned her back and began drying off. "What exactly do you mean by my 'spirit body'?"

"It's really very simple. The spirit body is an energy field surrounding the physical body. It responds to thoughts and feelings, our own and those of others. And its color reflects the energy that is collected and stored there."

"You can actually see it?"

"Yes, I can. When I arrived this morning I could tell by the darkness and density of your spirit body that your energy was blocked. You were obviously exhausted and depressed. You're a little stronger now, but we still have work to do. We must restore your power by building your inner strength and stamina. Put on your robe and come back downstairs for a healing ritual."

"Oh, please, Socorro. I'm not up for another magical ceremony!"

"It won't take long. And I promise it won't resemble anything that Juan put you through. His ceremony depleted your power. I'm trying to restore it."

"I know you are. And I appreciate your efforts. I really do. It's just that this is all so strange to me." She sighed. "Okay. I'm at my wits' end. I'll try anything to feel better."

* * *

"This is called a smudge stick," Socorro explained, lighting the bundle of dried sage and cedar. "Bathing in smoke is an ancient means of purification." She removed a crystal from the leather pouch and passed it through the smoke several times. Then she moved slowly around Lee, fanning the smoke from her feet to the top of her head. Socorro asked Lee to do the same

134

for her, before extinguishing the smoldering bundle in the abalone shell.

After spreading two blankets on the brick floor, Socorro instructed Lee to lie on her back. "Get comfortable," she said, covering Lee with a third blanket. "Are you warm enough?"

Lee nodded. Although she trusted Socorro, she couldn't help feeling apprehensive.

"The crystal will open your third eye and increase your visionary powers," Socorro said, placing the cool stone on Lee's forehead. "While all natural objects are manifestations of divine energy, crystals have the ability to generate that energy and pass it on to us."

"Juan's amulet had crystal stones," Lee said. "Sort of a reddish crystal. He said it was found only in the mountains of northern Mexico."

"Did he say what it was?"

"No, just that it was rare. Why?"

"My grandmother has spoken about a powerful red-colored crystal, found near a sacred mountain to the south—in Mexico. According to legend, this crystal has miraculous healing powers. It was said to have been used by Aztec priests to heal injured warriors after battle." She shrugged. "Who knows if the crystals ever existed? It may just be a legend. Still, I'd like to get a look at Juan's amulet. Tell me more about it. You said it was shaped like wings. Do you remember anything else?"

"Well, the stones were shaped like eyes. They seemed to glow, to deepen in color, especially when the candlelight hit them a certain way. Between the stones was a spiral design."

"The symbol of the north!" Socorro exclaimed. "Remember I said that the spiral is an ancient symbol representing the cycles of life and death. Did Juan happen to say where he got this amulet?"

"From his mother."

"Sinopa's amulet." Socorro's voice was grim. "It all fits. We have our work cut out for us, my friend. Let's get started."

Socorro was silent for the next few moments as she brushed the eagle feather back and forth across Lee's head and body. Then she took off her boots and sat cross-legged on the floor. "Close your eyes," she instructed, "and try to relax." She began beating a soft one-two-three rhythm on her drum.

After several minutes, she began to speak, her voice calm and soothing over the hypnotic beat of the drum. "Lee, I want you to envision a ball of golden light above your head. Now pull that light through the top of your head in a straight line down to your feet. See the light filling each toe, moving through your feet and into your ankles. That's good. Now bring the light up both legs. Feel it warm your calves, your knees, and your thighs. Bring it on up, into your buttocks and your belly. Take your time. See the light filling your chest. Feel its warmth. Now the light is moving into both arms, into your hands and each finger. It's traveling up your neck and filling your head, warming and healing you. That's it. Get a clear image of the light filling you—warming, healing and strengthening every cell of your body. Concentrate on this image for awhile." The drumming continued—ONE-two-three, ONE-two-three, ONE-two-three.

"Now, expand the light, extending it in all directions, about twenty inches beyond your physical body. Recognize this light as a field of energy, as your spirit body. Notice its brilliance. Feel its power. It is filling and surrounding you, healing and protecting you. Be with your spirit body for a few moments. Extend it out a few more inches. Good. Pull it back to where it was. Make your spirit body expand and contract for awhile, until you have a clear sense of it." The drumming continued for some time, as Lee did her best to follow Socorro's instructions.

"Your spirit body also acts as a psychic shield, my friend," Socorro continued. "Keep it brilliant. Keep it strong. Allow no negativity or evil to penetrate or weaken it." The drumming stopped.

"How do you feel?" Lee felt the crystal being removed from her forehead. She opened her eyes and turned her head to meet Socorro's warm and steady gaze.

"Pretty wiped out. But better than I did before you came. Thank you."

Socorro rose to her feet in a swift, graceful movement and put on her boots. "I'm happy to do whatever I can to help you," she said, returning the crystal, feather, smudge stick and abalone shell to her tote bag. "I will work with you again in the days to come, until you learn to cleanse and guard your spirit body by yourself."

She helped Lee to her feet and gave her a hug. "I must run," she said. "I'm meeting Dream Singer for lunch."

"Why do I know that name? You said that he's a medicine man?"

"He's also a well-known potter. We carry his work in the gallery. Dream Singer is an incredible man, a great teacher. Not to mention that he's the youngest eighty-six-year-old I've ever known. If I wasn't happily married, I'd run away with him in a minute."

Lee walked her to the front door. "Socorro, before you go, what can you tell me about ravens? Doctor Mallory said that they're associated with black magic."

Socorro shook her head. "That's only part of the story. Ravens have, indeed, always been associated with magic, both black and white. Apollo had his raven messenger, as did Merlin and many of the early Celtic wizards. As I said earlier, animals—all animals—are our teachers. They are neither good nor evil. They are just who they are. Raven medicine is magical and very powerful. Properly used, it is a healing medicine. Certainly, it can be used for evil ends. Those who are called by Raven must use great caution to use the magic only for the greatest good. I don't think that is the case with Señor Mascareñas. Take care, Lee."

"I will. Thanks again, Socorro. I do feel a little

stronger."

Socorro smiled. "I'll talk to you soon. Guard your
light, my friend. And stay clear of the spirit-sucker."
She walked through the courtyard and climbed into her
Jeep. "Don't forget to burn your candle," she yelled
through the open window before driving away.

Lee stood in the doorway, Socorro's warning echoing
in her ears. "Spirit-sucker...stay clear of the spirit-
sucker." Too late, Socorro, she thought. I couldn't
bring myself to tell you that your warning comes too
late, that I spent yesterday morning in Cavado—screwing the spirit-sucker. And none of your rituals can undo
that. Fighting back tears, she closed and locked the
door.

* * *

"Can I interrupt for a minute?" Julie stuck her head
into Lee's office. "I need your signature on a few
things."

Lee looked up from a stack of correspondence. She
shoved it off to one side of her cluttered desk. "Sure.
Come on in."

"I know you usually pay these bills," Julie said,
handing her a stack of checks. "But it's getting late in
the month, and I noticed that they were still sitting in
your 'in' box. So, I went ahead—"

"Oh God," Lee groaned, glancing up at the calendar.
"You're right. Thanks. The last week has really gotten
away from me."

"Anything else I can help you with?" Julie asked,
eyeing the disorganized state of Lee's desk. "I know
you haven't been feeling well."

Lee suddenly found herself near tears. "As a matter
of fact, you can. Most of this mess is just correspondence. A few queries from writers. Would you go
through it, take care of what you can, and organize the
rest into separate piles for me? I...I can't seem to get
anything accomplished this afternoon."

"Are you okay? You seem so upset."

"I guess I'm not completely recovered from that bug

I caught last week." She grabbed her purse and headed for the door. "When Annabel comes in, tell her that I went home."

"Have you seen a doctor?"

"There's not much they can do for this sort of thing. For a virus, I mean."

"Well, it might not hurt—"

"Thanks, Julie. I'll see you in the morning." She hurried out to her car.

* * *

Lee undressed and put on a warm-up suit and running shoes. She had at least an hour before Sara got home from school, time for a long walk. Maybe that would help to dispel the confusion and restlessness she was feeling. It sure couldn't hurt.

She walked around her house, following the faint circle drawn in the sand and locating the four rocks marking the directions of the medicine wheel. She stood for a moment, wondering if Socorro's efforts really could in any way affect Juan. Shaking her head in disbelief, she took off down the road.

* * *

By the time she got home, almost an hour later, Lee felt somewhat calmer. Socorro's spirit-sucker business had to be nonsense. Somehow, she had to put it all out of her mind and never see Juan again. And she would certainly never tell anyone about yesterday. There was no need to. It all seemed unreal now, anyway, like a dream. She would try to think of it that way—as just a romantic fantasy. Nick need never know. He'd be home in two days, and things would get back to normal.

As she walked into her brightly decorated living room, Lee was assailed by thoughts of Juan's dark, cluttered rooms. Vivid images flashed through her mind. Antique tables covered with an assortment of skulls, feathers, bones. Indian ceremonial paraphernalia. The worn buffalo skin rug. Bird wings moving on the wall as she rocked in Juan's embrace.

She leaned against a wall as the images of Juan grew

stronger—almost as though he were there in the room with her. She closed her eyes, feeling his arms around her and the smooth muscled texture of his naked back. Smelling the warm musky odor of his skin. Her eyes flew open and a nameless emotion, part fear, part sexual excitement, pricked her scalp. She felt her upper body flush and a warmth spread down her thighs.

"No!" she said aloud in a choked voice. "I can't let myself think about Juan. I have to get him out of my head and keep him out!"

Lee made a spur-of-the-moment decision to take Sara out for dinner and almost ran up the stairs. I'll visualize the golden light again, she thought, preparing to take her third shower of the day. If this keeps up, Nick will be complaining about the water bill.

Chapter 13

"*I* just love it here," Sara said, looking around the cozy, candle-lit room. "The Pink Adobe is my favorite restaurant in the world."

"I like it too," Lee said. She was determined to overcome her anxiety and spend some quality time with Sara. "And I'm glad we could get our usual table by the fireplace."

"That's right! We sat here, you and Dad and me, at my birthday dinner. I can't believe that's already been—let's see—almost three months ago! Wow, I've been fifteen for three months! Time really flies when you get older, doesn't it?"

Lee smiled. Sara looked so beautiful. And so grown up, Lee realized with a start. Sara really did look like a young woman tonight. There was just a trace of the child she had been only yesterday. Soon she would be gone, leading a life of her own. Oh God, Lee thought, what would life be like without Sara? How would she bear the lonely evenings when Nick was away on one of his trips?

Sara frowned at her across the table. "What is it?

You look like you're about to cry."

"It's nothing, baby," Lee said in an unsteady voice. "I was just realizing how much I'll miss you when you go away to college."

"Oh, Mom, that won't be for eons. I'm just a sophomore." She opened the menu. "Now, let's see. What looks the yummiest? Maybe the chicken enchiladas? Or...hey! How about shrimp Creole!"

* * *

Lee and Sara returned from dinner at eight-thirty. Lee felt better, considerably more relaxed. She realized what a comfort and anchor Sara was in her life.

"Thanks, Mom, that was great," Sara said, hanging her coat in the hall closet. "I'm stuffed. I probably gained five pounds."

"Me, too. I'd better walk an extra mile in the morning to undo the damage. Speaking of food, Mister hasn't had his dinner." Lee opened the front door and called, "Kitty, kitty," into the darkness.

When the cat didn't come running, she went to the back of the house and opened the sliding glass door that led to the redwood deck. "Mister? Kitty, kitty, kitty?"

She came back into the family room, frowning. "Sara, have you seen Mister? I can't find him."

"He's probably terrorizing mice in the arroyo." Sara kept her eyes on the television set. "Don't worry. He'll be crying at the door any minute. That cat never misses his dinner."

But Mister didn't respond to repeated calls as the hours passed. By bedtime, Lee felt heavy with apprehension. Sara joined her on the bedroom balcony. "This just isn't like him," Lee said. "He always comes home before bedtime."

"He'll be here in the morning," Sara said. "He's just out cattin' around somewhere."

"I hope you're right. But I worry about coyotes coming down from the hills after dark. They were really howling out there a few nights ago. And Mister's too fat to run very fast."

"I'm sure he's okay," Sara said, suddenly not sounding so sure. "Get some sleep, Mom."

Lee locked the door and reluctantly went to bed. She knew she had to get some rest. The emotional exhaustion she felt was taking its toll. After a few minutes of deep breathing exercises learned in yoga class, she fell into a restless sleep.

The next thing she knew, Sara was shaking her shoulder. "Mom! Mom, wake up! You're having a nightmare. Jeez, you scared me to death."

"What?" Lee looked around the dark room, trying to get her bearings. Her nightgown and hair were damp with perspiration.

"You were screaming. Are you okay? Are you awake now?"

"What time is it?" Lee fumbled for the switch on the bedside lamp.

"Twelve-fifteen," Sara said, looking at the numbers on the digital clock-radio. "That must have been some nightmare. I almost had a heart attack. I thought you were being murdered."

"Oh, honey, I'm sorry I woke you." Lee held her head with both hands. "My head is killing me. Would you get me a couple of aspirins?"

"I've never even heard you talk in your sleep before, much less scream. What were you dreaming about?" Sara asked, returning with the pills and a glass of water.

"Mister. Would you see if he's on the balcony?"

Sara turned on the balcony light and unlocked the sliding door. "Mister? Here, kitty, kitty."

Lee lay back on her pillow and closed her eyes. Then she smelled it. The sweating oil! She jumped out of bed, her heart pounding.

"Mister's not out there," Sara said. " But I'm sure he'll be back in the morning. What's the matter, Mom? Why are you looking like that?"

"Do you smell it?"

"What?"

"That strange odor. Can't you smell it?"

"I don't smell anything." Sara stared at her mother, a worried expression on her face.

Lee sat on the edge of the bed. "I don't smell it now, either. It must have been my imagination—probably triggered by the dream."

"Boy, that must have been some freaky dream."

"It was terrible. A huge black bird was attacking Mister. Then I became Mister. It caught him—or me—down in the arroyo. Only I was Mister." She shuddered. "It sounds crazy, I know. But it was so real." She managed a small apologetic smile. "But it was just a dream, a silly dream. Go back to sleep. I'm okay now."

"Well, if you're sure." Sara stood beside the bed, looking down at her mother, a slight frown on her face. "I think you've been working too hard, Mom. You've been really stressed lately."

"I'm fine, really," Lee said, reaching to squeeze Sara's hand. "Go back to bed."

Lee lay awake in the darkness. There wasn't any odor, she told herself. Sara didn't smell it. It was just my imagination working over-time. She closed her eyes, trying to shut off her thoughts. But the nightmare remained with her. The pain of talons ripping into her back—and the terrible sound of Mister's screams.

* * *

Mister didn't come home for breakfast. Lee walked around the outside of the house several times calling his name. She reluctantly left for work at eight-fifteen, realizing that she was already late for the weekly staff meeting.

At noon, she broke a lunch date to go home. Surely Mister would be there by now. He was probably sitting on the courtyard wall, waiting to be let into the house.

"Here, kitty, kitty," she called around the front of the house. She sat on a redwood bench in the courtyard, blinded by a rush of tears. "Oh, Mister," she whispered, "please come home." After a few moments she stood up. I've got to get a grip on myself and stop overreacting, she thought. Mister will come back. He probably just wandered too far and got lost. He was wearing his collar with our phone number on it. Surely someone will find him and give me a call. She went back into the house to grab a banana for lunch, before returning to the office.

* * *

There was still no sign of the cat when she got home late that afternoon. Heartsick, Lee climbed the stairs to her bedroom. She unlocked the sliding glass door and walked onto the balcony. "Mister, Mister," she called, her eyes searching the peaceful landscape. Santa Fe sparkled in the distance, bathed in warm October sunshine. "Oh, poor kitty," she whispered. "Where are you?" She grabbed her jacket and left the house, walking through the neighborhood and pausing frequently to call Mister's name.

* * *

She was in bed trying to concentrate on a book when the phone rang at nine-thirty that night. After a few minutes, Sara called down the hall, "Mom, it's Dad."

She braced herself and picked up the phone. "Hi," she said in what she hoped was a normal tone of voice.

"Hi, babe. How are you?"

"I'm okay. In bed reading. How's the experiment going?"

"So far, so good." His voice sounded tired. "Everything went off on schedule early Tuesday morning. I think we got some good data. We have another rocket launch scheduled for Monday."

"I'll keep my fingers crossed for you." She felt a pang of guilt as she realized how seldom Nick had entered into her thoughts during the week he had been gone.

"I meant to call last night, but I was going over the data and lost track of time. Then it was too late. I forgot about the four-hour time difference."

"That's okay, I knew you were busy."

"You sound depressed." He paused. "Sara told me

145

about Mister."

"I've looked everywhere for him. I'm afraid he's gone. I guess a coyote...or something...got him."

"That's too bad. I know how crazy you've always been about that cat."

"Yeah." Lee sighed into the receiver.

"Well, it was bound to happen one of these days. After all, Mister was getting old."

Lee felt a flash of annoyance. "That doesn't make it any easier," she snapped.

"No, I guess not." Another pause. "How are things at work?"

"Fine, everything is fine," she said, eager to hang up.

"Well, have a good weekend. I'll call the first part of next week."

"Okay." She took a deep breath and tried to soften the edge in her voice. "Don't work too hard."

She hung up and lay back on the pillows, trying not to cry. God, she dreaded Nick's return. She didn't know how she was going to face him.

Her feelings about Juan and what happened between them were a mystery to her, a jumbled mass of contradictions. One minute she felt normal, determined to put it all behind her. The next minute she was overwhelmed with feelings of desire, followed by shame and a deep, pervasive fear. She sat up, rubbing her temples. I don't know how I feel about anything, she thought. I can't seem to think straight anymore. I'm afraid Socorro's healing ceremony didn't take. She pressed her fingertips against the tight muscles along the back of her neck. I'm just wiped out. And Mister...Oh God, I can't bear to think about Mister. She buried her face in her pillow and cried.

* * *

Lee woke up before the alarm went off, put on her robe and slippers and went outside, calling Mister's name over the courtyard wall. After a few minutes, she was joined by Sara. "Still no sign of him?"

"No."

"I'm really sorry, Mom."

"Me too, baby." She put her arms around Sara. "How'd you sleep?"

"Fine. I got up early to do my hair a new way. I saw it in a magazine. You braid the back into three braids, then wind them around in a big loop."

Lee hugged her daughter close. "Sounds pretty exotic."

"I hope so. Maybe it'll make me look older. I'm sick of looking like a child. Gotta hurry." She squirmed out of Lee's embrace and dashed back into the house.

Lee made a complete circle around the house, calling Mister's name, before giving up and dressing for work.

* * *

"Look, kiddo," Annabel said, settling her plump frame into the chair in front of Lee's desk. "We have to talk. I'm worried about you and so is Julie. She said you were weepy when you left here yesterday. What's going on?"

Lee sighed. "My energy level is still low from that bug I caught last week. I'll be fine."

"Come on, partner. Don't pull that 'fine' crap with me. I know you pretty well, having worked with you five days a week for the past ten years. There's more going on with you than a virus." She studied Lee for a minute. "Is it Nick?"

"No. Nick and I are fine." She grimaced. "There's that word again. Nick and I are okay, the same as always. I'm just going through a little rough spot."

"Emotionally, you mean."

"It'll pass."

"Look, it would be understandable if you were suffering from some sort of burn out. You've worked your ass off here for years. And you almost never take a vacation."

"I took one last spring."

"Tagging along with Nick to some physicists' convention in San Diego doesn't count. You said yourself you never had a minute alone with him. Why don't you two take some real time off and just relax together? Not to hurt your feelings, but we could manage without you. Just barely, of course."

"To tell you the truth, I really don't want to spend time alone with Nick right now. I'm in such a funk I wouldn't be good company."

"Do you remember what a mess I was two summers ago? Snarling at everyone, crying at the drop of a hat, even threatening to divorce poor Milt. It felt like I was on an emotional roller coaster. And then there were the physical symptoms: hot flashes, night sweats, migraines. Also, I was absent-minded as hell. Couldn't seem to focus on anything."

Lee laughed. "Is this your subtle way of suggesting that I might be menopausal? I hate to remind you of this, but I'm nine years younger than you are."

"Some women go through the change at forty. Liz Eaton was just thirty-eight. I heard that she—"

"Annie, for heaven's sake! I had some kind of flu. It knocked me for a loop. And then Mister disappeared. Look, I appreciate your concern. If I don't feel better soon, I will take a few days off."

"Are you sure everything is okay between you and Nick? You never complain about it, but with all his traveling, it must get lonely—"

"You would have made a great therapist. But I already have a therapist. Stop worrying. My marriage is fine. My hormones are fine. Really. Now, get out of here. I have to interview that Arizona artist on the phone this morning, the one that shows at Wild West Gallery. The writer assigned to that story broke up with her boyfriend and left town. There's no time to reassign it, so I'll just write it myself."

"All right! Now you're sounding like your usual take-charge self." Annabel heaved herself out of the chair. "I'd better edit the two pieces that came in yesterday. Thank heavens this is Friday. I'm ready for the weekend. See you later." She left the office, closing the door behind her.

Lee shook her head. Annabel was a well-meaning person and a good friend. If only she didn't have such a big mouth. There was no way Lee could confide in her. It would be like putting an announcement in the newspaper.

She pulled out a notepad, intending to get the telephone interview over with. Reaching for the phone, she changed her mind. The interview could wait. First, she'd call a few of her neighbors. Maybe one of them had seen Mister.

* * *

"I'd appreciate it if you'd keep an eye out for him. No, he's never done this before. I know. Yes, I called the Blumbergs a minute ago. Well, thank you. I hope so, too. Good-bye."

Lee hung up the phone, feeling more depressed than ever. Just because no one had seen Mister didn't mean that he wasn't nearby, injured or...worse. After all, the houses in her neighborhood were situated on at least one-acre lots.

Fortifying herself with another cup of coffee, Lee called the artist in Tucson. Thirty minutes later she felt confident that she had enough information on the artist's background and work to write a respectable article. But the words wouldn't come.

Two hours later she was still struggling with the lead paragraph. Rereading what she had written, she groaned. "To hell with it!" she said, switching off the computer. Then she surprised herself by bursting into tears.

* * *

The next day was a Saturday. When the phone rang a little before noon, Lee was still moping around the house in her bathrobe. She'd been awake since early morning, unable to shake the depression that gripped her. Sara was spending the weekend with a girlfriend, and the house seemed unbearably empty. She sighed and picked up the receiver.

"Lee? Hi, it's me. Socorro."

"Oh, hi."

"I had hoped to hear you sounding better than that. What's going on?"

"I'm just down. Things haven't been going so well."

"Has Juan been harassing you?"

"I haven't heard from him."

"Then what's wrong?"

"My cat is missing. He's been gone since Wednesday night. Oh, Socorro, I'm just heartbroken. He was such a companion to me."

"Has he ever been gone this long before?"

"Never. Mister goes outside, but he always stays close to the house."

"Well, maybe he felt overdue for an adventure." Socorro's voice was thoughtful. "Cats sometimes need to just take off by themselves. Although they might live with us, animals have secret lives. They are a separate nation."

"I suppose so. But this is unlike Mister. I just know that something has happened to him."

"Are you sleeping?"

"Not well. I've been having really bad dreams. In fact, the night Mister disappeared I dreamed he was killed by a giant raven. And when I awoke I smelled Juan's sweating oil. Or at least I thought I did. Sara didn't smell it, so it must have been my imagination."

"Lee, I don't like the sound of this. Your defenses are being beaten down. You must get some rest so you aren't so vulnerable."

"I took a sleeping pill last night."

"That's the worst thing you can do. Drugs put a barrier between you and your Higher Self. They block your intuition, your inner knowing. Right now, you need all the spiritual and emotional support you can get."

"I sure need something. I'm in such a funk I can't even work. That's never happened to me before."

"You're grieving for your cat. Give yourself permission to do that. But stay connected to your center.

Meditate. Spend quiet time outdoors."

"Okay. Thanks, Socorro."

"Is your husband still gone?"

"Yes, for another week."

"Well, speaking of husbands, mine is waiting to take me to the Coyote Cafe. Howard and I always have a lunch date on Saturdays."

"That's nice," Lee said, feeling a twinge of envy. "Have a good time."

"We always do. I'll talk to you soon. Meanwhile, I'll send you energy—a big, golden wave of it. And I'll send good thoughts to Mister."

Lee smiled. "Thanks. Good-bye." She hung up the phone, feeling somewhat better. Socorro always had that effect on her.

* * *

Early the next morning, Lee took another walk. Socorro might be off the wall about some things, but she was certainly right about spending time outdoors. She was right about sleeping pills, too. Although Lee had awakened several times last night, she didn't feel drugged this morning. Her tight leg muscles complained as she left the dirt road and began jogging up a slight hill that marked the end of her property line.

Sometime later, after climbing out of the deep arroyo that ran behind her house, Lee paused to get her bearings. Suddenly a strip of red caught her eye—just ahead, dangling from a lower limb of a juniper. She rushed forward, knowing even before she picked it up that it was Mister's collar. The brass tag with his name and phone number dangled from the strip of red leather in her hand. "Oh, no," she cried aloud. "Mister, what happened to you?"

Images from her dream flooded her mind. Running. Gasping for breath. Heart pounding, a dull ache in her chest. Sharp, twisting pain as talons sunk into her back...into Mister's back...her back. Stop it! she ordered herself as she clutched the collar. Mister's collar came off. Somehow. That doesn't mean.... Unable to finish

151

the thought, she ran the rest of the way home.

The phone was ringing when she let herself in the front door. Lee hurried into the kitchen and picked up the receiver. "Hello?"

"I'm glad I caught you. I was about to hang up."

"Hi, Socorro. I was out walking."

"Did your cat come back?"

"No." She paused, swallowing back tears. "But I just found his collar."

"His collar? Where?"

"In the arroyo behind the house."

"Does it look like it was torn off?"

"No, just unbuckled. Oh, Socorro, I'm so upset. I keep remembering the dream I had about the raven catching him. It was as if I were Mister. I could feel his pain and terror..." Her voice broke.

"Listen to me, Lee." Socorro's voice was firm. "You mustn't allow your psychic shield to be so weak. Especially now. If Mister can, if he's still on the earth plane, he will return to you. In the meantime, you must focus your energies on strengthening yourself."

"I feel too depressed to focus on anything. And the thought of Mister lost or injured—"

"What have you eaten today?" Socorro interrupted.

"A piece of toast. Early this morning."

"Good. Don't eat anything else. But drink lots of fluids, water and juice. Herbal tea is fine. I'll pick you up about six o'clock tonight. Wear a warm jacket and hiking shoes."

"Why? What are you talking about?"

"Dream Singer is conducting an *inipi* in the mountains tonight. I want you to come with me. It's a powerful cleansing ceremony, more healing than any I could conduct. I think it's just what you need."

"Oh, no. Absolutely not. Please, no more ceremonies."

"Your spirit is under attack, Lee. You have a real fight on your hands, and you need help. Will you allow me to help you?"

"Oh, God." Lee's voice was little more than a whimper.

"Good. Now, you will need to prepare yourself. Rest this afternoon. Visualize and strengthen your psychic shield. Take a long shower about five-thirty. Dress warmly. Oh, one more thing, you'll need to bring something for your Give-Away."

"My 'Give-Away'?"

"It's an integral part of Native American ceremony. Before asking for something from Great Mystery, which is the unknowable aspect of the universe, we prepare by giving something to it. A Give-Away symbolizes the harmonious give and take in all of nature."

"But what should I give?"

"A packet of American Spirit tobacco would be fine. You can get it at the Market Place on Alameda. But it has to be all-natural American Spirit, the pow-wow blend."

"Did you say 'pow-wow blend'? That sounds like it should be illegal."

Socorro laughed. "Don't worry. It's just tobacco blended right here in Santa Fe with red willow, sage and spearmint. All perfectly legal. Okay, I've got to run now. I'll pick you up at six o'clock."

"Wait a minute. What am I letting myself in for? I've never heard of an ini—what did you call it?"

"*Inipi.* That's a Lakota word meaning sweat lodge ceremony. See you tonight." The line went dead before Lee could respond.

* * *

Sara was sprawled across her bed, head hanging over the side and hair trailing down to the carpet, talking on the phone. Lee stuck her head around the door just before six o'clock. "Bye, sweetie. My friend will be picking me up in a minute."

"Just a minute," Sara put her hand over the phone. "Where did you say you're going?"

Lee hesitated. She hated being dishonest with her daughter, but a sweat lodge ceremony would be difficult to explain. And it would probably get back to Nick. That would never do. "Just over to a friend's house," she said, carefully choosing her words. "She's having a little get-together and insisted that I come along. I don't think she has a phone. Don't worry if I'm not home by your bedtime."

"Okay, see you later." Sara resumed her telephone conversation. "Okay, Wendy. I'm back."

"I've locked all the doors," Lee continued, "and turned on the outside lights. I know I've told you this before, but Sara—honey, are you listening? Don't ever open the door to anyone you don't know when you're here alone."

Sara giggled into the phone.

"Did you hear what I said? If anyone you don't know comes to the door—"

"Right. I heard you, Mom. I'll be fine. I've been baby sitting for little kids for over a year now, remember? I can certainly take care of myself. Don't worry. Good-bye."

Lee blew her a kiss and walked out of the room. "Mom's really uptight lately," she heard Sara say as she started down the hall. "Acting totally weird. Who knows? Maybe it's that change of life thing. Doesn't that happen around forty?"

* * *

"You said this takes place up in the mountains? Where exactly are we going?" Lee fastened her seat belt as Socorro backed her Jeep out of the driveway and drove down the dirt road toward town. "I have to admit I'm a little nervous about this."

Socorro gave Lee a reassuring look. "I know. And I'm honored by your trust in coming with me tonight. It's not far. We go up Hyde Park Road toward the ski basin, then take a dirt road for about three miles. Dream Singer bought a few acres up there years ago and built a little house. Of course his land is worth a fortune now. Some developer just made him an incredible offer. He wasn't interested. In fact, he told the guy to get off his property or he'd sic Howler on him." She grinned. "I'll bet that was a hasty exit. Howler is 90 percent timber wolf."

"We're going to be sweating with wolves? Socorro, I—"

"Don't worry. Howler won't hurt you. He's an excellent judge of character. He's also a real addition to the ceremony. Sits guard outside the lodge during the ceremony."

"Wonderful." Lee closed her eyes. Her empty stomach rumbled, and her head was starting to throb. "I'm starving," she said. "Why did you tell me not to eat anything today?"

"Because an *inipi* is a spiritual rite of purification, it's traditional to fast for at least a day beforehand. Besides, the heat is easier to take on an empty stomach."

"Does it really get that hot?"

"You bet. Dream Singer has been heating lava rocks for several hours now in a ritual fire. The rocks will be brought in one at a time and placed in a pit in the center of the lodge. Be prepared to endure some serious heat."

"I don't know, Socorro. I'm having second thoughts about this. Frankly, it doesn't sound like much fun."

"It isn't supposed to be fun. It's a very serious and sacred ceremony. It builds endurance and strength. Like most things in life from which we benefit, it's not easy. That reminds me, did you bring tobacco for your Give-Away?"

"Yes. I ran out and bought a couple of packets. I felt like a kid, sneaking it into my shopping basket along with low-fat yogurt, rice cakes and mineral water. But the check-out clerk didn't bat an eye."

"Why should he? Tobacco has been used ceremonially by Native Americans since prehistoric times."

"Why? I mean, why tobacco?"

"Because it has an affinity for spirit stronger than any other herb. The tobacco plant is awake in more worlds than one."

"I don't understand."

"Because of its multi-dimensional nature, tobacco is able to translate what's in your heart and communicate that to the spirit world. Dream Singer says it's like a telephone line to God."

"But you don't smoke, do you?"

"Only during ceremonies. That reminds me, did you drink plenty of fluids this afternoon?"

"I slosh when I walk."

"Good. I don't want you to get too dehydrated." Socorro turned off the paved road onto an unmarked dirtroad. Expertly navigating the sharp curves with one hand, she reached under the seat and pulled out a bottle of spring water. "Here, drink some more while I give you a little background on what you're about to experience."

Lee forced down half the bottle while Socorro continued. "The sweat lodge ceremony is an ancient method of cleansing both the body and the mind. It's been practiced by Native Americans—from the Eskimos to the Aztecs—for thousands of years. According to Lakota tradition, the sweat lodge and instructions for using it were brought to the people by *Pte Ska Win*, the Sacred White Buffalo Calf Maiden. The ceremony varies only slightly from tribe to tribe. Actually, the Lakota, or Sioux, language was adopted by the Indian Unity Movement in the early 1970s to be used during prayer and inter-tribal ceremony. So most of the Indian words you'll hear tonight will be in Lakota."

"Do I have to say anything?"

"You will be asked to state your reason for participating, or what you hope to gain from the experience. You can say as little or as much as you wish. Remember that the entire ceremony is a prayer. Anything divulged by participants within a lodge is held in strictest confidence. Anyway, it's pitch black inside, which provides a feeling of anonymity. It's a symbolic return to the safety of the womb. You don't suffer from claustrophobia, do you?"

"Not ordinarily. How long does it last?"

"Usually a couple of hours."

Lee jerked her head to stare at Socorro. "A couple of hours? Inside a dark little sauna? You're kidding!"

"I've done sweats that have lasted up to three and a half hours. It depends on how many people attend and how many rocks are brought in."

Lee took several more swallows of water and leaned her head back against the seat. She closed her eyes and tried to ignore the queasy feeling in her stomach. All of this because of Juan Mascareñas. Damn him! She envisioned his face, seeing again the intensity in his black eyes as he pulled her close...remembering the feel of his naked chest.

She jerked her head upright and opened her eyes. Bring on the heat, she thought. If the only way to get that bastard out of my system is to sweat him out, then I guess that's what I'll have to do.

Chapter 14

"*L*ooks like a good crowd," Socorro said, pulling the Jeep up beside a dozen or so randomly parked cars and pickups. "I see that Crow Dog is here. He's an Apache silversmith and a cousin of mine by marriage. And that BMW belongs to Emma Feldman. You know Emma, don't you? She owns Santa Fe Gourmet."

"I don't really know her, although we've met a couple of times. She's on the Board of the Santa Fe Symphony. I'm surprised that she'd be here."

"Emma's a regular at Dream Singer's sweats. She's been one of his followers for years. A funny, warm-hearted woman. She describes herself as a Jewish princess who moved to Santa Fe and became an Indian."

Socorro opened the Jeep door and slid out. "Leave your purse here," she said. "You won't need it. Just bring your tobacco. If you'll help me get some things out of the back, I'll lock up."

Lee stuck the packet of tobacco in her jacket pocket and got out, feeling a bit like she'd landed on an alien planet and was leaving the safety of the spaceship. Socorro handed her a large paper sack. "Here, you carry the food, and I'll get the other sack."

"Food?"

"I brought a couple dozen burritos and some apple cider. Oh, can you grab those paper plates? It's traditional to have a potlatch, or 'feast of giving', after an *inipi*."

"What's in the other sack?"

"Our sweat dresses and towels. All-women or all-men ceremonies are usually performed in the nude, but this is a mixed lodge. Dream Singer insists on modesty."

"Good."

"There's a tepee by the lodge where we can change. Come on, it's about a quarter of a mile up that path."

They walked a short distance and paused at the top of a hill. Below them spread a panoramic view of Santa Fe, the Española Valley and, far to the west, the ancient Jémez Mountains. "Look at that sunset," Lee said. "It looks like a painted backdrop. The colors are so incredible."

"The sun rises and sets in beauty," Socorro said softly. "I think of it as a daily reminder of how we should fill the hours in between."

Lee felt deeply touched. She nodded her head, not trusting herself to speak. The two women stood shoulder to shoulder for several moments, watching the crimson sky fade into a brilliant golden glow.

When Socorro continued down the path, she moved at a surprising pace. Lee, doing her best to keep up, was short of breath when they finally came to a clearing in the trees.

About fifteen people were standing around an open fire. Although most of them were Native American, Lee saw Emma Feldman talking to another Anglo woman who looked vaguely familiar. Both women wore sleeveless dresses. In spite of the cool evening air, the men were clad only in shorts or bathing trunks. A few had towels draped around their necks. A short distance away was a blanket-covered dome about ten feet in diameter and four feet high. That must be the sweat lodge, Lee realized with a growing feeling of dread. How are all those people going to fit into that tiny space?

Her eye was drawn to an elderly man kneeling in front of a rock-rimmed mound of dirt about two feet away from the opening to the lodge. He was dressed in faded blue jeans, cut off several inches above his bony knees. Thin white braids hung half-way down his back. Lee watched as, lips moving silently, he plugged small bundles of what looked like sage into the eye-sockets of a buffalo skull. Then he unwrapped a carved red pipe stone pipe from a length of buckskin and propped it up against one of the horns.

"Dream Singer is preparing the altar," Socorro said. "We must dress. Hurry." She headed toward a tepee perched on the top of a nearby knoll. Lee hurried after her, lugging the sack.

"Take off your underwear too," Socorro instructed as they ducked through the flap of the tepee. "You don't want to wear any more than you have to. And I brought some rubber thongs for you. It's too dark to walk around outside bare-footed."

The only light in the tepee came from a kerosene lantern on a narrow table that was laden with an assortment of covered dishes and bottles of water and juice. The floor was covered with blankets.

As Socorro unpacked the burritos and cider, Lee pulled two rumpled cotton knit sundresses from the sack. She undressed quickly and pulled one of the dresses over her head. When she turned, Socorro was nude, braiding her long black hair into a single braid. Lee couldn't help but envy her friend's full-breasted, slender figure. Fabulous muscle tone. Socorro was one of those women who looked as good undressed as dressed.

Out of the corner of her eye, Lee saw something

large and grey bound through the opening into the tepee. Before she could move, the wolf was upon her, its nose pressed into her crotch. She gasped.

Socorro laughed. "Hello, Howler," she said. "I was wondering where you were. This is my friend, Lee. She has a good heart, although it's not very strong tonight. I'm afraid you haven't helped. Come here."

The wolf raised its head and studied Lee with intelligent yellow eyes before turning to Socorro, who bent to press her cheek against his powerful muzzle. Howler opened his mouth and gently took the lower part of Socorro's face between his jaws, making a soft whining sound in the back of his throat. After a moment, he released her. Moving toward the tepee opening, the wolf yapped several times, the last yap ending in a melodious howl. Then he was gone.

"That's an impressive animal," Lee said weakly.

"He was telling us to hurry," Socorro said, reaching for her dress. "Wolves don't often bark. But they love to talk. Do you have your tobacco? Good. Now, drink some more water while you have the chance."

"I don't suppose there's a ladies room around here."

Socorro snorted. "We'll stop behind a bush on the way back to the lodge. At least that way we don't have to worry about your urine falling into the wrong hands!"

* * *

They were almost to the lodge when the drumming started. "It's beginning," Socorro said. "Stay close and enter the lodge behind me. Remember that I am right beside you. When the heat becomes too much, cup your hands around your mouth and nose and put your face down close to the earth. The air will be a little cooler there."

"Oh, God..."

"There's a reason why this ceremony is considered sacred, Lee. Just as there's a reason for you to be here tonight. It's a profound experience. You'll be fine. Trust me. I'm psychic, remember?"

"You'd better be. Oh, no. I have to pee again."

"Squat right here. No one can see you. But hurry."

* * *

Moments later, Lee stood between Socorro and a heavyset Indian woman as one by one the group placed their Give-Aways—packets of tobacco, several crystals, beaded medicine pouches and small pieces of decorated pottery—around the buffalo skull on the earthen altar. They formed a semi-circle around the dying fire.

After a few moments, Dream Singer signaled for the drumming to stop. He stood still, gazing into the glowing embers that covered red-hot volcanic rocks. Although his face and neck were etched with deep lines, he appeared at least twenty years younger than his eighty-six years. He looked up with kind eyes.

"We have gathered here to perform an *inipi*, a sacred rite of purification," he said in a strong, clear voice. "We ask *Wakan Tanka*, Great Spirit and Source of All, to strengthen and purify us in body, mind and spirit. We thank Father Sky and Mother Earth for our many blessings. We pray for all forms of life—the plant people, the winged people, the four-legged people, the six-legged, and last of all, we pray for us two-legged people. Give us the courage, strength and wisdom, *Wakan Tanka*, to endure the unendurable. We ask the hot steam, which is the breath of *Tunkashila*, our Grandfather, to cleanse us of all sorrow, resentment and fear. We come ready to receive the gifts offered by this sacred ceremony. We come ready to learn whatever we need to know. *Hetch etu aloh*. It is so."

An enthusiastic response of "*Ho, hetch etu aloh*," sounded from the group. Lee saw Emma break out of the circle and move to the entrance of the lodge. She carried an abalone shell, which contained a smoking smudge stick. At least that's familiar, Lee thought, remembering that Socorro had "smudged" them both with sage smoke when she'd come to the house last week.

The women lined up first. One by one, they turned in

a slow circle, pausing to acknowledge the four directions, as Emma waved the smudge stick from their heads to their feet. Lee noted that the women all bent to kiss the ground, before disappearing through the small opening of the sweat lodge. Heart pounding, she fell into line behind Socorro.

"Crawl into the lodge clockwise," Socorro whispered. "Keep coming until you bump into me." A moment later she was out of sight.

Lee met Emma's eyes and tried to return her encouraging smile before turning in a slow circle. Taking a final deep breath of cool, pine-scented air, she dropped to her knees, kissed the ground and crawled into the lodge.

The first thing that hit her was the absolute blackness. She paused for a moment, feeling disoriented. The space seemed airless. There was a gritty taste of dust in her mouth. It was like being buried alive. She instantly thrust the thought away. Back to the womb. Isn't that what Socorro said? Mother Earth. Yanking on her skirt to clear her knees, she felt her way along the blanket-covered floor. "Socorro?" Her voice was a choked whisper.

"Right here."

Lee felt a hand on her shoulder, guiding her forward. She reached out, felt Socorro's bare thigh and scrambled close to her. Hiking her dress up, she arranged herself in a cross-legged position.

"You okay?"

"I don't know. It's pitch black in here."

"The darkness is a necessary part of this ceremony. It represents our ignorance. Also, being deprived of the sense of sight sharpens our ability to hear whatever messages Spirit may send to us."

The only message I'm getting is that I'm nuts to be doing this, Lee thought as someone brushed against her right knee and settled close beside her. She felt penned in, trapped in the suffocating darkness. And more than half of the people were still outside, waiting to come in.

How could they all fit? "There's not enough air in here," she whispered frantically. "I already feel like I can't breathe."

"That's just anxiety." Socorro's soft voice was calm and reassuring. "Take long, slow breaths."

"What if I can't do this? What if I have to get out of here?"

"You just say *mitakuye oyas'in*, which literally means 'all my relations', and the flap will be opened to let you out."

"Ma-tah-ka-way what?"

"Just remember 'all my relations'. Calm yourself. I'm right here. I will get you out if necessary."

Lee closed her eyes and took a long deep breath. When she opened her eyes, she was relieved to see a few stars shining through the open flap about eight feet to her left. The view was soon blocked by another dark silhouette crawling through the small opening. There were soft sounds of movement. Someone cleared his throat. She leaned toward Socorro. "When do they bring in the rocks?"

"The fire tender will bring them to the entrance of the lodge after everyone is inside. Dream Singer will then use a pair of deer antlers to place them in the pit."

"Where's the pit?"

"Right in front of us, in the center of the lodge."

Lee was alarmed to hear that the steaming rocks would be so close. She tried to scoot further back, but was already up against the willow support of the structure. At that moment, she heard Dream Singer's voice from inside the lodge.

"Crow Dog honors us by serving as fire tender tonight. May his benefits from the ceremony be many. Ho, Crow Dog."

The medicine man was answered by a chorus of "Ho!"

"Bring in the first seven rocks, Crow Dog," he yelled cheerfully. "We have work to do."

A glowing football-sized rock appeared at the

entrance to the lodge. Lee could faintly make out
Dream Singer's slender frame as he transferred the rock,
which made a slight crackling sound, into the center of
the pit—just inches from her knees. The rock was
joined by six others and reverently sprinkled with sage.
More red-hot rocks then joined the first seven. When
the pit was more than half filled, the door flap was
closed.

Lee hugged her knees, pulling as far away from the
heat as possible. The rocks provided a dim light, just
enough for her to see how tightly packed the lodge was.
Women were crowded together on the north-facing side.
The men, having entered last, took up the remaining
space. If anyone faints in here, they won't have enough
room to fall over, she thought. Unless they pitch face-
forward into the pit.

"The fire pit represents the sun, the great giver of life
and energy," Dream Singer said, interrupting her
thoughts. "The *inipi*, the lodge, stands for *Unchi*,
Grandmother Earth, the Turtle Island we live on. In our
ceremony tonight we utilize the four great powers—
earth, water, fire and air. We sit on the earth, our
Mother who sustains and nourishes us. These ancient
rocks, *Tunkayatakapaka*, honor us tonight by joining
with fire and water in a trinity of power." He sprinkled
a handful of herbs over the glowing rocks, filling the
already steaming lodge with a sharp, pungent fragrance.

There was a low murmur of approval and shouts of
"Ho to the Earth! Ho to our Mother! Ho to our brothers, the rocks!" Lee swallowed several times, trying not
to choke on the smell.

"We use water to call forth the Thunderbeings,"
Dream Singer continued, as he poured a ladle of water
from a large bucket onto the hissing rocks. "Ho to the
Thunderbeings!"

A cloud of searing steam exploded through the lodge.
Lee gasped and turned her head away, but there was no
escaping the brutal heat that seared her nostrils and
lungs. Even her nipples were stinging. She felt her

pores open and sweat begin to run down her face, chest and back.

Dream Singer's "Ho" was answered by a chorus of voices, including Socorro's. How can they speak? Lee wondered as she buried her head between her arms. It was all she could do to keep breathing.

"We welcome the steam," continued Dream Singer, "as a gift from the rocks heated in *peta owihankeshni*, the fire with no end. We ask it to purify us so that we may live as *Wakan Tanka* wills." He poured another ladle of water on the rocks. "There will be four rounds of prayers," Dream Singer said, "honoring the four directions. At the end of the rounds we will pass the *chanunpa*, the sacred pipe. But first we sing to welcome the spirits and announce our intentions."

Someone in the lodge began to beat a drum and the singing started, a haunting, chant-like melody in what Lee assumed to be the Lakota tongue. She could pick out Socorro's clear strong voice. Beautiful, she thought, hugging her knees to her chest and swaying slightly to the sound. For some reason, the song made her want to cry. She wished she knew the words so she could join in.

When the drumming and the singing had died down, Dream Singer asked the participants to state their intentions or what they were "sweating for." One by one, prayers were voiced, each prayer ending in a fresh wave of steam. Lee tried to ignore the increasing heat by concentrating on what was being said. One man prayed for a son in prison, another man asked for strength to control his alcoholism. A woman prayed for wisdom and patience in dealing with her children. The next voice, a woman's, asked that a terminally ill friend be granted an "easy passing." The prayers went on and on. Someone, the voice sounded like that of a young girl, delivered a tearful plea for an end to pollution and the survival of the rain forests. At the end of each prayer, Dream Singer poured another ladle of water on the hissing rocks.

Jann Arrington Wolcott

By the time it was Lee's turn to speak, she wasn't
sure that she could. Sweat was cascading down her
forehead and into her eyes; her tongue felt as if it filled
her entire mouth. Socorro patted her leg encouragingly.

"I'm here tonight..." She paused and tried to swallow.

"Louder," someone said. "I can't hear you."

"I came to this sweat tonight to ask for strength," she
said. "I had an experience.... I've been going through a
very difficult time." Suddenly, to her surprise, Lee
began to cry. She felt Socorro's arm around her shaking
shoulders. "I'm sorry," she said, "I can't..."

"Take your time, sister," Dream Singer said. "We
are here with you, to add our prayers to yours."

Sobbing, Lee wiped at her face. Tears and sweat
flowed together down her cheeks and dripped onto her
chest. "Thank you," she was able to say. "I need your
prayers. I'm going through a very frightening thing. I
feel weak, out of control—unable to trust myself." She
took a deep shuttering breath. "I feel very confused. I
ask for clarity. And courage. Thank you for letting me
join you tonight."

"Ho!" Dream Singer honored Lee's prayer with
another ladle of water. This time Lee almost welcomed
the wave of heat that enveloped her. She felt light-
headed and weak, but somehow stronger. After
Socorro's prayers, which included one for a friend in
trouble, Lee added her own "Ho!" to the group chorus
and just barely noticed the blast of steam that followed.

Soon the round of individual prayers was completed.
Dream Singer opened the flap and Lee felt a welcome
rush of cool night air hit her wet skin.

"I'm proud of you, my friend," whispered Socorro.

"Is it over?"

"No. There's still quite a ways to go. Each of the
four directions must be honored. But after each round
the door flap is opened for a few minutes."

"I didn't know it was possible to sweat like this."

"You're doing fine. As Dream Singer says, anything

worth wanting is worth sweating for."

"Can I have a drink of water?"

"A water bottle will be passed around half-way through the ceremony."

The flap closed and the drumming started. Several ladles of water were splashed onto the rocks, which responded each time with a loud hissing sound and an explosion of steam. "The rocks sing," said Dream Singer. "Let us join them." Another Lakota song filled the lodge. This time, Lee found herself humming along.

"The east is the place of illumination," Dream Singer said, sprinkling sage and water on the still-glowing rocks. It seemed to Lee that the resulting heat was even more intense than it had been before. Her entire body was drenched in sweat.

"It is from the medicine power of the east that we seek wisdom and spiritual vision," Dream Singer continued. "The season of the east is spring, a time of rebirth and new beginnings. The animal of the east is the eagle, messenger of visions."

Time became distorted for Lee as the prayers and songs honoring the east continued. Disconnecting from the discomfort of her body, she began sinking deep within herself. Soon she was only vaguely aware of what was going on in the lodge. At one point, she was surprised to find herself singing aloud, chanting the ancient words. How can I be singing with them? she wondered. I don't know the words. But I do. Yes— incredibly—I do.

Waves of heat. Endless heat. Endless ceremony. Now honoring the south. She suddenly remembered Juan questioning her about the direction of her door that led into the spirit world. She had told him that it faced the south. "The south corresponds to fire and strong emotions," he had replied, "as well as to innocence and trust." He had taken advantage of her innocence and trust. Drugged her...seduced her.... But was it really that simple? Lee had to admit that she'd wanted Juan as much as he'd wanted her. Wiping at the steady stream of sweat from her forehead, she stared into the glowing pit. It seemed as though she saw a face in one of the rocks. She closed her eyes for a moment, then opened them. The face was still there. A thunderbeing? No, that was the steam. My brain is cooked, she thought. I'm seeing things. Must be completely dehydrated.... She dropped her head and bent toward her lap.

She felt Socorro grab her left hand and force it under the blankets they were sitting on. Suddenly she felt the coolness of dirt. Ah, she thought, wonderful. Mother Earth. She stuck her other hand under the blanket and pressed them both flat against the bare ground. Then she pressed her cooled hands to her face.

"Put your face down," Socorro whispered. "Cup your hands over your face and breath slowly through your mouth."

Lee bent down further, twisting in her cramped space to do as Socorro suggested. The air was cooler there. She pressed her lips against the cold hard earth.

Mercifully, the door flap was opened. Cool, fresh air washed over her like a wave of happiness. The woman to her right handed her a large plastic bottle filled with water. Lee drank deeply, greedily, letting the water run down her chin.

"Not too much," Socorro said. "You might get sick." She took the bottle from Lee. After taking a couple of swallows herself, she passed it on.

Lee groaned aloud as fresh glowing rocks were added to those already in the pit. God help us, she thought, as the door flap was pulled down. We're being roasted alive. For a moment she thought of Sara, at home alone, and of Nick, thousands of miles and another world away from this sweat lodge. If they could see her now...sealed inside this sweltering hut.... If Annabel could see her.... Her thoughts blurred in the onslaught of heat, distracted by remotely familiar songs and chants.

Dream Singer's voice, as strong as it was when the ceremony first started, broke through the wet haze that enveloped Lee. "The medicine power of the west is that of introspection, of knowing yourself," she heard him say. "It corresponds to the autumn, to the middle years of our lives when we assimilate those lessons learned in our youth. The color of the west is black. The animal of this direction is the bear. Bear goes within, to the dream lodge, in deep hibernation. But when threatened, he rises up and walks like a two-legged being. There are times in our lives when we, like our brother the bear, must stand tall and be willing to fight."

Lee heard a loud ringing in her ears. The glow of the fire pit receded, becoming smaller and smaller until it was gone.

* * *

She was waist-deep in a gently flowing stream. Long black strands of her freshly washed hair clung to her bare shoulders and breasts. She could see her tanned doeskin garments where she had left them, draped over a sour-berry bush on the nearby bank.

Bending her knees, she lowered herself into the cool water. She watched her hair float out on each side of her face, as the soft current tried to take it downstream. Birds were singing in the nearby trees. The sun felt hot on her face. All was in harmony.

Suddenly she heard a commotion on the bank— branches breaking and a frantic snuffling, growling sound. The birds stopped singing and took to the air. She froze, every sense alert.

A bear cub broke through the brush and splashed into the water, not twenty feet away. Close on its heels was a pack of six adult wolves. They stopped at the water's edge.

Without hesitation she rose up out of the water and scrambled onto the bank. "Scatter!" she yelled at the surprised hunting party. "Go from here!"

The wolves studied her for a moment. They began to growl and whine. She knew that they were waiting for a signal from their pack leader, a huge grey beast. His mind was easy to read as he decided to challenge her. He would not be cheated. The bear cub was his.

Placing herself between the pack and the terrified cub, she gathered her power. At that moment, she heard a loud crashing through the bushes. Seconds later an enormous brown bear charged into view. With a furious roar, the mother grizzly rose on her hind legs.

In moments the wolves were gone. The bear started toward her. She stood very still. I am friend! She formed the thought and hurled it into the bear's mind. The bear continued to come. I wish your cub no harm. I am friend! She repeated the message with all the force of her will, staring up at the towering beast who was now less than ten feet away. She tried to ignore the four-inch teeth and deadly claws.

The bear stopped. It studied her for a moment before dropping to all fours. Turning its massive head, the mother grizzly growled instructions to her cub and lumbered back into the bushes. The cub came splashing out of the water. Giving her a curious sideways look, it scampered after its mother. She stood alone and naked on the bank. For the first time since emerging from the stream, she felt the chill morning air on her wet skin. She began to shiver.

* * *

"Lee? How are you doing?" The whispered voice seemed to be coming from far away. Someone was shaking her arm. Must get my garment from the bush, she thought. Must wrap my hair in a drying fur....

"Lee!"

"What?" Lee was shocked to find herself in darkness. She was wet, dripping wet. And cold. The sweat lodge! I'm still here, she thought. But how can that be? I was somewhere else. In a river. Facing a bear—an unbelievably huge, brown bear. Was it a dream? No, not a dream. It was like the others. A memory. God help me, she thought. They were all memories.

"Are you all right?" Socorro's voice sounded alarmed.

Lee noticed that the entrance flap was open. Cool incoming air caressed her drenched skin. "I...I don't

171

know. I guess so. Is it over?"

"Almost. Just the round to the north. And the passing of the pipe. Sure you're okay?"

The flap dropped. Any reply Lee might have made would have been drowned out in the drumming and singing that honored the direction of the north.

"After the springtime of the east, the summer of the south, and the autumn of the west, we arrive on the sacred wheel of life, at the winter season of the north." Dream Singer doused the still glowing rocks with water.

Lee felt her pores open again as hot steam filled the lodge. How long can a person continue to sweat like this? she wondered, hugging her slick arms. It's hard to believe that there's any water left in my body.

"The medicine power of the north is wisdom," Dream Singer's voice continued. "Throughout nature it is a time for rest and renewal—in preparation for rebirth, the next turn of the wheel of life. The color of the north is white, and its medicine animal is the buffalo."

I can't take much more of this, Lee thought, cramming her hands under the blankets to cool them. It's got to end soon or they're going to be carrying me out of here. She pressed her hands against her face, wiping away the sweat.

As though she'd read her mind, Socorro felt for Lee's arm, then grabbed her hand. "Hang on," she whispered, giving it an encouraging squeeze. "We're almost there."

Sometime later—ten minutes? An hour? Lee had lost all sense of time—Dream Singer passed the pipe. "As we smoke the pipe let us remember that all that exists is alive and related," he said. "We all share a common source, a common breath. The sacred tobacco smoke is breath made visible. White Buffalo Calf Maiden gave the gift of the pipe to our forefathers so that we might never forget our connection to all forms of life, to all our relations. As we dedicate our prayers and actions to the good of all, we ask the smoke to carry our prayers to all realms of the spirit world."

The remaining water in the pail was poured on the

rocks as the pipe was passed clockwise around the lodge. Through the steam Lee could see a quick flare as it was frequently relighted. "How do I do this?" she whispered to Socorro, pushing her wet hair away from her face.

"When it comes to you, grasp the stem with your right hand and the bowl with your left. They are also passing a cigarette lighter. I will help you light it if the pipe has gone out. It's hard to keep it lit at this altitude."

When the two-foot-long pipe was passed to her, Lee held it gingerly and tentatively inhaled. Thick sweet smoke filled her mouth. She exhaled and passed it, along with the lighter, to Socorro.

After the pipe had made the complete round, Dream Singer's voice again filled the lodge. "We have been purified," he said. "This sacred ceremony teaches that hardship and discomfort are only obstacles to be overcome on the spiritual path. Now, giving thanks for that lesson, let us go forth and live as *Wakan Tanka* wills."

The flap was opened. One after another, the participants began to crawl from the lodge and into the cool night air. Lee's hands and feet felt slightly numb. Her dress was plastered to her body. Surprised that she had the strength to move, she followed close behind Socorro, pulling herself toward the opening. Finally, her head was free, and she was outside. Socorro helped her to her feet and gave her a hug before turning to Dream Singer.

"It was a good sweat," she said to the medicine man.

Dream Singer nodded. "A good hot lodge." His intense gaze fell on Lee. "Your first?" he asked.

"Yes." In spite of her exhaustion, Lee was experiencing a strange exhilaration. She felt refreshed, lighter in spirit as well as body. "It was...quite an experience."

"Take her to the tepee," Dream Singer instructed Socorro. "She needs fluids. First a glass of water, then juice and some food." He turned to Lee. "The weakness will pass. Honor and bless your body for the hardship that it has endured. Treat yourself gently. Go now, and walk your path in life with firm steps."

"Thank you," Lee murmured. She felt Socorro's arm around her waist. Walking together wordlessly, the two women headed up the hill.

After she had toweled off, dressed, and gulped down a large glass of water, Lee was surprised to find that she was hungry. "When do we eat?" she asked Socorro, who was unwrapping food and setting out paper plates.

"As soon as Dream Singer prepares the spirit plate."

"What's that?"

"An offering of food to the spirits that aided us in the lodge," Socorro said, removing Saran Wrap from a large fruit salad. "Here he is now."

Dream Singer and the other men joined the women in the tepee. The group stood in silence as the medicine man placed a small portion of each available food on a paper plate. "We share our food with the Grandmothers and Grandfathers who shared their energies with us tonight. After they have partaken of its essence, may it be enjoyed by our brothers and sisters, the animals of this forest. *Wash Tay*. It is good." The medicine man left the tepee.

"Where's he going?" Lee whispered to Socorro.

"To put the plate outside, as an offering. Let's get in line. I want a piece of Emma's crab quiche before it's all gone."

Realizing that she was famished, Lee loaded her plate with a large serving of tamale pie, a rolled chicken taco and a hunk of fried bread.

Socorro grinned, watching her. "You have proven yourself tonight," she said, filling her own plate. "Now, if ever your courage waivers, you will remember what you endured in the *inipi*. That will remind you of your strength."

"Speaking of courage, I had a strange experience in there. It was sort of like a dream, but different. I could have sworn that I was living it."

"Tell me about it." Socorro guided them to a small army cot where they sat down.

"Well, I was standing up to both a pack of wolves and a grizzly bear. It was as though I could communicate with them telepathically." She stared down at her plate. "I must have dozed off. I mean, that's the only rational explanation."

Socorro shook her head. "It's not unusual to receive a vision in the lodge. The experience is, in many ways, a descent into the subconscious. It can reveal things to us that we need to know about ourselves."

"How long were we in there? I lost all concept of time."

"Over two and a half hours," Socorro said, glancing at her watch. "It's almost ten o'clock."

"You're kidding. No wonder I was seeing things." She ate a large bite of the spicy tamale pie. "You know, I'm curious about something. We entered the lodge in a clockwise direction, and the entire ceremony followed that pattern: starting with the round dedicated to the east, moving to the south, the west and, finally, to the north."

"That's right. Ceremonies are usually conducted in a clockwise—or sunwise—direction, following the natural order of things."

"Juan invoked the spirits of the four directions during his awakening ceremony. But he did everything in a counterclockwise motion."

Socorro lowered the bite of quiche she was about to put in her mouth. "Well, that removes any doubts about his intentions," she said. "Moving counterclockwise, or against the turning of the earth, is a traditional occult method of summoning negative energies."

"Negative energies?"

"Black magic, Lee. Juan was working black magic."

* * *

Sara's bedroom light was still on by the time Lee got home.

She hurried down the hall, not wanting to be seen in her wrecked condition. "I'm home, honey," she called, and headed for the bathroom.

Moments later, Sara was knocking at the bathroom

door. Lee came out, dressed in a robe with a towel hastily wrapped around her head. "What are you doing up?" she asked her daughter. "You need to get to sleep."

Sara stared at Lee. "Jeez, what happened to you?"

"What do you mean?"

"Your face. It's covered in dirt! Mom, where have you been?"

Lee ran her hands over her face, feeling the grit that was stuck on her cheeks. "We were outside, sitting around a campfire. The wind came up. I guess—"

"You even have dirt under your fingernails," Sara interrupted. "And you look all flushed or something."

"I told you, I was sitting on the ground around a hot campfire. Now, back to bed. You have school tomorrow." Lee blew her a kiss and closed the bathroom door.

A close-up look in the bathroom mirror explained Sara's shocked reaction to her appearance. Lee's face was streaked with dirt, a result, she realized, of pressing her damp hands against the cool earth and then wiping sweat from her face. When she removed the towel from her head, her hair was matted flat and stiff with sweat.

On her way to the shower, she stepped onto the bathroom scales. One hundred and sixteen. No wonder I feel so much lighter, she thought. I sweated off close to six pounds of water. Talk about a quick weight loss treatment. She stepped into the shower stall, marveling that she could look so soiled, yet feel so cleansed.

Chapter 15

*L*ee awoke early the next morning, feeling rested and rejuvenated. She'd almost forgotten what a good night's sleep felt like. It might take awhile to assimilate last night's sweat lodge experience, but the immediate results were certainly impressive. Maybe she could get some work done today.

While dressing for work, Lee found herself mentally outlining her upcoming editorial on the pros and cons of growth in Santa Fe. Better add a quote from the mayor. She'd give her a call this morning, right after the staff meeting. She hurried downstairs to join Sara for breakfast.

* * *

She was in her study writing when the phone rang at nine o'clock that night. Should she answer it? It might be Juan. But if it was, she certainly didn't want Sara to answer. She picked up the receiver.

"Lee? How're you doing, babe?"

"Oh, Nick. It's good to hear your voice. I'm doing fine. I've had a very productive day. In fact, I'm still working, on an article to round out the January issue. One of our writers left town rather abruptly."

"Well, it's good to hear you sounding like yourself again." He hesitated. "Did Mister come home?"

"No. I've about given up hope. I found his collar in the arroyo behind the house yesterday morning."

"Just his collar? That's odd."

"Yeah. Odd. It's really hard, not knowing what happened to him."

"I know. But try not to dwell on it. It's good to keep busy." When Lee didn't respond, he changed the subject. "Did you have a good weekend?"

"I kept busy."

"Good. Sara okay?"

"Just fine."

"Well, give her my love. We're planning the final launch early Wednesday morning. Then I'll need a day to look at the data. I probably won't get a chance to call again. The next few days will be pretty hectic."

"When will you be home?"

"Friday night, around nine-thirty. If there's any delay, I'll have one of the secretaries in the office get word to you."

"Okay. Hope it goes well."

"Thanks, babe. Hold down the fort."

"I will. I've had plenty of practice." Instantly regretting her sarcasm, Lee tried to soften her tone. "Take care of yourself, Nick."

"You, too. See you Friday."

Lee hung up the phone and turned out the light. For once she was glad that Nick was so involved in his work. *I guess I should also be grateful that he takes me so much for granted,* she thought ruefully. *It makes deceit so much easier.*

* * *

For the second morning in a row, Lee awoke feeling refreshed. She lay in bed for several moments, thinking about her sweat lodge experience. *I have to hand it to Socorro,* she thought. *The ceremony seems to have* worked wonders for me. I feel much stronger, both emotionally and physically. No wonder Native Americans have been doing it for thousands of years. I'd like to discuss it with Nick, but I'm afraid that's out of the question. How could I explain my motivation? She tossed the covers back and stood up, doing several minutes of slow yoga bends before taking a shower.

* * *

Lee was in the garage emptying trash into large plastic garbage bags when she heard the telephone ringing. By the time she got back in the house, the answering machine had picked it up. She froze when she heard Juan's deep voice leaving a taped message.

"Where are you, *querida*? I trust that you are on your way. I have a strong need to see you. I'll be waiting."

Lee felt stunned. How dare he leave such a message on her answering machine! Did he know that her husband was out of town? No, of course not. How could he know that? She hit the replay button.

The sound of his voice, intimate and seductive, went through her like an electric shock. "I'll be waiting." Her hand was shaking as she hit the replay button a third time.

She sat on a stool at the snack bar for a moment, her face buried in her hands. "No!" she said out loud. "He can wait until hell freezes over." She erased the message and hurried upstairs to get her purse and coat. Just as she was leaving the house, the telephone rang again.

The answering machine picked it up on the fourth ring.

"Lee? It's me, Socorro."

Lee grabbed the receiver. "Hi. I'm here."

"What's wrong? You sound upset."

"Juan just called. I didn't talk to him, but he left a message on my machine that he was waiting for me to return to Cavado."

"I'm not surprised. *Brujos* don't give up easily. How have you felt since the sweat?"

"Much better. I've actually been able to concentrate

179

on getting this issue of the magazine out on time."

"Good girl. Listen, we need to talk. Could you drop by the gallery sometime today?"

"I should be able to leave the office a little early today. How about four o'clock?"

"Great. See you then."

* * *

Lee turned off Paseo de Peralta onto Canyon Road. Once a prehistoric Indian trail, the narrow picturesque street had evolved in recent years into a major art center. She drove slowly past the centuries-old adobe buildings, remembering when many were private residences. Now they were almost all converted into art galleries, boutiques or restaurants.

A red Mercedes drove out of the small parking lot in front of Socorro's gallery. Must be my lucky day, Lee thought, pulling into the empty space. Parking was always at a premium on Canyon Road. Lee walked through the antique wooden doors into a large, well-lighted room. She walked around a small group of people who were examining a display of pueblo pottery and Navajo rugs. In a far corner, Socorro was chatting with a man in buckskin who looked as though he'd just stepped out of an old Western movie. She waved Lee over.

"Lee, I want you to meet Martin—better known as Mountain Man Murphy. We sell his wooden sculptures as fast as he can turn them out. My friend, Lee Lindsay."

"You're a real looker," the heavily bearded artist grinned, putting a burly arm around Lee's shoulder. "Married?"

"Yes, she's married," said Socorro with an exasperated laugh. "Now get out of here, Mountain. Go transform that inexhaustible energy into something I can sell."

"This lady is a slave driver," he said, releasing Lee and bending to kiss Socorro's cheek. "Nice meeting you, Lee. Let me know if you're ever not married."

With a wave, he was out the door.

"Let's go into my office," Socorro said. She motioned to a young girl behind the counter. "Hold down the fort, Marilyn. I'll be back in a few minutes. Buzz me if Mrs. Wyatt comes back. I think she's really interested in that McBride painting."

Lee followed her into a cozy room decorated with a beige leather sofa and a gorgeous antique oak desk. Colorful Navajo rugs hung on the walls and accented the ochre Saltillo tile floor. Red geraniums bloomed in a south-facing window sill. "This is a beautiful place," Lee said, looking around.

"Doesn't it have a marvelous energy? It was originally part of a huge hacienda built by Don Pedro Gaspar y Romero in the mid-seventeenth century. We bought it from one of his descendants. Some of the original adobe walls are three feet thick." She perched on the edge of the desk. "Have a seat."

Lee sunk into the sofa. "What's up? You said you had something to tell me."

"I had an interesting conversation with my uncle, Luis Tafoya, last night. Luis is a Deputy Sheriff with the Rio Arriba Sheriff's Department. Actually, he's retired, but he talked them into hiring him back part-time, to answer the phone and things like that. I asked him about Juan Mascareñas."

Lee tensed. "And?"

"The name rang a bell with Uncle Luis. He remembered an incident involving Juan many years ago, when Juan was a student at the University of New Mexico. Some investigation."

"What kind of investigation?"

"Uncle Luis couldn't remember the details. But he promised to look it up in the police files. Tomorrow's my day off. I'm going to meet him for lunch in Española." She paused for a minute. "You know, I just had an idea. Maybe after lunch, I'll drive on up to Cavado. I could find some excuse to talk to Juan and just check him out. See what kind of feelings I pick up.

I'd sure like a clearer reading on him."

"But you've said that it would be dangerous to go back there."

"Yes, it certainly would be, for you. But Juan doesn't know me. And I'd be on guard. I know how to protect myself against his magic."

"But what excuse—?"

"I don't know. I could come up with something." She shrugged. "It's just a thought. I may not have time tomorrow. There are always a million things to do on my rare days off. For instance, I need to swing by the pueblo and check on my grandmother. She was fighting a cold last week, and her aura looked a little dark." She studied Lee for a moment, a satisfied expression on her face. "Speaking of auras, yours looks a heck of a lot brighter. It has from the moment you crawled out of the sweat lodge."

"Well, I certainly feel better. I think you Native Americans are really onto something. Have there been any medical studies about the benefits of sweats?"

"I doubt it. You palefaces are generally slow to learn. But, I'm beginning to think there's real hope for you."

Lee laughed and stood up. "Thanks. I mean it, Socorro. I don't know what I would have done without your support the last couple of weeks. Now, I'll do you a favor and be on my way. I know what it's like to run a business."

Socorro walked her to the front door of the gallery. "I'll call you later this week. With any luck, I'll have something concrete on the *brujo*." Her expression turned serious. "Keep your psychic shield strong, my friend. I still sense great danger around you."

"But I feel—"

"I know that you're feeling better. But you're not out of the woods yet. You must continue to protect yourself. Burn your candle. And always guard—"

"I know." Lee smiled. "Guard my light." She gave Socorro a hug. "You do the same."

Lee walked past a boisterous group of tourists in the parking lot and got into her car. I wonder what Socorro would say if she knew I'd had sex with Juan, she thought. And how great it was—how I keep reliving it over and over again in my mind. She'd probably have me sweating every night for a month. Actually, I wish I could tell her. Maybe someday I will. But right now, I don't want to admit to anyone how weak I was. Not until I've come to terms with it myself.

Pulling out of the parking lot and heading toward town, Lee tried to refocus her thoughts. It's best not to think about Juan right now, she told herself. That just messes up my head. I certainly have other things to concentrate on, like the editorial I need to write tonight. But first, I'd better stop by the grocery store. We need milk and eggs. Let's see, what else? Beer for Nick. Her mind went instantly to Cavado. She saw Juan walking toward her, carrying a bottle of beer. His naked body...

"Stop it!" She startled herself by saying the words out loud. Consciously ignoring the flush she felt spreading across her chest, she forced her thoughts back to her grocery list.

* * *

Lee held her breath each time the telephone rang that night, but there was no further word from Juan. She told herself that she was relieved. Obviously, he'd gotten the message. What had happened between them could never happen again.

* * *

A few minutes past midnight on Thursday night, Lee awoke and sat up in bed, her heart pounding wildly. She turned on the light. Another nightmare. Something terrifying...horrible. But now it was gone. It had involved Juan. That was all she could remember.

She got up for a glass of water, trying not to cry. Oh, God, the dreams were starting again. She'd been so hopeful that they were over, that the sweat lodge had put a stop to them. What if they never went away? What if...hold it, she ordered herself. Everyone has dreams. Calm down and go back to bed.

Lee tossed and turned for over an hour, unable to relax enough to get back to sleep. Although her mind had blocked the content of the nightmare, her body couldn't forget it. Damn, she thought, finally throwing back the covers and getting out of bed. I give up. I can lie here all night, or I can take a sleeping pill. Reluctantly, she decided on the pill.

* * *

"Mom?" Sara gently shook Lee's shoulder, pulling her out of a drugged sleep. "Aren't you going to work? Kevin's picking me up for school any minute."

Lee forced her eyes open. "What time is it?"

"Seven-thirty. Didn't your alarm go off?"

"I'm doing some writing here at home this morning, so I didn't set it. Thanks for waking me though. I need to get up. Boy, I'm groggy. I had a rough night."

"How come?"

"Just bad dreams."

Sara frowned. "Like the one you had about Mister?"

"I can't remember. But I woke up and had a hard time getting back to sleep."

"Maybe you should be taking vitamins or hormones or something."

"Hormones? Have you been talking to Annabel?"

"What?"

"Never mind. Don't worry, honey. I'm fine. Have a good day."

Lee lay in bed for awhile after Sara left, feeling drugged and depressed. Finally she got up and splashed cold water on her face. Then she put on her robe and walked outside to get the morning paper.

The morning was overcast, with thick clouds rolling across the mountains like dark smoke. The weather certainly suits my mood, she thought grimly, as she hurried back into the house. She turned on the burner under the tea pot and removed the rubber band from the rolled newspaper. Sighing, she sat down at the kitchen table.

It took a moment for her mind to register what she was seeing. She blinked, then gasped as she stared at the front page of **The Santa Fe New Mexican**. The caption under a photo of a familiar face read, "Socorro Tafoya-Hall, Santa Fe Gallery Owner, Dead at 36. Story on Page B4." She brought her hand up to cover her mouth, staring in disbelief, then quickly turned to the obituary section and read:

Socorro Tafoya-Hall, 36, prominent Santa Fean and co-owner of Galería de Canyon Road was pronounced dead at Saint Vincent Hospital at nine-thirty Wednesday night. Preliminary examination indicated cerebrovascular hemorrhage, according to hospital spokesman Dr. Joseph Romero. An autopsy is scheduled. Tafoya-Hall is survived by her hus-band, Howard J. Hall, stepson, Chad Hall, a grandmother, Yolanda Tafoya of Santa Clara Pueblo, an uncle, Luis Tafoya of Española, and cousins Lydia and Maria Trujillo of Santa Fe. Memorial services will be announced at a later date.

"No!" Lee's voice echoed in her ears. She reread the short announcement, then sat stunned at the kitchen table. Gradually, she became aware of the shrill whistle of the tea kettle and rose automatically to turn off the gas.

Shock gave way to sorrow and Lee began to sob. Poor Socorro! She was so sweet and funny. So beauti-ful. How could she be dead? Cerebrovascular hemorrhage. But how can that be? I was with her, the day before yesterday. She was fine, she was.... Lee was washed by a fresh wave of horror. It was difficult to breathe. Did Socorro go to Cavado after she met her uncle in Española? Oh no! she thought, springing to her feet. Did Socorro go to see Juan?

Stop it, stop it, she ordered herself. Don't think crazy

thoughts. Socorro had a stroke. People die of strokes all the time. Juan didn't have anything to do with it. She paced back and forth through the kitchen, talking to herself. But Socorro was so young—only thirty-six! And she wasn't sick. She was so vibrant, so alive. Lee remembered the expression on Socorro's face the last time they met. She had looked so worried, as she warned Lee of possible danger. Danger from Juan. Now she's the one who's dead. "Oh, God," Lee moaned, tears flowing down her cheeks.

She ran down the hall to her study and grabbed the phone book. "Doctor Mallory," she whispered, frantically turning the pages. "Be there," she breathed as she punched in the number. "Please be there."

Chapter 16

"*J*ust take your time, Lee. Sit back and relax for a minute."

She took a deep breath and leaned back into the soft cushions of the sofa. "Thanks for working me in again, Doctor Mallory."

"No problem. I had a cancellation this morning." He sat quietly, watching her. "Now, are you ready to tell me what's going on? I'm assuming that this is related to your visit two weeks ago."

"Yes. I guess you know about Socorro."

Mallory nodded, his round face turning sad. "It was quite a shock. My wife is taking it hard."

"The newspaper said it was a stroke. But I don't believe that. I saw her Wednesday morning, and she was just fine."

"Apparently it happened right out of the blue. Edie talked to Howard, Socorro's husband, this morning. He said they were having dinner with friends when she just collapsed. Absolutely no warning. Poor Howard." Mallory shook his head. "Terrible thing."

"She was only thirty-six years old."

"I know. Well, unfortunately, these things do happen. Probably a congenital weakness. I guess the autopsy will give us the answer." He reached inside the candy dish on his desk. "Join me?" Lee shook her head and watched him unwrap a piece of peppermint candy and put it in his mouth. He sucked on it for a moment, studying her. "Obviously, you followed my suggestion and talked to Socorro about your experience in Cavado."

"Yes, I did. In fact, we spent quite a lot of time together in the last two weeks. We became good friends." Lee's voice broke. She grabbed a tissue from a box on the end table and wiped at tears that ran down her cheeks. When she was able to speak again she continued. "Socorro was so supportive. She conducted a healing ritual for me at my house and even took me to a Native American sweat lodge ceremony. I visited her again at her gallery on Tuesday morning. Although I hadn't known her very long, I feel a terrible sense of loss."

"Socorro was a warm, generous person, easy to like. I'm not surprised that you two hit it off. It's only natural that you would feel shocked and saddened at the news. I am too." He studied her for a moment. "But, somehow, I don't think you're here just to discuss Socorro's death. Am I right?"

Lee put her head in her hands, too overcome by emotion to speak. "There's more," she finally said. "A lot more."

"Tell me about it."

"I'm not sure where to begin."

"Just take it from our last meeting." He reached for his notepad. "Let's see, that was on Friday, exactly two weeks ago."

She took a deep breath. "Everything feels all jumbled together in my head. I'm having trouble keeping things in order. Let's see. Juan called me that Friday night, right after I saw you."

"How did he get your home phone number?"

"I don't know. That's a mystery too. He said he called the office and told the receptionist he needed to reach me. But Julie denies ever speaking to him."

"Okay, go on."

"Well, he said he wanted to see me again. It was eerie. He seemed to know that I was alone. And he knew that I'd been sick. He said it was from the awakening ceremony."

"Wait a minute. Did he mention your illness first, or did you?"

Lee frowned, trying to remember. "I don't know. Maybe I did. He said I would feel better after he shook my sweat blanket to the four directions or something like that. Something about scattering my fears."

"Did he say when he planned to do that?"

"In two days. When the moon was full."

"Go on."

"He talked about the ceremony, saying that it had been very powerful. He denied drugging me."

"You confronted him about that?"

"Yes. And he said something about it being my own power that I had felt, not drugs."

"Interesting. Anything else?"

"He insisted that I return to Cavado. I told him I couldn't, that I didn't want to go through with the next ceremony."

"How'd he take that?"

"He let it drop. Said something about not rushing me. But he kept insisting that he had to see me again. Something about unfinished business."

Mallory snorted. "Persistent, isn't he?"

"I went back," Lee said in a small voice. "The next Tuesday morning."

Mallory's eyebrows shot up. "You did? Tell me about it."

"First, let me explain why, if I can." She spent the next fifteen minutes describing her lunch with Socorro and her strange experience while meditating with the candle. Mallory sat quietly, nodding occasionally and taking notes on a yellow legal pad balanced in his lap.

"I decided the only way to get to the bottom of this past-life thing, to put it to rest, was to talk to Juan again. So, I went back." She took a deep breath and forced herself to give a brief but truthful description of her return visit to Cavado.

Mallory looked grim by the time she finished. "How did you feel afterward?" he asked. "After having had sex with Juan?"

"Confused. Guilty, of course. And frightened when he started talking about taking me to Mexico." She stared at her lap. "But before that, while we were..." She looked up at him with an expression of wonder. "I have to admit that it was fantastic. The most exciting sexual experience I've ever had."

"Okay, we'll come back to that later. Go on."

"Well, then Socorro called after I got home from Cavado, insisting that she had to see me the next morning. You see, she was trying so hard to help me..." Lee stopped, unable to go on.

"Just take your time," Mallory said. "I know this is difficult."

Lee blew her nose and swallowed hard. "Socorro had been to Santa Clara pueblo to visit her grandmother, and had some news about Juan or, at least, about his mother." Lee paused. "Socorro's grandmother said that Juan's mother, Sinopa Mascareñas, was a *bruja*—one of the most notorious witches in local history. It had even been rumored that Sinopa had murdered Juan's father when he objected to her practicing black magic. Juan did tell me that his father died before he was born. And she was also supposed to have done away with some woman in Cavado after bewitching her husband. Nothing was ever proven, of course. But Socorro felt certain that Juan's mother had passed her powers on to him. Especially after I told her that Juan was wearing Sinopa's amulet. She warned me to stay away from Cavado. She was afraid that Juan might be a spirit-sucker."

"A what?"

"A spirit-sucker. A sorcerer or *brujo*, who can steal someone else's spirit or will."

"Suck it right out of them, huh? Pretty obscene image. Go on. Tell me more."

"Well, actually, Socorro concluded that Juan wasn't after my spirit. Because apparently *brujos* use sex to work that particular bit of magic. And Socorro didn't know that I'd had sex with Juan. I...I didn't tell her that I'd been back to Cavado. Socorro spent most of the morning with me, constructing a medicine wheel around my house and instructing me on how to strengthen my psychic shield."

"Your psychic shield?"

"Socorro maintained that we have a spirit body, an energy field that surrounds our physical body. When it's strong and healthy, it acts as a shield to protect us from psychic attack."

Mallory smiled. "I see. Naturally one would need a spirit shield for protection against a spirit-sucker." He shook his head. "Socorro and her psychic realms. Go on."

"Last Sunday, Socorro took me to a sweat lodge ceremony. That was quite an experience—almost three hours of utter darkness and intense heat. But it seemed to work wonders. I felt much better for several days afterwards."

"I've never tried that. I'm a little embarrassed to admit that I suffer from claustrophobia. I know, shrink, heal thyself." He shuddered. "Just the thought of being confined like that upsets me. But I have to say, I find the possible psychological benefits of the ceremony intriguing. As a matter of fact, I know a clinical psychologist in northern California who attended several sweat lodge ceremonies and was so impressed by the emotional breakthroughs she witnessed that she gave up her conventional practice. Now she just takes patients to sweats. She maintains that two hours in a sweat lodge can accomplish more than two years in therapy." He shrugged. "I guess it's something you need to experience to really understand."

"I would say so."

"Well, so you sweated and felt better. Then what?"

"Juan called Tuesday morning and left a message on my answering machine wondering where I was. He wanted me to go back to Cavado."

"Did you?"

"No."

"Did you want to?"

Lee was quiet for a minute. "Part of me did. As I said, the sex with Juan was incredible. I try not to remember how incredible."

"And the other part of you?"

"That part feels guilty as hell. And frightened. Very frightened." Lee shook her head. "There are so many loose ends, so much that I don't understand."

"Go on."

"Tuesday morning Socorro called and asked me to drop by her gallery. When I got there, she said that her uncle, who's a deputy sheriff in Arriba County, thought he remembered an investigation years ago—something that involved Juan at UNM. He promised to check the records. Socorro was planning to meet him in Española for lunch the next day and get the story." She hesitated. "There's something else, something that's really making me crazy. Socorro mentioned that she might go to Cavado herself. To check Juan out."

"Did she?"

"I don't know. That was the last time we spoke." Lee paused for a moment. "I need help, Doctor Mallory. I feel like I'm losing my grip on reality. I'm weepy and absent-minded, even at work. Annabel, my partner, had a little talk with me last week, suggesting that I take some time off. But one of the worst things is the dreams. I've been having such terrible dreams."

Lee described her nightmare about the raven killing Mister. "When I woke up, I smelled the sweating oil again. But Sara didn't smell it. So, I convinced myself it was just my imagination. But, that very night, Mister disappeared. He went out and never came home. I found his collar in an arroyo, but not a trace of him." She rubbed at the tears that rolled down her cheeks. "That's quite a coincidence, don't you think?"

"This has been a very difficult time for you, Lee. You've been under a lot of stress. And stress can do all kinds of things. It can certainly cause olfactory illusions."

"That's all you think the sweating oil odor was? An olfactory illusion?"

"Lee, you had just awakened from a nightmare—"

"My life is becoming a nightmare! Look what happened to Socorro!"

"Are you saying that you think there's some connection between Juan and Socorro's death?"

"Yes! I mean—oh, God—I keep trying to convince myself that there can't be a connection—that it's crazy to believe that Juan killed Socorro or Mister. But, down deep..." She took a breath, trying to steady her voice, then looked into Mallory's eyes. "All right. Let me describe the demented thoughts I've been having, and then you can just go ahead and fill out the papers to have me committed. What if Juan killed Mister, somehow, to punish me for refusing to run away to Mexico with him? And then, realizing that Socorro was on to him, maybe he did away with her, too. What if Socorro was right? What if he really is a *brujo*?" Her voice broke and fresh tears streamed down her face. "While I thought he was making love to me, maybe he was just sucking out my spirit." Lee grabbed another tissue and wiped her eyes. "I'm really frightened, Doctor Mallory," she whispered. "What's happening to me? Am I going crazy?"

"I certainly don't think you're going crazy. You've been through some extremely stressful situations and they're taking their toll. Let's just backtrack and re-examine some of these things." He leaned back in his chair. "We'll start with your first meeting with Socorro. You said that she felt certain, even then, that Juan was a *brujo.*"

"Yes, and she called Cavado a 'vortex of evil energy', or something like that. She talked about wanting to consult with her spirit guides and advised me to keep candles burning in my room at night."

Mallory shook his head. "Well, I warned you that Socorro considers—" He stopped, then corrected himself— "considered herself to be a psychic. I expected you to take all that with a grain of salt. Was Juan's awakening ceremony familiar to her?"

"No, she didn't have much to say about that. Except that his counterclockwise motions indicated that he was working with negative energies. And I couldn't find anything like Juan's ceremony in any of the books I read at the library." She paused, trying to organize her thoughts. "Anyway, Socorro called later to say that she was going to Santa Clara to visit her aunt. She suspected that if Juan was a *brujo*, her aunt would have heard of him. Then she asked me if I'd left anything, any clothing or personal item, in Cavado. She said that *brujos* need something belonging to a person in order to put a spell on them. She really sounded worried when I told her that I'd used Juan's portable toilet. She seemed to think that urine, in combination with my sweat on the blanket, would make for a first-class spell."

"Okay, let's stop right there for a minute. You have to see that Socorro, well-meaning though she was, planted the unsettling idea of a magic spell in your head the first time you met with her. Even though you rejected the idea on an intellectual level, it began to work on you emotionally. That led to your 'past-life' experience while you were meditating. You were already pretty upset and susceptible to this reincarnation and witch-spell business. You were nicely set up to overreact to a particularly vivid dream."

"But I've had other so-called dreams since then—all of them as real as memories. I had one after returning to Cavado and another one during the sweat lodge ceremony."

"Vivid dreams are a common reaction to stress, the mind's way of letting off steam. Speaking of steam, how long did you say you were in that sweat lodge?"

"About two and a half hours."

"Good grief. That would cause severe dehydration, not to mention exhaustion. You probably passed out at some point and began to dream."

"I know that's the logical explanation. But something tells me that it's not that simple. Doctor Mallory, how can you be so certain that Juan doesn't have supernatural powers?"

"Lee, these guys, *brujos*, if you will, have power only over the people who believe in that power. Of course, that can be deadly. Tell a believer in voodoo that a death spell has been placed on him—or a Native American that his spirit has been stolen—and he's apt to lie down and die. But the whole thing relies on the power of suggestion, not the supernatural. As far as Socorro's death is concerned, medical evidence points to a stroke. And there's no real reason to believe otherwise. Is there?"

"I told you, I just feel—"

"I know what you feel, Lee. But let's just look at the facts. At the medical evidence. That points to a stroke. Doesn't it?"

Lee leaned her head back against the sofa pillow and closed her eyes. "I guess so," she replied in a tired voice.

"Okay, so Juan called you, insisting that you return to Cavado. And even though you hadn't originally planned to, you went back to see him. Let's talk about why."

"I told you, I wanted to question him about some of the things he'd said. About his claim to have known me in a past lifetime!"

"Were you aware then of how attracted you were to him?"

Lee frowned. "No. Well, at least I didn't admit it to myself at the time. I was outraged at the idea of having been drugged during the interview. I wanted to confront him about that. But I was also intrigued by his references to reincarnation. Especially after my meditation dream. I wanted him to tell me more about our so-called past life together. Although I was frightened of him, I wanted some answers."

"So you arrived loaded for bear." Mallory leaned forward in his chair. "And?"

"And it just happened. I walked in the door and he started kissing me." She hesitated. "One thing very quickly led to another. I don't understand it at all. He didn't really force me. He didn't have to. The truth is I wanted him more than I've ever wanted anyone. I've never felt that kind of passion before."

"You didn't eat or drink anything?"

"Not until afterward. After we'd rolled around on the buffalo skin a second time. Then we had a beer."

"A beer?"

"Yes."

"Ah," Mallory said with a raised eyebrow. "*Brujo* brew?"

Lee managed a small smile. "Apparently. The point is, I wasn't drugged this time. And I don't think there was time for him to hypnotize me."

"It wouldn't take long. Especially if you'd been hypnotized once before." He reached for another mint. "Got to kick this nasty habit before all my teeth fall out." He unwrapped it and rolled it around in his mouth with a thoughtful expression on his face. "Well, did our medicine man offer any more karmic info?"

Lee ignored the sarcasm. "He did talk a little bit about a past life we'd shared—as prehistoric Indians living on a mesa near Los Alamos. According to Juan, I was a medicine woman. That would explain the dreams I've been having."

"I can give you more rational explanations, Lee. What other details did he offer about this 'past life'?"

"Well, I think he implied that he had been my mentor as well as my lover. But maybe that's just my impression from my dreams."

"Anything more?"

"Let's see. He did say that I was rather amply built in those days—something else I'd noticed in my candle-meditation dream."

Mallory rolled his eyes. "Too many buffalo burgers? I'm sorry. Go on."

"He mostly talked about this lifetime, about helping me to get in touch with my medicine power and with the earth. He said he would help me remember how to communicate with plants and animals."

"That fits in with the animistic American Indian belief system. Animism assumes that everything in nature has a soul as well as a physical nature. Plants, animals, rocks, wind, rain—everything has its own spirit. It's an ancient belief, perhaps the origin of all religion." Mallory frowned. "But wait. Didn't you tell me that the Mascareñases were Spanish? I'd expect Juan to be Roman Catholic."

"His mother was an Indian. Juan said that he'd studied with her people in the mountains of northwestern Mexico."

"Do you remember what tribe? Were they Yaqui Indians?"

"Yes, Yaqui, I'm sure that's what he said. Why?"

He made a quick note on his pad. "The Yaquis are an interesting tribe, rumored to have strange powers. I suspect that many of their religious ceremonies involve mind-altering drugs. Remember the books by Carlos Castaneda that came out in the late 60s, early 70s?"

"Yes, but I didn't read them."

"Well, Castaneda was a graduate student in anthro-pology who spent more than five years with a Yaqui sorcerer. As a matter of fact, the sorcerer's name was Don Juan. Don Juan Matus. Anyway, this old Indian had some incredible powers, including the ability to switch to a completely different reality whenever the mood hit him. According to Castaneda, that is. I have to point out that some people believe Castaneda was actually writing fiction. Anyway, his books came out in the middle of the hippie era and were very popular with college students looking for an excuse to stay stoned. If Juan is half-Yaqui, that sheds another light on this." He made some more notes on the legal pad, then looked up at her. "What else did he say about his mother?"

"Just that she had been an exceptional woman. Powerful, I think he said. She's been dead for a long time. He didn't volunteer anything about her being a sorceress who passed her powers onto him. But according to Socorro—"

"Well, let's keep in mind that Socorro was part of the Indian culture. And, being a psychic, she had her own particular view of reality." He paused. "Let's talk some more about your feelings after having had sex with Juan."

She looked down at her hands clutched together in her lap. "I can't believe it happened. It's like some kind of erotic dream." She bit her lip to stop it from quivering, then continued in a strained voice. "Nick and I have a long history of mutual trust in our marriage. We made a pact years ago to trust each other and not give in to jealous fantasies while we're apart. That was the only way we could survive his frequent traveling."

She blinked back tears before continuing. "I've never been unfaithful to Nick before. It just never seemed worth the guilt and risk." She shook her head. "And now, after eighteen years of marriage, it's finally happened. And with a *curandero*, or whatever the hell he is. I just hope he doesn't have any sexually transmitted diseases."

"That's certainly a concern these days. I would advise an AIDS test in three months. And, of course, report any unusual physical symptoms to your gynecologist." He hesitated. "Is pregnancy a concern?"

"No, thank God. I had a tubal ligation after a miscarriage years ago."

"I take it you don't plan to tell Nick about any of this. Is he still out of town?"

Lee sighed. "He gets home tonight." She ran her

fingers through her hair. "God, no, I'll never tell Nick. What could I possibly say? 'Welcome home, dear. Sit down, I have something to tell you. You know how you've always encouraged me to develop my own interests? Well, I'm having an interesting little affair with a *brujo*. I peed in his pot, he collected my sweat and said some magic words, and now I'm in his power. By the way, we were Indian lovers in a past life, when I had long black hair and a weight problem. I'll be back whenever the spell wears off or I finish my graduate work in Mexico—Witchcraft 40l. Don't try to stop me because I think he's already killed Mister and Socorro. You don't want to make him mad'." She grimaced. "I can just imagine how understanding Nick would be."

Mallory smiled. "At least you haven't lost your sense of humor. That's an encouraging sign." His expression became serious again. "I agree that there's nothing to be gained by discussing this affair with Nick. Assuming that you still value your marriage."

"Of course, I do! I love Nick. I have a very good life. This thing—whatever it is—with Juan can't really be considered an affair. It's just a...I don't know what it is. Temporary insanity. It won't happen again, and it certainly is no reason to break up my marriage!"

"Okay, okay, calm down. I agree that it isn't. I just wanted you to verbalize that. You have to keep what's real and important straight in your mind. You don't have much time to pull yourself together, if Nick's returning tonight."

Lee groaned. "I know. I can't tell you how I dread seeing him." She turned her wedding ring on her finger and looked up, her expression almost hopeful. "But surely everything will get back to normal then. It'll have to. Nick wouldn't tolerate a disruptive spirit-sucker in his orderly world."

"I'm sure he wouldn't." Mallory looked at the clock on the wall above her head. "I'm afraid our time's up. I suggest that you go home and relax. Try not to dwell on upsetting thoughts. You're not going crazy. Some quality time with Nick this weekend would also be good medicine." He gave her shoulder a reassuring pat as he walked her to the door. "And remember, I'm just a phone call away."

Chapter 17

*I*t was raining when Lee left Mallory's office. She turned the collar up on her jacket and dashed to her car. Like most New Mexicans, she expected the sun to shine and rarely carried an umbrella.

She sat in the car, trying to organize her thoughts. It was ten-thirty. The morning was already shot. She'd have to work until six o'clock to get caught up. That would still give her a couple of hours to pull herself together before Nick got home. God knows, she'd need it.

She talked to herself as she drove to the office. Mallory was right. She was in a vulnerable state of mind and had simply overreacted to Socorro's death. That was certainly understandable. But enough was enough. It was time to get a grip on herself. She couldn't afford to dwell on what had happened with Juan. It was just one of those things, a mistake that was best forgotten.

She cringed, trying to imagine Annabel's reaction to her choice of Juan as a lover. She would love it. "He's a what?" she would ask incredulously. "A *curandero*? How kinky! I knew it. You're definitely menopausal." No, she could never discuss this with anyone but Mallory. She couldn't risk having it ever get back to Nick. Cold fear washed through her. Dear God, Nick must never find out.

* * *

Lee was sipping wine and watching flames dance in the stuccoed fireplace when she heard the thump of the garage door closing. She stood, tucking her shirt into her skirt. There. Everything was neatly in place. Almost everything. Lee glanced at the empty chair where Mister should have been curled up by the fire and felt a familiar ache.

She heard the door burst open and Nick's footsteps in the hall. "I'm home," he called.

Lee took a deep breath and stood up to meet him.

"Hi, babe," he said, dropping his suitcases and holding out his arms.

She put on a welcoming smile and walked into his embrace. "How was your flight?"

"Too long," he said, kissing her forehead. "And there was a crying baby behind me all the way from Salt Lake City." He hugged her hard. "It's been a very long day."

"Leave your bags here and come sit down. How about a drink? Sara, Daddy's home," Lee called as she and Nick walked arm in arm down the hall.

"I could use a Jack Daniels. On the rocks. Well, there's my girl." Nick held out his arms to Sara who came down the stairs, dressed in a nightgown and robe. "What? No date on a Friday night?"

"Kevin's sick," Sara said. "The doctor thinks it's strep. They did a throat culture this afternoon."

"See why you're not allowed to kiss boys?" Nick teased, hugging his daughter. "They carry germs."

The three of them went into the living room where Nick collapsed into his leather recliner. "Well, every-thing went off on schedule," he said, stretching his legs out in front of him. "I think we got good data this time. Oh, thanks," he said to Lee as she handed him his drink.

"What kind of data?" Sara asked, making room for Lee to sit beside her on the sofa.

"We launched a rocket from Poker Flats, just north of Fairbanks. The payload on that rocket was an electron accelerator that I helped design."

"I don't understand," Sara said. "Why are you accelerating electrons?"

Nick savored a swallow of his drink before answering. "Well, sweetheart, we're trying to understand more about auroral processes."

"Auroral processes?"

"You know, the aurora borealis. I've shown you pictures of them from other trips."

"Oh, yeah, the northern lights."

"That's right. We're studying the aurora in order to understand how the sun interacts with the earth's magnetic field. Even small solar changes could influence the weather here on earth. If our technique works, it could help predict global weather change."

"You mean like the next ice age?"

"Or its opposite, the greenhouse effect. Either one could be catastrophic. Whatever the future holds for us on this poor mistreated planet, we need to be prepared."

"Your work is really important, isn't it, Dad?"

"I believe that it is. Otherwise, I wouldn't work so hard at it. I really don't like being away from you and your mom so much, you know."

Sara jumped up and flung herself into Nick's arms. "I'm so proud to have you for a dad," she said, burrowing her face into his shoulder. "Really, really proud."

Watching Nick over the edge of her wine glass, Lee was surprised to see his eyes fill with tears. He didn't often display his softer side. "I'm proud of you, too, princess," he said to Sara in a husky voice.

Lee felt on the verge of tears herself. She drained her wine glass and escaped into the kitchen to refill it. You're doing fine, she told herself, leaning against the refrigerator. Relax. Just act normal. And for God's sake, stop sniveling. She stayed in the kitchen as long as she felt she could without attracting attention.

"When are you taking us to Alaska?" Lee heard Sara ask as she returned to her chair. "Mom and I are ready for one of those king crab pig-outs."

"Right," said Lee, chiming in. "We sure are."

"Well, one of these days we'll have to arrange that." Nick swirled his drink in the glass, looking at Lee. "So tell me, what went on here while I was slaving away in the frozen north?"

"Well, you know that Mister disappeared," Sara said with a worried glance at her mother. "It's been pretty depressing, especially for Mom. He was really her buddy."

"I know. Well, we'll just have to get Mom a new kitten to cheer her up."

Lee forced herself to smile. "I think you'd better scoot off to bed, young lady. It's almost eleven o'clock and you're going shopping in Albuquerque with Wendy tomorrow."

"Yeah, I'm about ready to turn in myself," Nick said with a meaningful look at Lee. "How about you, babe?"

* * *

Nick enveloped her in an affectionate hug when she came to bed. "It's good to be home," he said, reaching under her pajama top to fondle her breast.

Lee felt her body tense. I don't think I can pull this off, she thought. But I have to. I have to act normal. She turned her face toward his and dutifully returned his kiss. As Nick stroked her, Lee closed her eyes and allowed her mind to float.

Suddenly, she was back in Cavado, lying on the buffalo skin rug. Juan's face came into focus above her, his features shadowed by the flickering candlelight. His head lowered. His mouth claimed hers. It was his hands that moved over her breasts and down her body, his knee that deftly parted her thighs. She pressed against him, smelling the tantalizing warmth of his skin as his strong naked body covered hers.

Once again, Lee was gripped by an alien and over-whelming desire. She moaned, abandoning herself to the heat that raged through her. Her body seemed to have a will of its own—a raw, savage need. She dug her fingernails into his back, ignoring his startled cry. With a quick impatient thrust of her body she rolled him over, straddling him. Eyes still tightly closed, Lee rode her wild passion to its climax.

* * *

Nick lay stunned for several moments after she rolled off and away from him. When he finally spoke, he sounded dazed. "Wow!" He took a long, deep breath. "You were—Jesus—incredible. What got into you? You've never responded like that before." He reached for her across the rumpled sheets. "Honey? It was great. Fantastic. Why are you crying?"

* * *

Nick still had his head partly buried under his pillow when Lee rolled out of bed early the next morning. She slipped into a jogging suit and tiptoed into the bathroom to brush her teeth and hair. Carrying her walking shoes and socks, she eased the bedroom door shut. Moments later she was walking down the dirt road away from the house.

The sun was peeking over the Sangre de Cristos, bathing the foothills below in soft shafts of golden light. Lee zipped her parka all the way up and pushed her hands into the pockets. She was glad she'd forced herself up and out of doors. Maybe the exercise and brisk morning air would help to clear her head. Anyway, it was better than lying in bed staring at the ceiling. She stopped, startled, as a flock of birds rose in swirling unison from a gnarled *piñon* tree just ahead.

Suddenly, Juan's voice echoed in her head. *"I want to teach you to talk to the birds again, Lee."* Talk to the birds? She frowned, remembering the dream she'd had after returning from Cavado. In that dream she had somehow communicated with a crow. She had called the crow "Bright Eyes" when she'd sent it for help after her fall.

Lee began walking rapidly, lost in thought. Her passionate love-making last night had been as much of a surprise to her as it had been to Nick. Thank God he couldn't know what was going on in her head. Awake or asleep, her mind was never free of Juan. Last night was no exception. She tried to reconstruct the final dream that had jolted her awake, leaving her with a pounding heart and a body clammy with sweat. It involved Juan, that much she knew for sure. She stopped walking as memories of the dream broke free and flooded her mind.

She had been in Juan's embrace, lying in a dark, shadowy place. She remembered his urgent half-Spanish whispers in her ear and the feel of his warm breath on her neck. Then someone had called her name. Socorro! It had been Socorro's voice, calling her from somewhere in the shadows. She'd tried to answer, but Juan's hand had clamped over her mouth, cutting her off. Then Juan had spoken in Spanish to Socorro, his voice a low, menacing snarl. Then they were flying, hurtling through black space. She had clung to Juan, burying her face in his shoulder.... The dream-memory drifted away like a ribbon of smoke.

What had Juan said to Socorro? *"Tu eres una,"* you are a—what was the word?—*"molestia"*? Something like that. You are a—what?—to me. Then, *"Tu vas a morir."* The words seem to echo in her mind. You're going.... *"Morir"*? The word sounded threatening, but she couldn't quite place it. She would have to look it up in her Spanish dictionary as soon as she got home. Feeling uneasy, the peace of the still morning disturbed by the memory of her dream, she turned and started back at a trot.

As she jogged down a hill, Lee lost her balance, sliding on some loose rock. She landed on one knee, catching herself with her open hands. Rising to her feet, she felt a sharp pain in her right ankle. Cautiously, she put her weight on it. It was okay. Just twisted a little, not really sprained. A sand-colored lizard raised its head from a nearby rock. It raced toward her, not stopping until it was inches from her foot. Lee thought of the lizard on her pottery candle and recalled Socorro's words when she'd presented it to her. *"The lizard is a survivor. We can all learn a lesson from her."*

Lee bent down and studied the lizard who rested near her foot. It seemed to be watching her, too. Finally, it blinked a tiny yellow eye and darted away. She stood and brushed herself off. Walking gingerly, she started home.

* * *

The smell of muffins baking greeted Lee when she opened the front door. She discovered Nick in the kitchen, dressed in jeans and his old grey sweatshirt with University of Colorado in faded letters across the back. Lee stood quietly in the doorway, watching him spoon dough into a muffin tin. She shook her head fondly. Nick loved that old sweatshirt. Several times over the years he had prevented her from turning it into a dust rag. "I see the master chef is at work," she said.

He smiled at her over his shoulder. "Apple bran muffins. The first batch is almost ready. I'm about to scramble some eggs to go with them."

"I think I'll just stick with coffee. Thanks, anyway."

He turned to look at her. "Eat something, babe. You've lost weight lately. I don't want you just disappearing on me."

"I haven't had much of an appetite lately."

He grinned. "Maybe not for food. I have to say, you really knocked my socks off last night."

Lee felt herself flush. "As I remember, your socks were already off," she said, turning away from him to pour a cup of coffee. She felt eager to change the subject. "Maybe I will have a muffin."

Nick watched her as she set the table for two. "How was your walk?" he asked. "I was surprised to find you gone when I got up."

"I woke up early and thought I might as well get some exercise. It's a beautiful morning."

"Oh, Julie, your receptionist, called a few minutes ago. To invite us to brunch at her house tomorrow. Is she still married to what's-his-name? The would-be playwright with the phony Russian accent?"

"Boris. They're in the process of divorce."

"That's too bad. I'll miss his verbal attacks on my work at social gatherings. What a pain in the ass. I remember your office Christmas party, when he ganged up on me with that little prick who always wears a beret—"

"Allen. Why can't you remember his name? He's been writing for us for three years. You've met him several times."

Nick shook his head. "Those free-lance writers all run together in my head. I can't keep them straight. They're all self-centered underachievers who expect to be recognized as great talents someday."

"I hate it when you make generalizations like that," she snapped. "May I remind you that I was once a free-lance writer? Look, let's make a deal. You don't make fun of my co-workers, and I won't make fun of yours. I'm referring to those brilliant overachievers with Einstein hairdos whose idea of party conversation is a heated debate about the nature of quasi-stellar objects."

Nick grimaced. "Ouch. Okay. It's a deal."

"Well, what did you tell Julie?"

"I told her you'd call her back." He poured milk into the bowl of eggs and beat the mixture with a fork. "I'd be happy to escort you if you want to go. I know you were disappointed about my missing the Buchanans' party. I don't want to be the bad guy again."

Lee was quiet for a moment, considering the invitation. It would probably be a good idea to go, to be with people. She didn't want to spend an entire weekend at home with Nick. Not yet. Not until she could come to terms with what had happened in Cavado. Juan's face, with his intense, brooding expression, his compelling eyes, leapt into her mind. And his body, his strong, hard body....

"Well?"

She jumped at the sound of Nick's voice. "What?"

"I said, do you want to go to the brunch?"

"I guess so. If you're up to it. I know you're tired from your trip."

"It might be fun. Besides, I haven't had a date with my best girl in some time."

Lee had trouble meeting Nick's eyes. She unfolded the newspaper and pretended to be engrossed in the front page.

* * *

After breakfast, Lee hurried up the stairs and closed herself in her study. She took her Spanish-English dictionary off the shelf. "*Molestia*"—she was certain that was one of the words Juan had said to Socorro in her dream. "*Tu eres una molestia para mi.*"

She found it: "*Molestia*: a nuisance or annoyance." You are a nuisance to me. And what was the rest of it? "*Tu vas a morir.*" You are going to—she looked up the word—die. *You are going to die!*

Shocked, Lee threw the dictionary on the floor. She dropped into her chair and leaned over, holding her stomach. For a moment she thought she might be sick. Her mind raced. How could she dream words she didn't even know? She had studied Spanish long ago, in high school, but hadn't retained very much. Of course, she heard a lot of Spanish spoken around town. I must remember more than I think I do, she tried to assure herself. Those words were just buried in my subconscious. That's the only possible answer!

Still, no matter how hard she tried to talk herself out of it as the day wore on, Lee couldn't shake a growing feeling of apprehension. Nick must have noticed her preoccupation. She caught him watching her out of the corner of his eye as she worked around the house, trying to keep busy.

* * *

They sat down to dinner alone that night. Sara
wasn't due back from Albuquerque until nine o'clock.
Lee looked up from her salad to find Nick watching her
with a worried expression on his face. He put his fork
down and leaned back in his chair, frowning. "Okay,
what's going on? You haven't been yourself since I got
back."

"Really? I'm sorry, I guess I have been a little
stressed. But it's nothing to be concerned about. It'll
pass."

"I know you're mourning for Mister. But I get the
feeling that it's more than that." He sipped his wine,
watching her. "You were upset when I left last week. Is
it still that Cavado business?"

Lee looked down at her plate. The soggy alfalfa
sprouts looked like little white worms. She felt a twinge
of nausea. "No. It's just a combination of things. I
don't know. Maybe I'm pre-menopausal."

"Seriously? Are you having female problems?"

"No, I was joking. It's just that I've felt a little
overwhelmed, at work and in general." She took a sip of
wine, trying to swallow the lump that was forming in her
throat. "But, as I said, it'll pass. Doctor Mallory said
that..." She broke off as his fork stopped midway to his
mouth.

"Mallory? You saw Mallory while I was gone?"

"Yes, I did. I just hadn't gotten around to mentioning
it." Her scalp prickled as she struggled to get on safer
ground. "I felt I needed to touch base with him. I
hadn't seen him in a couple of years, you know. And,
well, I was upset about that interview in Cavado. I
couldn't understand how I had let it get so out of hand."
She swallowed hard. "I decided to talk it over with
Doctor Mallory. I thought he'd make me feel better, and
he did."

"When did you see him?"

"Friday before last." She hesitated. "And again
yesterday."

"You saw him twice while I was gone? It sounds to

me like you were more than a little depressed."

"The second time I was really upset about Mister, and—"

"Pardon me, but I just don't buy this. I think there's something you aren't telling me. People don't normally go running off to a shrink just because their cat disappears."

Lee blinked back angry tears. "This may be hard for you to understand, Nick, but some perfectly normal people are really attached to their pets. Mister may have been just a cat to you, but, damn it, I loved him. At least he was here all the time."

"Unlike me, you mean. Look, I'm sorry about Mister. I know he was important to you." He reached across the table and covered her hand with his. "I don't mean to be insensitive about it." He patted her hand. "What did Mallory have to say about the Cavado creep?"

"Well," Lee hesitated. Then she took a deep breath and freed her hand to pick up her wine glass. "He thinks maybe Juan drugged and hypnotized me."

"What?" Nick's outburst caused Lee to jerk and splash red wine into her salad bowl. "Drugged you? Did I hear you right?"

"You don't have to yell."

"Let me get this straight. Mallory thinks this weirdo drugged you? How? And what do you mean hypnotized?"

Lee explained Mallory's theory to Nick, wanting to kick herself for allowing the conversation to take this turn. "He said it would have been very easy for Juan to put marijuana or something in my tea. And he said that it might have made me sick afterwards. Remember? I thought I had the flu."

"Jesus Christ!" Nick snatched his napkin out of his lap and slapped it on the table. "You didn't call the police?"

"The police?" Lee clutched her hands together in her lap. "Are you serious?"

"You're damned right I'm serious!"

"Nick, calm down. Listen to me. I didn't consider calling the police because that would have blown it up into a big deal. It might have even gotten into the newspapers, and that would have been very embarrassing. I don't want anyone else to know about this." She glared at him. "Do you?"

He stared back at her for a moment. "No, I guess not. But if this guy really did that, he shouldn't be running around loose! He's dangerous. Anything could have happened to you!"

"Well, nothing terrible did. He didn't hurt me." She drained her wine glass.

"That's a matter of opinion. You've been moping around, depressed as hell. You've been to see a shrink. Twice. I would call that hurting you." Nick's face was flushed with anger. He poured more wine into both their glasses. "I think I'll pay that sneaky bastard a visit. I'll show him what to do with his sweating oil."

"No! Don't do that." She put her hand on his arm. "Please. That would only make me feel worse. I just want to put the whole thing behind me. I would like very much to forget it."

Nick stared into space, eyes narrowed. "I knew it was completely unlike you to go along with that awakening ceremony bullshit, but it never occurred to me—"

"It's over now. Let's just forget it." Lee felt a wave of exhaustion. "Promise me."

"Maybe I should discuss this with Doctor Mallory. See if he doesn't agree that this guy should be investigated."

"No! We don't know for sure that I was drugged. That's just Mallory's theory. And it doesn't really matter now because it's over, and we're going to forget it. Okay? Okay?"

Nick looked at her for a long moment, his face flushed with indignation. "No, it's not okay with me. Not by a long shot. But I don't want to upset you any more than you already are. If you're sure you don't want me to—"

"I'm sure!"

"Then I guess I don't have any choice but to drop it. But it galls me to see that bastard go unpunished." He pushed his plate away. "I've lost my appetite. Come on, I'll help you straighten up the kitchen. Then I'm going upstairs. I need to spend a couple of hours on the computer."

"Tonight? Nick, it's Saturday night."

"I have a lot of data to organize before the Monday morning staff meeting." He stood and started clearing the table.

"Don't bother," she said. "I'll take care of this."

"Lee, I want to help—"

"Just leave me alone. Go on and organize your data."

Nick started to speak, then changed his mind and walked out of the room.

Lee put her head down on the table and let the tears come. You can't help, Nick, she thought. I'm afraid no one can help me now.

* * *

Later, in bed that night, Nick reached for Lee. "Don't pull away from me, babe," he said. "I didn't mean to make you angry tonight. It's just that I'm worried about you. You're acting strange as hell. You're so strung out—"

"Please, Nick. I can't talk about it. I mean, there's really nothing to talk about. I'm not angry. I'm just tired. I'll feel better in the morning. Let's go to sleep."

He sighed. "Okay. Sleep well." Soon afterwards he rolled onto his side and fell asleep.

Lee lay stiffly on her side of the bed, far from Nick, staring at the ceiling. When she closed her eyes, erotic images of Juan invaded her mind. She shuddered with guilty desire and buried her face in the pillow.

Chapter 18

*L*ee sat at her makeup table in her underwear the next morning, trying to pull herself together for Julie's brunch. Peering critically at her reflection in the magnifying side of the mirror, she was alarmed by what she saw. She looked pale and tired. And the skin under her eyes was unusually puffy. I've got to lay off the wine, she thought, reaching for a small jar of eye cream. As she patted the cream under her eyes, she tried to remember how many glasses she'd had last night. At least three, maybe four. It was dangerous to use booze to escape from reality. Her alcoholic father had certainly taught her that.

She was smoothing makeup under her eyes when Nick walked in, carrying a cup of coffee. He leaned against the wall, watching her. "You are a veritable vision, Scarlett mah deah," he said, twirling an imaginary moustache and launching into his Rhett Butler imitation.

Lee forced the expected response. "Why, ah declare, sir, how you do run on." She felt a sharp stab of nostalgia. The corny Rhett and Scarlett exchange was a ritual that remained from the early days of their marriage. Years ago, the game would end with Nick sweeping her up in his arms and carrying her off to bed. Now, they just stuck to the timeworn dialogue. She turned back to the mirror, feeling depressed.

"May ah lace yore corset, mah lovely?"

"Oh, fiddle de dee," Lee said, struggling to play along. "I burned that ol' thing along with mah bra." She smoothed blusher along her cheekbones and stood up, walking past him into her walk-in closet to get a dress.

Her eyes fell on the blouse she had worn when she returned to Cavado. Suddenly she was reliving the moment when Juan unbuttoned it, slipped it from her shoulders and tossed it on the floor. She closed her eyes and felt his warm lips on her neck and her shoulders, his hands cupping her buttocks, pulling her closer. She shuddered, feeling her nipples grow hard. Lost in the memory, she began to stroke her breasts.

"Babe?" Nick's voice shocked her back to the present. "What are you doing in there? Get a move on. It's after eleven."

She snatched a denim dress off its hanger. Then she took several deep breaths, fighting to regain some composure before returning to the bedroom.

* * *

"Hi, come in!" They were greeted at the door by Julie, dressed in a long corduroy skirt and cowboy boots, her sweater covered with strands of turquoise beads. "I'm glad you could come on such short notice. I just had this sudden urge to throw a party. I hope you're hungry." She slipped her arm through Nick's and escorted them inside.

Indian rugs and art posters competed for wall space in the cheerfully cluttered living room. Lee estimated at least forty guests crammed into the small town house. Quite a spur-of-the-moment Sunday brunch. A handsome young man sat by the fireplace, singing and strumming a guitar. His music was almost drowned out by the loud conversation and outbursts of laughter. Lee, scanning the crowd for familiar faces, stumbled over a stack of books protruding from under an end table.

"Oops, be careful," Julie said, grabbing Lee's arm. "You'll have to excuse the mess." She rolled her eyes and repositioned a silver comb into the side of her wild mane of salt and pepper hair. "My cleaning lady couldn't make it yesterday. She found her boyfriend drinking with another woman at The Bull Ring and took an axe to the hood of his car. Then she slugged a policeman who tried to interfere. Now she's in jail, can you believe it?" she laughed merrily. "Oh, excuse me, there's the doorbell. Help yourselves to margaritas in the kitchen."

"She can afford a cleaning lady?" Nick asked in a low voice. "How much are you paying Julie?"

"Not nearly as much as she's worth. Oh, there's Alessandro and P.J. waving to us. You remember them from the Garretts' Fourth of July barbecue. They own an antique shop on Canyon Road. P.J. used to be a female impersonator in San Francisco."

Nick groaned. "So now he's impersonating a male in Santa Fe?" Lee shot him a warning look.

"I'm sorry. I'll behave myself. But I'm going to need several margaritas to get through this, I can tell. And a bowl of posole. Can I get a margarita for you?"

"No. But I'd like some mineral water if she has it."

"Okay. Here goes. If I don't come back, you'll know that Allen has me cornered again, trying to save the world from science." He moved away through the crowd, toward the kitchen.

As she was maneuvering her way across the room, Lee stopped. Several women directly in front of her were discussing Socorro's death. "According to Leona, Socorro collapsed right after dinner," one of them said. "They were still sitting at the table, drinking coffee, when the poor thing just keeled over. Like she'd been shot. Can you imagine? The last thing in the world you'd expect to happen. Why, I saw her in her gallery early last week, looking absolutely smashing..."

Lee turned, desperate to escape the upsetting narrative, only to run into Annabel.

"Hi," she said. "Some party, huh? I understand that Julie just came into some money. A grandmother or something. Let's hope it isn't enough for her to retire on. We'd have a hell of a time replacing her."

Lee nodded her agreement, thankful for a change of subject.

"I was just talking to Leona," Annabel continued. "She was with Socorro Tafoya-Hall, when she died last week. You know, the owner of Galería de Canyon Road. You've met her, haven't you? They started advertising with us about a year ago. Anyway, she was a full-blooded Indian—high cheekbones, long black hair, and thin to boot. Looked a little like Cher. And she was so young! I doubt that she was even forty. Anyway, Leona was having dinner with Socorro when she just dropped dead. Right at the table." Annabel's voice dropped to a confidential tone. "I guess it was absolutely grisly. Leona said Socorro suddenly grabbed her head with both hands. Her mouth was moving but no words were coming out. Then the poor thing's eyes started to bulge and—"

"Stop it!" Lee's voice rose. "I can't listen to this! Damn it, Annie, I just can't listen—" She had a glimpse of Annabel's shocked face just before she whirled and bumped into an aproned woman carrying a tray of enchiladas. The noisy room hushed in fascination.

Horrified, Lee ran through the staring crowd and out the front door. She was leaning against her car, shaking uncontrollably when Nick arrived running.

"Lee? Are you all right? What on earth happened? Annabel rushed up to me and said that you just suddenly went to pieces."

"Take me home, Nick. Please, take me home."

* * *

Lee went straight to her room. Nick followed close

behind. "It's just a headache," she said, lying down on the bed. "I think I'm getting a migraine. Would you get me a tranquilizer? Maybe I can sleep it off."

Nick returned from the bathroom with a pill and glass of water. "Thanks," she said. "I'm so embarrassed. I didn't mean to cause a scene. Annabel was just babbling on and on—you know how she does—and all of a sudden I felt very sick. If I can just lie here quietly for awhile, I'll be all right." She swallowed the pill.

"Lee, you haven't had a migraine in years. I think you need a thorough medical checkup."

"I had one last month, remember? The doctor said I was in great shape."

"Well, you aren't now." He looked down at her with a concerned expression. "Maybe you have some sort of hormone imbalance. That might explain—"

"Maybe so." She closed her eyes. "I'll have it checked out if I'm not better soon."

He looked somewhat relieved. "Okay. Just rest for awhile. And I wouldn't worry about hurting Annabel's feelings, She's about as sensitive as a warthog."

Lee smiled weakly and tried to change the subject. "Sara's spending the afternoon with Wendy. I don't expect her home before five o'clock. I imagine you can use some quiet, uninterrupted time."

"I do need to spend another hour or so on the Alaska data," he said. "But first, I want to put a fresh coat of wax on the Volvo. This weather can't last. It'll be snowing before we know it."

He left the room. Moments later, Lee heard the door to the garage open and close. I can't believe I went to pieces like that, she thought. And in front of all those people. I'll have to call Julie later and apologize. And hope Annabel will forgive me for screaming at her. Now she'll be convinced that I'm going bonkers. She closed her eyes, but images of Socorro—of her last dreadful moments as described by Annabel—tortured her mind.

That's probably Annabel, she thought, when the

phone rang moments later. Might as well get the
apology over with. Blame it on a migraine. Or rampag-
ing hormones. She lifted the receiver.

"Lee? I could wait no longer to hear your voice."

"Juan?" Her voice was a horrified whisper.

"I must see you. Come tomorrow."

"No! No, I can't come. I can't talk. My husband is
here. I have to hang up."

"Tomorrow. I will be waiting." The line went dead.

Lee banged the receiver down. I can't believe this,
she thought. That he would dare call here on a Sunday
afternoon. Nick could have picked up the phone! If he
had heard.... She shuddered. I have to put a stop to this
once and for all. Juan has got to leave me alone. She
curled up, clutching Nick's pillow. After awhile, the pill
did its work and she drifted into a light sleep.

When she awoke, she felt a little stronger. It's up to
me, she told herself, to get out of this mess. Somehow, I
have to get it through Juan's thick head that it's over
between us. I have to make him listen to reason.
Obviously, that can't be done over the telephone. I
guess I'm going to have to see him again. Just one last
time. To make certain that he understands the situation.
I'll scare him. I'll tell him that Nick's threatening to call
the police.

She forced herself up and into a hot shower. By the
time she was dressed and downstairs preparing dinner,
Lee had almost convinced herself that the nightmare
would soon be over. Enough of this *brujo* nonsense, she
thought, putting a frozen quiche into the oven. Juan is
just a man. I can handle him. I can make him accept the
fact that it's over between us. She repressed a warning
stab of uncertainty and even managed a smile for Nick
when he came into the kitchen a short time later.

"Ummm, something smells good. Did I hear Sara
come home a few minutes ago?"

Lee nodded. "She's in her room. On the phone, I
imagine."

"Of course." He leaned against the counter, watching

her. "You look better. Headache gone?"

"Just about. The little nap I took did the trick. Sara," she called up the stairs. "Will you come down and make a salad, please?"

"Did you hurt yourself?" Nick asked. "You're limping a little, favoring your left leg."

"I am?" She frowned, then shrugged. "Oh, it's nothing. I just twisted my ankle on my walk yesterday morning." She executed a graceful pirouette on the smooth tile floor. "See, no harm done."

"I'm relieved to see you acting more like your old self," Nick said. "You've really had me worried."

"Well, stop worrying. I'm fine. End of discussion." She busied herself setting the table. "Have you unpacked from your trip?"

"Yeah. While you were napping. I have a couple of sweaters and a sports coat that need to go to the cleaners. Could you drop them off for me tomorrow?"

"Sure," she said. "I'm not going into the office. Things are under control there. The next issue of the magazine is ready to go to the printers. I think I'll give myself the day off. There's a little personal business I need to take care of."

Chapter 19

Slamming the car door behind her, Lee marched resolutely up the dirt path leading to the small adobe house. She squared her shoulders and rapped sharply on the front door.

"At last," Juan said, opening the door. His shirt was unbuttoned almost to the waist. "I have been expecting you." He pulled her inside the darkened room and closed the door. Lee stood still, feeling her courage waiver. Eerie shapes and shadows appeared to be moving, closing in. She straightened her shoulders, determined to maintain her composure.

"Juan," she began in a firm voice, "We have to talk." She stiffened as she felt him slide her woolen wrap off her shoulders. Then, before she could resist, he pulled her into his arms.

"Let me go! I can't—"

His lips closed on hers, cutting off her words and speaking directly to her body. She pushed against his chest with her palms. "Listen to me! I came here to—"

"I know why you came. I feel your need." He pulled

221

her buttocks hard against him. "And you can feel mine, can't you?"

She twisted frantically in his embrace, aware of his erection pushing against her stomach.

"Don't fight me, *querida*." He held her fast. "You're still trying to fight me."

Lee had an image of a fly ensnared in a spider web, becoming more hopelessly trapped with each frantic movement. She made an anguished sound.

"Look at me," he said. His voice was soft but insistent. "I want you to look at me."

She stared at the wooden floor instead, her heart hammering in her chest. His hands moving on her back seemed to burn through her blouse. Again, she tried to push him away. But his power was too great. Slowly, she lifted her head. Her eyes traveled up his partially exposed chest and lingered on the amulet that dangled from the chain around his neck. The stones eyes seemed to glow with a light of their own.

She heard Juan's voice as if from a distance. "Let go of your fears, Lee," he said. "Let yourself come into your power."

She tore her gaze from the amulet and met his eyes. The passion she saw there almost caused her knees to buckle. "No!" she said, wrenching her eyes from his and turning her face toward the door. "Please, don't."

His grip tightened around her waist and his free hand gently clasped her chin, bringing her face toward his. "Trust me," he whispered. His voice wrapped around her like soft silk cords. "What is happening is meant to be."

Lee stared up at him like a rabbit mesmerized by a bright light. She felt her strength and will drain away, exposing her raw physical need. Her body seemed to have a will of its own and, in spite of her fears, it ached to press against his. "What have you done to me?" she moaned.

"Shhhhh. Later," he whispered. "We will talk later." She felt his fingers at her chest, unbuttoning her blouse.

"I can wait no longer to touch you."

* * *

Lee lay exhausted in Juan's arms on the buffalo skin. She felt the soft tickle of fur beneath her naked buttocks as she buried her face against his neck. She caressed his chest, gently trailing her fingers through the soft, dark hair. As she moved her hand toward his throat, her fingers touched the amulet. She jerked them away. The amulet felt hot, almost too hot to touch.

Juan turned and slid his leg over her hip, pinning her against him. He kissed her forehead and stroked her back. Far removed from the outside world, Lee sighed and closed her eyes.

* * *

She awoke with a start, shocked by her surroundings. It hadn't been a dream. It had happened again! She bolted upright, finding that she was alone. The room felt stuffy and uncomfortably warm. Glancing at the wood-burning stove in the corner, Lee felt a wave of panic. What if she was trapped, locked inside this dark, suffocating place? No one knew she was there. No one would know where to look for her!

Suddenly, from the other room, she heard the soft creak of the front door. She rose to her feet, clutching a blanket around her. In a moment, Juan appeared in the doorway, fully dressed and wearing a sheepskin jacket.

"You are awake," he said, smiling at her.

"Yes." She was uncomfortably aware of her nakedness. "Where were you?"

"I stepped outside for a moment." He moved close to her and stroked the side of her neck. "What's wrong, *querida*? You look upset."

"Everything's wrong. I feel so strange, so lost." She let him draw her into his arms and rested her cheek on his shoulder.

"You are not lost, *mi vida*. You are beginning to find your true self."

"How did you get up and dress without waking me?"

He laughed softly. "I can be as quiet as a shadow

when I want to be."

She took a deep breath and raised her head to look at him. "Juan," she blurted, "did you know that Socorro died last week?"

He seemed to freeze for an instant, before bending his head to kiss her shoulder. "Who?" He continued to slide his lips up the side of her neck.

"Socorro Tafoya-Hall." Lee felt her stomach twist into a tight fist. "She was a friend of mine."

"I know little of life outside of Cavado," he said, releasing her. He took off his jacket and hung it on a wooden peg. "You sound as though I should know this woman."

"I thought you might have heard of her. She was an Indian from Santa Clara." Lee shivered.

"You are cold. Come, wrap the blanket around you and sit by the stove." He led her to the sofa and sat close beside her, one arm around her shoulders. He slid his other hand beneath the blanket and began to caress her breast. Lee pulled back. It was now or never.

"Juan, I have to talk to you. I came here today to talk. Not to..." She squirmed as his hand moved down across her naked stomach. "Don't, please. I don't know what kind of power you have over me, but I can't—"

"Don't you?"

"What?"

"Don't you know what kind of power I have over you?" His finger traced slow circles around her navel.

She turned to look at his face. A smile played across his lips. A memory of Mister toying with a captured mouse sprang to Lee's mind. "How can I get through to you, damn it?" she blurted. "I cannot continue to do this!"

Juan frowned and withdrew his hand from under the blanket. "You are blocking your memory of what is between us! When will you allow yourself to understand?"

"What you don't seem to understand is that I'm a married woman! My husband is already very upset about my first visit here—about the awakening ceremony. He's threatened to go to the police."

A muscle near the corner of Juan's left eye twitched. "The police? Why?"

"He thinks you drugged me during our interview." Lee could feel cold sweat on her palms. "I...I can't see you again. That's what I came here today to tell you."

"You think you can walk away from me so easily?"

"Why won't you face reality? Our relationship has no future. You must know that. I love my family, my daughter...and my husband."

His hands gripped her shoulders, roughly turning her to face him. "Your love belongs to me! You are mine. You have always been mine." His eyes glittered with a dark intensity. They burned into hers, scattering her thoughts and forcing her compliance. With a sinking heart, Lee felt her resolve desert her once again. She didn't even protest when he yanked the blanket from her naked shoulders.

* * *

It was late afternoon when she pulled into the parking lot of the City Different Cleaning Company and reached into the back seat for the clothes she had collected early that morning. She stared, frowning at the small pile. What happened to Nick's navy sweater? She twisted around in her seat to search the floor board, certain that she had put the sweater with the other items to be cleaned. "It's not here," she mumbled to herself. "But I distinctly remember.... God, what's happening to me? Am I losing my mind?"

Chapter 20

"Mom?" Sara stared at Lee in amazement. They were alone in the kitchen, cleaning up after dinner. Nick had excused himself immediately after eating to work on a report that was due in the morning. "Do you realize that you just put the salt shaker in the refrigerator? You've been totally spaced out all night. What's wrong?"

Abashed, Lee retrieved the salt shaker. "Nothing."

"I don't think you've heard a word I've said."

"What?"

"You weren't listening, were you?"

"I'm sorry. I guess my mind was wandering. What is it?"

"Oh, nothing important. Just that my entire life is coming apart, and my mother obviously doesn't give a rat's ass!" Sara's eyes shone with angry tears.

"Watch your language, young lady! And don't speak to me in that tone of voice."

"I can't talk to you at all lately!" Sara wailed. "I can't trust Wendy. You don't listen..."

"What on earth are you talking about? Sara, stop crying and tell me what's going on."

"Are you sure you're interested?" Sara grabbed a paper napkin and wiped her eyes.

"Of course I'm interested. What's wrong?"

"I just found out that my best friend in the whole world is trying to steal my boyfriend."

"Wendy? Wendy's interested in Kevin?"

"More than interested! She has a serious case of the hots for him! The mere fact that we've been best friends since the fourth grade doesn't count for anything. I'm so mad I could just die. I'll never, ever trust her again. And then, tonight, when I tried to talk to you about it, you acted like you were on Mars or something." Fresh tears started to flow.

"I'm sorry, Sara," Lee said wearily. "I know I've been preoccupied lately. But that doesn't mean I'm not interested in your problems. I'm always here for you."

"Not lately, you're not."

Lee sagged under a wave of exhaustion. "Look, honey, can we talk about this tomorrow? I really can't—"

"Oh, terrific! Just forget it! It's only my life!" Sara whirled and ran up the stairs. Lee heard her bedroom door slam. She sighed and finished clearing the kitchen counter. Leaving the dirty dishes in the sink, she went upstairs to her bathroom.

Sitting at her dressing table, she stared into space as the tub filled with hot water. She'd spend some time talking to Sara tomorrow. Just not tonight. Dear God, not tonight. She slipped out of her clothes and into her bath.

Eyes closed, she leaned her head back against an inflated bath pillow. The hours she had spent with Juan began replaying in her mind. She'd been a fool to think that she could control the situation, that she could simply tell Juan good-bye and be done with it. *Brujo* or not, he had a fierce hold on her. Socorro hadn't been exaggerating when she said that Lee was in "deep shit."

And crawling out wasn't going to be easy.

It doesn't make sense, she thought. How can I be afraid of Juan and so attracted to him at the same time? What kind of power does he have over me? There's the sex, obviously. But is it more than that? Am I, as Socorro believed, under some kind of spell? She dismissed the thought, determined not to think about Socorro. Then her thoughts returned, as they always did now, to Juan.

Was he really someone she had known and loved in a past lifetime? Was that the reason for this obsession? Sinking deeper into the fragrant, steaming water, Lee admitted to herself that only one thing was certain. Whatever the truth of the situation was, she was in over her head.

* * *

Nick was sitting at his desk, reading a thick report titled "Experimental Ionospheric Observations and Theory," when Lee came out of the bathroom in her nightgown. "I was beginning to think you'd drowned in there," he said, glancing up.

"I was just draining off negative energy."

"What?"

"Never mind." She turned down the bed and crawled in.

"Is your headache back?"

"I'm just tired."

"You were so distant during dinner—"

"Nick, I said I'm just tired! Stop interrogating me!"

"Interrogating you? Is that what you think I'm doing? You're my wife, damn it. And I'm worried sick about you. What am I supposed to do? Just keep my mouth shut? Not ask any questions?"

"Just let me sleep. Please. I'll feel better in the morning."

"That's what you keep saying." He sighed. "Okay, I'll drop it. I've got another hour or so of reading here. Will the light bother you?"

"No. I'll wear my mask. Goodnight." She adjusted

a black satin sleep mask across her eyes and quickly fell asleep.

* * *

A freezing wind whistled and moaned beyond the blanket-covered doorway. She crouched closer to the warmth of the open fire, spreading her sacred objects on the hard-packed dirt floor. She picked up the three clear crystals that symbolized light, fire, and truth, and put them inside her medicine bundle. They would strengthen her magic. And she would need prayer sticks, she remembered, reaching for two pieces of wood, carved from a tree struck by lightning and decorated with emblems of Father Sun and Mother Earth.

Her thunder-speaker. She mustn't forget that. The flat piece of wood—set with sacred blue stones and attached to a length of rope woven from the hair of ancient Holy Ones—reproduced the sound of thunder when whirled above the head, driving away sickness. She added it to the items in the bundle.

Sacred snakes, carefully carved from a river tree and painted in the colors of the four directions—white for north, yellow for east, red for south and black for west— felt warm, almost alive, to her touch. She murmured with satisfaction. Their magic would be strong tonight. She laid them beside a delicate pink and white spirit shell from the endless waters that lay far to the west.

Finally she selected the spear-shaped leaves and small red berries that would be boiled for tea and made into medicine paste. It was all assembled, everything needed for a curing chant. She stood slowly, painfully, supporting her weight on her left leg, and reached for her walking stick that leaned against the mud-plastered wall. It was time to dress.

She pulled a soft doeskin ceremonial garment over her head, adjusting the bear teeth that decorated the neckline. Then she tied skunk fur pelts over her moccasins for protection from any evil that might be released during the ceremony. For added strength, she posi-

229

tioned an eagle feather in the leather band around her forehead.

She spoke softly to a large grey wolf that was sleeping close to the fire. "Accompany me to the great cave, Wind Runner," she said, wrapping herself in a long fur cape. "I will need the medicine of your keen senses tonight." The wolf yawned and rose to its feet.

Carrying her medicine bundle, she stepped out into the cold night. Snowflakes hit her face as she slowly made her way, bent against the blowing wind, along the narrow path. The wolf followed closely behind. She could hear the soft beat of medicine drums as she approached the ceremonial cave. Iatik, Great Mother of All, be with me tonight, she prayed. Help me restore the son of Miwana to harmony with the earth and heavens.

A small figure wrapped in brown fur lay on a flat stone in the center of the cave. A whispering group of women gathered around him, one of them crying. They fell silent and drew back, heads lowered in respect, as she entered the cave. A handful of men, faces blackened with ashes, sat around an open fire beating a soft rhythm on their drums.

The child opened his eyes and began to cry as she approached him. Then he started to cough, a dry, wheezing sound that wracked his thin frame. Drops of perspiration glistened on his flushed face. He has the coughing sickness, she thought with a sinking heart. She was going to need her strongest magic to save this little one. He was too young, and already very weak. It was going to be a long night. She gently touched her hand to his hot forehead, then blew three purifying breaths across his face to cleanse away all traces of evil winds. The child began a thin wailing. Chanting softly, she opened her medicine bundle.

* * *

Lee woke up, chilled and trembling. She ripped off her sleep mask and lay shivering in the darkness, her heart hammering in her chest. Another dream. And the most realistic one yet. A sick child, a cave, a big dog—

or was it a wolf? And she was there. She was really there! I don't know what's going on, she thought frantically, but something really frightening is happening to me.

She raised her head and looked at the clock. Twelve-fifteen. All right, just calm down, she told herself, turning over her damp pillow. There's no reason to be this unnerved by a dream. She tried to relax by matching Nick's slow, deep breathing, but when she closed her eyes a high-pitched, wailing cry echoed in her mind—accompanied by a soft, rhythmic sound like distant drumbeats. Cold panic rose in her throat. She shuddered and moved close to Nick, fitting her body against his comforting warmth.

* * *

Lee turned off the alarm and groaned. Morning already. She used to wake up eager to face the day. Now it was a real effort to drag herself into work. But she had to go in. She'd been out of the office too often lately. She automatically looked at the foot of the bed and felt a lump in her throat. There would never be another cat like Mister.

* * *

"Oh, Julie," Lee said, stopping by the front desk, "I meant to call you yesterday. I owe you an apology for leaving your party on Sunday. All of a sudden, I felt really ill. There were so many people I couldn't find you. Please forgive me."

Julie looked uncomfortable. "Of course I forgive you. But I was worried. Are you feeling okay now?"

"Yes. It was just a migraine. Is Annabel in yet?"

"She's meeting with a new advertiser this morning, that Thai restaurant on Cerrillos Road. I expect her around nine-thirty."

"Okay. I need to talk to her when she comes in." She hurried into her office and closed the door.

* * *

As Lee sorted through memos and miscellaneous correspondence, her thoughts kept returning to the dream she'd had the night before. She had been sitting in some kind of hut, on a dirt floor, gathering a peculiar bunch of things—decorated sticks, rocks and a sea shell—and tying them into a leather pouch. Lee sat back in her chair, remembering a cold walk through wind and snow to a fire-lit cave, and the expression of fear on a small face staring up at her from a mound of dark fur. She could still hear the child's hacking cough and shrill, haunting cry. A realistic dream? Or was it a past-life memory? She knew what Juan would say.

She buried her face in her hands. I'm really worried about myself, she thought. And I don't know what to do. Call Doctor Mallory again? He'd attribute my dreams to exhaustion and an impressionable state of mind. Just a reaction to Juan's reincarnation line of bull. No, she decided. No need to take up more of Mallory's time. He's done all he can for me.

Her thoughts turned to Socorro and their last meeting. Did she indeed go to Cavado? Her husband might know. But Lee didn't want to bother the poor man with questions at a time like this. He must be devastated. Besides, what could she say without sounding like a lunatic? If she admitted her suspicions, he'd think she was deranged.

But if Socorro did go to Cavado, then Juan had lied about not knowing her. Lee stopped cold. Wait a minute. Socorro's uncle—the Deputy Sheriff! He was going to do some checking on Juan, something about an investigation years ago. My God, she thought, how could I have forgotten about that? Somehow, with all that's happened, it completely went out of my head. I've got to talk to the uncle, find out what he discovered. And besides, he might know if Socorro went to Cavado. But what was his name? Leroy? No. Luis. Luis Tafoya. She grabbed the phone book and looked up the number of the Rio Arriba County Sheriff's Department.

After several frustrating transfers, she was connected to the correct office. "May I speak to Deputy Sheriff Tafoya, please?"

"Speaking." The voice was gruff.

"Deputy Tafoya, my name is Lee Lindsay. I was a friend of your niece, Socorro. The last time I talked to her she said that you might have some information about a man I met in Cavado. Juan Mascareñas."

"You the one that owns that magazine? Santa Fe—?"

"**Santa Fe Today**. That's right. Did Socorro talk to you about me?"

"She just said that you'd had a little run-in with Mascareñas."

"I guess you could call it that." She hesitated, unwilling to volunteer any more information than she had to. "I interviewed Mr. Mascareñas for an article. Afterwards, I had some questions about him." She cleared her throat. "First let me say how sorry I am about Socorro. She was a wonderful person."

"Yes, she was. It was a terrible shock. Very unexpected."

"I saw her the day before she died. She said she was going to see you, that you were going to check the records. Something about an investigation years ago, involving Mr. Mascareñas. I'm very curious. Did you find anything?"

"Just a minute. What did you say your name was?"

"Lee. Lee Lindsay."

"Okay, just checking. That is the name I'd written down. Have to be careful, giving out information over the phone. Yes, I located that file. Let me get it." Lee was put on hold for several minutes. "Sorry to keep you waiting. I had to take another call."

"Then there was an investigation?"

"In 1962. But it didn't amount to much. Mascareñas was questioned in connection with a missing person. Let's see, it was a twenty-year-old woman from California named Susan Miller. She was a student at the University of New Mexico when Mascareñas was there and, from all accounts, she was his girlfriend. They both dropped out of school suddenly, in the middle of a semester. According to the girl's friends, they were headed for Mexico."

"Mexico?" Lee felt the muscles in her stomach tense.

"According to the report, the Miller woman told her roommate that she and Mascareñas were going to spend some time studying a tribe of Indians in the mountains near Chihuahua. She was never heard from again. Her family alerted the Mexican police, hired a private investigator, did everything possible."

"She was never found?"

"Not as far as I know."

"But Juan came back."

"Yes, he did, two years later. But the girl wasn't with him. Mascareñas claimed to have no idea where she was. His story was that she had jilted him for another man after they arrived in Chihuahua. But he stayed on in Mexico, traveling alone, until he learned that his mother was sick."

"Sinopa Mascareñas?"

"That's right. She died shortly after he got home." There was a short pause. "Sinopa Mascareñas. Man, she was really something. I met her right after I joined the department, more than forty years ago. But that's another story."

"I'd like to hear it."

"Well, as I remember, several villagers from Cavado came in, insisting that Sinopa be arrested. Her husband, Don Gregorio, had died a few days before and they were convinced that she'd killed him. They still weren't satisfied, even after old Doc Lopez diagnosed the cause of death as natural—a stroke or something."

Lee swallowed hard. "Did you say a stroke?"

"I think so. If my memory serves me. It was a long time ago. Anyway, I went out to Cavado and talked to Sinopa. I'll never forget her. She was beautiful. Black eyes that looked right through you. And all that hair hanging down past her waist. But she was very—what is the word?—haughty. She was very haughty. Cold as ice. It was easy to see how the rumors got started."

"What rumors?"

"Well, the villagers in Cavado were apparently terrified of her. Said that she had supernatural powers."

"You mean they thought she was a witch?"

"I guess so. There's a lot of superstition in those little mountain villages. And they don't take easily to outsiders. If I remember correctly, Don Gregorio met Sinopa and married her in Mexico. The villagers were upset when he brought her home to Cavado. It had been assumed that he would marry one of the local girls. So, of course, there was a lot of jealousy and resentment. That's human nature."

"I suppose so."

"It didn't end with Don Gregorio's death, though. There was more trouble concerning Sinopa, several years later. I remember that the villagers were up in arms again. Some nonsense about her having put a death hex on a woman whose husband she'd seduced."

"What happened?"

"Nothing. There was no evidence. As I said, there's a lot of ignorance and superstition in Cavado. Those folks are still living in the Dark Ages. But I got sidetracked. Back to Juan and the Miller woman. He swore that he had no idea where she was. Seemed genuinely shocked that she was missing. There was no reason not to believe him. A girl like that, one who would run off to Mexico, no telling what kind of trouble she got into. You know, young people get into drugs and disappear all the time. Especially in Mexico. Anything could have happened to her down there after she left Mascareñas."

"So you think he was telling the truth? That she left him for another man?"

"As I said, there was no reason not to believe his story."

"You told Socorro all this?"

"Yes. She had already heard the stories about Sinopa from my mother, her grandmother. And based on that, she was ready to believe the worst about Juan. Socorro was always quick to jump to conclusions. And—I'm not sure how to put this—but from the time she was a child she had some very strange ideas. Used to talk to invisible people. Spirit guides she called them."

"Deputy Tafoya, do you know if Socorro drove up to Cavado after she left you?"

"No. Why would she do that?"

"Well, she mentioned to me that she might."

"I doubt it. She was in a rush to leave the restaurant, talking about all the things she had to do. I remember her saying that Howard was taking her to a dinner party that night." He paused. "That's where she—"

"I know. Well, thank you."

"You're welcome. I hope I've been of some help. As I said, as far as I know, Mascareñas was innocent of any crime. And I've never heard of any other problems concerning him. I asked around after Socorro contacted me. I learned that he's a *curandero*—no doubt he learned some healing skills from his mother—and he apparently leads a quiet life in Cavado. The villagers seem to think highly of him. After all, the Mascareñases are an old and respected family in these parts." He hesitated. "But Socorro indicated that he'd given you some trouble. Did you want to file a complaint?"

"No. I was just curious about him."

"Well, is there anything else I can do for you?"

"I guess not. Thank you for your time. Oh, if you remember anything else about this case, would you let me know? You can reach me at the magazine office."

"Okay, I'll make a note of it. As I said, I hadn't heard anything at all about Mascareñas for the past thirty years, until Socorro brought his name up. Of course, that doesn't surprise me. Those villagers tend to keep to themselves. They don't like the law involved in their affairs."

"I see. Well, thanks for your time. Good-bye." Lee replaced the receiver.

That's that, she thought. A dead end. Tafoya obviously believes that Juan was innocent of any wrongdoing. But I doubt that he succeeded in convincing Socorro of that. Damn. I should have asked if he had the results of her autopsy. I don't want to bother him again. Maybe Doctor Mallory has some information by now. I'll call him later this morning.

Her thoughts returned to Juan. The more she learned about him, the more of a mystery he seemed. What was he doing at that very moment? Was he at home in his grandfather's *hacienda*? Or was he already at his "office," treating a villager with herbs and mumbo-jumbo? He had spoken so matter-of-factly about removing spells cast by those with the "evil eye."

Rising abruptly, Lee paced around her office. I can't let myself dwell on this, she scolded herself. Mallory is right. I have to keep a grip on reality. I don't believe in witchcraft, at least the rational part of my mind doesn't. Socorro died of a stroke. And what happened between Juan and me has nothing to do with the supernatural. Juan is an attractive, sexy man. That's all. I can't excuse my infidelity with fanciful theories about witchcraft and reincarnation.

"Lee?"

She whirled around to see Annabel standing in the doorway. "Damn! You scared me."

"Sorry. What were you doing? Standing at the window talking to yourself?"

"You might have knocked."

"Well, excuse me." Annabel's feelings were clearly hurt. "I knew you were alone. Julie said you wanted to see me."

"Oh, Annie. I'm sorry. I did want to see you, to apologize for the way I acted at Julie's brunch. And I didn't mean to snap at you just now." Lee's eyes filled with tears.

Annabel rushed forward to give Lee a hug. "It's okay," she said. "I know you're going through a rough time. I only wish you'd let me help."

"You can't. I'm just tired. I really haven't been sleeping well."

"Are you having night sweats?"

Lee moved out of Annabel's embrace. "No. Well, not exactly." She reached for a tissue and blew her nose. "Please, I'll be all right. Just bear with me."

"What else can I do? We're partners, remember? That reminds me, are you ready for the Writer's Group luncheon today?"

"Oh, God. No! That's today?"

"Lee, you're scheduled to give the pep talk."

"I completely forgot! I can't believe it. I...I've just lost track of the days. I haven't prepared anything to say. What time is it? Oh hell! It's only an hour away! What am I going to do?"

"You're going to go home."

"Go home? What do you—"

"Lee, calm down. Listen to me. I want you to go home. Call your gynecologist and make an appointment for a checkup. Then go to bed and get some rest. I'll cover for you at the luncheon. I hate public speaking, but I can do it. I'll give them the old 'perseverance counts' routine."

"Oh, thank you. I'm so sorry, Annie. I'm a real mess lately, aren't I?"

"It happens to the best of us," Annabel said, giving Lee another hug.

* * *

Lee was surprised to see Nick's car in the garage when she got home a short time later. She found him upstairs, lying in bed with a washcloth across his forehead.

"Nick? What's wrong?"

"I don't know." His voice sounded strained. "I just suddenly got sick. What are you doing home?"

"I decided to work here this afternoon. When did you get sick? You seemed fine when you left this morning."

"I know. But halfway through the division meeting I got dizzy. Felt so lightheaded I thought I was gonna keel over." He looked at her with glazed eyes. "Must be one of those viruses going around."

Lee sat on the bed beside him and felt his forehead. "You're burning up," she said. "Let me get the thermometer."

"No, don't bother. I took some aspirin. I just want to sleep for awhile. Close the drapes, will you?"

"Sure. I'll be back to check on you in a little while. Go to sleep." She drew the draperies and straightened the blankets around him. "I thought you were immune to flu bugs."

"Must be some Alaskan super-virus. Don't get too close to me. I'll be okay after a little rest."

She left the room, closing the door behind her. It was really unusual for Nick to be sick, she thought, as she went down the stairs. She couldn't remember the last time he had missed work because of illness.

He slept fitfully for several hours. Lee checked on him periodically, slipping quietly into the bedroom. She stood by the bed, watching as he tossed and turned, throwing back the blankets and winding himself up in the sheet.

* * *

Lee was in her study in the late afternoon when she heard Nick cry out. She rushed into the bedroom to find him half out of bed, his arms thrashing through the air as though fending off an invisible attacker. His eyes were open and he was making loud incoherent noises.

"Nick! What is it?" As soon as she spoke the words she smelled it. The sweating oil. "Oh, my God," she whispered.

"No! Get away from me!" Nick's voice was high pitched and frantic.

She grabbed him by the shoulders. "Nick! It's me! Wake up!" The odor made her want to gag.

He jerked away violently, banging his head against the headboard. His eyes were unfocused and wild with fright. A trickle of saliva ran down one side of his mouth, and his breath came in ragged gasps. He was shaking his head from side to side.

"Honey, wake up. Please. You're having a nightmare." Lee stared at him in horror. She had never before seen Nick frightened. The cringing, babbling man before her was a stranger. The odor grew stronger. Forcing herself to ignore it, she touched the back of her hand to his feverish forehead. Hot. So terribly hot. "Nick! Please. Wake up!"

Gradually, his eyes focused on her. "Lee? What...?" She put her arm beneath his neck, helping him to lie down. "I'm here. It's all right. You're just feverish, and you were having a nightmare."

She pulled the blankets up around his shoulders. "Let me wet this washcloth for you and bring you some more aspirin. Don't try to talk. Just relax. I'll be right back."

Lee ran down the hall and into the kitchen. She flipped through the Rolodex and dialed Dr. Zimmerman's office. "I need to talk to the doctor," she said to his receptionist. "My husband is very sick."

She was transferred to a nurse, who promised to have the doctor return her call as soon as possible. Lee poured orange juice into a glass, grabbed the aspirin bottle and rushed back to the bedroom. The odor was gone.

* * *

Dr. Zimmerman, who lived several houses down the road, agreed to stop by to see Nick on his way home that evening. Lee breathed a sigh of relief when the doorbell rang at six-fifteen. "That's the doctor," she said to Sara. "I'll get it." She opened the front door.

"Doctor Zimmerman, come in. Thank you for coming. I know you don't usually make house calls."

"No, I don't. No time for that these days, I'm afraid. But you convinced me this is a special circumstance. And it is on my way home. How's Nick?"

"He's asleep again. He's been sleeping most of the day. I'm really worried. I've never seen him like this. You know Nick. He never allows himself to get sick."

"Your husband may have the constitution of an ox, but there are some formidable viruses going around. Has he been traveling?"

"Yes. He just got home Friday from Alaska. Do you think he might have been exposed to something there?"

"Could be. Let's wake him up and find out what we're up against."

Nick looked startled to find Dr. Zimmerman sitting on the bed beside him. He lifted his head, then collapsed back onto the pillow. "My head," he moaned.

"Okay, just relax," said the doctor. "Open up so we can take your temperature." He inserted a thermometer into Nick's mouth and took out his stethoscope. "Now let's see what's going on here."

Lee watched anxiously from the edge of the bed as Dr. Zimmerman listened to Nick's chest and heart, peered into the pupils of his eyes and prodded along his abdomen. He removed the thermometer and held it up to read. "Any vomiting or diarrhea?"

Nick shook his head.

"Well, you're playing host to a real doozie of a bug. I'm pretty sure it's a virus, in which case, all we can do is wait it out." He began gathering his instruments into his black leather bag. "Your lungs sound fine, but you're running a fever of almost a hundred and three. That's high for an adult, and accounts for that headache. I want to hear from you tomorrow. If you're any worse, I'll schedule you for some tests." He made some quick notes on a pad while he talked. "Chances are, though, this thing will run its course in a few days. Drink plenty of liquids, take aspirin for the fever, and plan on being out of commission for awhile."

"Thanks for coming by, Doc." Nick's voice was a weak whisper.

Lee closed the bedroom door and walked the doctor to the front door. "Maybe I overreacted this afternoon, but I was really frightened. He was having a terrible nightmare. In fact, I thought he was delirious. I had a hard time waking him up. He seemed to think he was being attacked by something."

"That was the fever," Dr. Zimmerman said as he struggled into his coat. "A high fever like that is dangerous. Keep an eye on it. Give him aspirin until it breaks. And call me if it climbs any higher. Goodnight."

"Goodnight. And thanks again." She closed the door firmly against the chilly night air and walked down the hall. Sara was waiting in the doorway of her room, obviously alarmed. "Mom, I thought I should just stay out of the way. What did the doctor say? Is Dad going to be okay?"

"Yes. Of course he is, honey." Lee drew her daughter into her arms and hugged her. "Of course he is."

* * *

Later that night, Lee was awakened by a hoarse cry and thrashing beside her in the darkness. "Nick?" She sat up, reaching for the bedside light. "What—?" She broke off as she smelled the odor of sweating oil again—stronger than ever. At the same time she heard Nick hit the floor with a loud thud. She scrambled to the end of the bed and stared down in horror.

He was rolling back and forth on the carpet, partially wrapped in the sheet. His eyes were wide with fear, his face flushed and anguished. "It's chasing me, coming closer," he whimpered. "Please, no."

She jumped out of the bed and knelt beside him. "Nick, wake up!" She shook his shoulder. "It's just a dream," she said, talking to herself as much as to her husband. "That's all it can be!"

He looked at her with unseeing eyes. "Wings," he whispered hoarsely. "Giant wings."

Lee felt an icy splash of shock. "What?" she whispered. "Nick, what did you say?"

His eyelids fluttered closed as he slipped into a deep sleep. "Stop it!" she cried. "Don't hurt him. Please don't hurt him." She knelt beside her husband, sobbing. After a while, she became aware of a ringing in her ears and a chilling cold spreading through her body. The odor was gone. Lee forced herself to rise. Realizing that she couldn't get Nick back into bed by herself, she decided to make him as comfortable as possible on the floor. She slipped a pillow under his head and covered him with blankets before turning out the light. She sat beside him in the darkness for a moment. Then, with sudden inspiration, she scrambled to her feet.

"Candlelight," she murmured to herself. "We need candlelight." She hit the light switch, then fumbled through her nightstand drawer for a book of matches. Finally she managed to light the blue stoneware candle on her nightstand.

"Oh, Socorro," she whispered, "I hope you were right about the power of this candle. We need all the protection we can get."

She pushed a bedroom chair close to the side of the bed, turned off the light and sat down, wrapping the comforter around her. Hours later, she was still huddled in the chair, listening to night noises and watching the candlelight dance across her sleeping husband's face.

* * *

She had just dozed off near dawn when she heard Nick struggling to sit up on the floor. He needed her help to get to the bathroom and then back into bed. She gave him three aspirins and wiped his face with a cool washcloth before getting into bed beside him. She curled up against his broad back and slipped an arm around his waist. Then, hugging his feverish body, she fell into a light sleep.

* * *

Nick's condition seemed to be the same when he awoke several hours later. Although his temperature continued to hover near 103 degrees, it didn't rise any higher. He slept through the morning, waking at noon to sip orange juice and swallow a little chicken broth. "You look pretty beat yourself, babe," he said, squeezing her hand. "Don't worry, I'm going to be fine."

"I know you are. Doctor Zimmerman said it will just take a few days. In the meantime, you're to rest and let me pamper you. I'm taking time off from work until you're well."

"Really? Are you sure you can do that? I know how

hard—"

"I can do it. We have a very competent staff. The magazine is in good hands." She brushed a strand of hair back from his damp forehead. "And so are you."

He smiled weakly and nodded. Then he turned bloodshot eyes toward her nightstand. "That candle," he whispered. "Why is it burning in the daytime?"

"It...it was a gift from a friend. I just thought it might improve the atmosphere in here a little. You know, create a nice, restful mood. Besides, you know I look younger in candlelight. Now go back to sleep."

"Yes, nurse," he whispered, closing his eyes.

Lee sat on the bed beside him, watching him sleep. She bit her lower lip, trying to hold back tears. Nick's getting better, she told herself. He's going to be all right. The odor was just in my mind. That's what Doctor Mallory would say. Another hysterical reaction. That's all it could possibly be.

* * *

Lee realized that she was in no condition to confront her suspicions about Nick's illness. She hid behind a detached routine that afternoon, keeping too busy to think. Mechanically, she reorganized her file cabinet. Something kept nagging at her as she worked, circling in the back of her consciousness but keeping just out of reach. She was on her way into the bedroom to check on Nick when it hit her. In a flash she realized what had been playing hide-and-seek in her mind.

Nick's sweater! His missing sweater. She *had* put it in the back seat of her car along with the rest of the things to go to the cleaners. She knew she had. Early Monday morning, before she went to Cavado. Before she made love with Juan again. And then had gone to sleep.

She remembered waking alone in the dark room before Juan had come in from outside. What had he been doing out there? Oh, dear God, what was Juan doing while she slept? Did he take Nick's sweater from the car?

At that moment, she recalled Socorro's voice, confirming her worst fears: *"Brujos need something belonging to a person in order to cast a spell on them. A personal object, an article of clothing..."*

"No," she whispered to herself. "No, it can't be. It's the flu—just a virus. I have to stop giving in to crazy thoughts." She leaned against the wall for support as Nick's choked voice echoed in her mind. *"Wings...giant wings!"*

Rushing back into her study, she closed the door and quickly dialed Mallory's number.

"I'm sorry," his secretary said. "He's with a patient."

"This is Lee Lindsay. I really need to talk to him. As soon as possible. Please. Tell him that it's urgent."

"Your phone number?"

"999-6538."

"I'll give him the message."

Lee hung up the phone and paced around the room. She wasn't sure why she was calling Mallory. He didn't believe in witchcraft. Did she? Was she finally convinced? No. Yes. I don't know, she thought. I don't know anything anymore. I just have to talk to someone. And now that Socorro is gone, Mallory is the only one I can trust.

Less than an hour later, the phone rang. "Lee? What's up?"

"Doctor Mallory, I have to talk to you."

"Okay. I have a few minutes until my next patient. What's going on?"

"It's Nick. He's very sick. He's feverish and having nightmares. About some kind of bird. I think it's a giant bird—like the one in my dreams. And I smelled the sweating oil again. I know you think I'm imagining that. But I'm telling you, it was there! I lit Socorro's candle, and I think he's a little better now, but I'm terrified that—"

"Hold on a minute. Just slow down. Nick is ill? Has he seen a doctor?"

"Yes. Doctor Zimmerman was here last night. He

thinks it's just a virus. But he's wrong. There's more to it than that."

"Why?"

"I went back to Cavado. The day before yesterday. I went to tell Juan to stop calling me, to let him know that Nick was threatening to go to the police."

"Nick knows what's going on?"

"Oh, God no. Only that I saw you while he was in Alaska. And that you think Juan drugged and hypnotized me. He really hit the roof over that."

"But he doesn't know that you've seen Juan again? I mean, after the awakening ceremony?"

"Of course not! I haven't gone that crazy."

"Okay, so you went back to Cavado. Did you convince Juan to leave you alone?"

Lee hesitated, feeling hot shame wash over her. "No."

"What does this have to do with Nick being ill?"

"I think Juan stole one of Nick's sweaters out of my car while I was there." She fought to keep her voice steady. "And now he's using it to cause the illness. Remember, Socorro said—"

"I think you'd better come in to see me. Can you come after five today?"

"No, I really can't. Not today. I'm afraid to leave Nick. He's still running a fever, and—"

"Okay, then listen to me. Nick is going to be fine. If Frank Zimmerman said it was just a virus, that's all it is. Now what were you saying about a candle?"

"Socorro gave me a candle that she had blessed by a medicine man to weaken Juan's magic. It's been burning since last night."

"I'm going to be frank with you, Lee. I'm more concerned about you than I am about Nick. Have you been getting any sleep?"

"Not much. Could you prescribe something for me? I took my last sleeping pill a few nights ago. I don't like to take them, but I'm desperate. I keep having these dreams—" Her voice broke.

"All right. I'll call something in to the drugstore on Saint Francis Drive. But I don't want you to start relying on pills to sleep. They can exacerbate depression and seriously impair your judgment."

"I'll be careful. I know I must sound deranged, calling you like this. I just—"

"Lee, listen to me. You're exhausted. It's easy to overreact when you're under a lot of stress. Just don't let your imagination run away with you. You've been doing that lately."

"You really think that's all it is?"

"I'm sure of it."

"Oh, before you hang up, what about Socorro's autopsy report? Do they know yet what killed her?"

"Still no word. I'll see what I can find out and get back to you. I looked for you yesterday at her memorial service."

"It was yesterday?"

"Yes. It was announced in Monday's paper."

"I didn't read the paper on Monday. There's been too much going on. Oh, damn. I should have been at the service."

"Don't, Lee. No guilt trips. You don't need any more burdens. You've got your hands full. Socorro would understand."

"I guess you're right. If anyone could understand, it would be Socorro. But I wish I'd—"

"You've got to try to take it easy," he interrupted, "or you're going to get sick too. Keep things in perspective, and stop dwelling on this witchcraft business."

"I'll try."

"Nick's going to be fine. Believe it."

"You always manage to make me feel sane again. At least while I'm talking to you."

"You are sane. But you're on overload. Serious overload. I have to go now, but I want to talk to you again soon. Take care of yourself."

"Good-bye, Doctor Mallory." Lee hung up the phone and rested her head in her arms on top of the desk. She was unable to control the tears that dripped onto the polished wood.

Before long, she sat up and reached for a tissue. Enough of this, she thought, wiping her eyes and blowing her nose. I have to stay in control, keep a cool head. Otherwise—Mallory's right—I'm going to make myself sick. And what would happen then? Who would keep the candle burning?

Chapter 21

By Thursday morning Nick's temperature was almost normal and he was hungry. Lee put orange juice and two bran muffins on a wooden tray and carried it into the bedroom. She fluffed pillows behind his head and helped him sit up in bed. "A sure sign of recovery," she said, placing the tray on his lap. "You can't keep a good appetite down for long."

Nick gave her a weak smile. Lee was struck by how old he looked. The skin on his face was pale and slack, his three-day-old beard sprinkled with grey. When had his face started to sag? She felt a rush of affection for him and bent to kiss his cheek.

"Well, well," he said, raising one eyebrow. "I really like all of this attention. Maybe I should get sick more often."

"Don't you dare. Now eat your breakfast." She pulled the chair closer to the bed and sat down, facing him. "Nick?"

"Hmmm?" He drained the glass of orange juice and bit into a muffin.

"You've been having nightmares. Do you remember them?"

"Nightmares?" He stopped chewing and frowned.

"Yes, when you were running a high fever. They seemed pretty bad. I was wondering if you remembered what they were about."

Nick shook his head. "You know I hardly ever remember dreams."

"Don't you remember waking up on the floor night before last? I had to leave you there for part of the night, because you fell out of bed during a bad dream."

"No kidding?" He shook his head and took another bite of muffin. "I have no memory of it."

"I was just curious, that's all." She pointed to his empty glass. "How about some more juice?"

"Later. Thanks, babe. I've got to call the office." He took his last bite of muffin and reached for the phone. "What is today? Thursday? God, I've lost most of the week." He punched in numbers and, cradling the phone under his chin, pointed to his briefcase on the desk. "Would you hand that to me? Diane? Hi, it's me. Back from the dead. Well, almost, anyway." He winked at Lee as she lifted the tray from his lap. "What went on in the division meeting yesterday?"

Lee shook her head and left the room. As she walked down the hall, she could hear Nick giving his secretary brisk instructions. Nice try, Juan, she thought grimly, but no cigar.

* * *

The phone rang while Lee was fixing Nick's lunch. She heard him answer it in the bedroom. "Hello? Hello? Is anyone there?"

Moments later, she walked in, carrying a tray. "Here you are, tuna salad with lettuce." She waited for him to clear newspapers to one side before placing the tray on his lap. "Who was on the phone?"

"I don't know," Nick looked at her over the top of the half-glasses he wore for reading. "Must have been a wrong number. They hung up without saying anything."

"That's annoying." She straightened the comforter at the foot of the bed. "I'm brewing some herbal tea for you."

"I'd rather have a beer. Do we have any cold in the fridge?"

"I think so. You really are feeling better, aren't you?"

"Still a little weak when I stand up. But definitely on the mend. I'll be able to go into work tomorrow." He took a bite of his sandwich.

"I don't think you should," she said. "You've really been sick. Don't rush it. You don't want a relapse."

"I'll be fine. There's an important meeting scheduled for tomorrow morning. And Hans Kresny—I've told you about him, he's with the Department of Energy in Washington—he's arriving to talk about next month's experiment. I need to be there. Don't worry, I'll take it easy."

"Sure you will. You're a workaholic, Doctor Lindsay."

"It runs in the family. Now, how about that beer?"

The phone rang again as Lee was walking into the kitchen. She heard Nick's annoyed demand, "Hello? Who is this, dammit! Hello?" She stopped in her tracks. Juan! she thought wildly. That's Juan. I know it is! He's hoping I'll answer the phone.

She opened the refrigerator door and grabbed a beer for Nick. This can't go on, she thought. I'll call that crazy bastard and tell him never to call here again. I'll threaten him.... Where did I put his number? I guess I could always try the yellow pages. Under "B" for *brujo*. Damn him! She took a deep breath and tried to compose herself. Then she hurried down the hall, carrying Nick's beer.

* * *

Half an hour later, Lee peeked in at the sprawled figure in the bed. Nick was sleeping on his stomach, snoring softly. She quietly closed the bedroom door and tiptoed into her study. She flipped through her notebook until she found Juan's number. Taking a deep breath to steady herself, she dialed.

He answered on the third ring.

"Juan! Now listen here—"

"Lee." His voice was soft and intimate. "How are you, *querida*? I've missed you. Do you know how much I've missed you?"

She felt her knees go weak. "It *was* you calling here, wasn't it?"

"I wanted to hear your voice."

"What the hell are you trying to do? That was my husband who answered the phone!"

"Ah, yes. Your husband. How is he?"

She hesitated. "He's been sick."

"He is recovering?"

"Yes, he's recovering. She spoke rapidly, keeping her voice low. "Listen, I can't talk. I just want to tell you to stop calling. I mean it. I don't know what Nick would do if—"

"I must see you. Come to me tomorrow."

"No!" She exhaled a soft, exasperated breath. "I can't do that! I don't know what to do about you, Juan, about this whole crazy situation. I know it has to end. I promise myself I'll never see you again, but then I hear your voice, and I can't think straight."

"You don't need to think, my love. We both know what you need. I'll expect you in the morning."

"I said no! I can't." She pressed her forehead against the cool wall, forcing herself to think about Nick's missing sweater and his sudden illness. And Susan Miller. She wanted to ask Juan about the disappearance of his old girl friend and to judge his reaction for herself. "But I do have to talk to you," she heard herself say. "For my sanity's sake, I need answers. About a lot of things. Will you come here, to Santa Fe? I could meet you somewhere—for coffee."

"Coffee?" He laughed softly. "You are afraid to return to Cavado? You are afraid of me, Lee?"

"Yes, I'm afraid of you! I'm afraid of what happens

to me when I'm with you. I can't trust myself. I can't seem to stop myself—"

"That's because you don't want to stop yourself. What is between us is too strong. Don't fight it. I will be waiting here for you tomorrow. *Adios, mi vida*." The line went dead.

* * *

Sara rushed into the kitchen a few minutes after four o'clock, her face flushed with excitement. "Hi, Mom," she said, jolting Lee out of her reverie. "I'm home. But I've gotta hurry and get dressed. Wendy's having everyone over at her house for hamburgers before the dance." She paused. "That's okay, isn't it? Please say yes! I can't let Kevin go without me!"

"Wait a minute," Lee said, trying to cover her confusion. She glanced at the clock on the wall, shocked to realize that she'd been sitting at the kitchen table, staring into space, for over an hour. She felt like she'd been asleep. "Slow down. Now, what's going on?"

"The dance is tonight! The Halloween dance." Sara looked at her mother in amazement. "Don't tell me you forgot that tonight's Halloween?"

"It is?" Lee groaned. "Oh, no. I don't have any candy for trick-or-treaters. I'll have to go to the store." She stood, wincing as a sharp pain shot through her right ankle.

"What's the matter?"

"I hurt my ankle a few days ago. It still bothers me, off and on. Now, let me get this straight. You're planning to have dinner at Wendy's, then go on to the dance with Kevin from there?"

"Yeah. Is it okay?"

"Sure, that's fine. Does this mean that you've worked things out with Wendy?"

"I guess so. She swore to God that she's not after Kevin. I'm keeping a close eye on her though."

"I'm glad you talked it through with her, honey. Friendships are very important."

Lee started down the hall, limping slightly. That's strange, she thought, my ankle felt fine this morning. She grabbed her purse off the kitchen counter and a jacket from the hall coat closet. "I won't be gone long. Go ahead and get dressed. But don't play your stereo. Dad's asleep."

"Oh, wow. I've been so excited about tonight I forgot to ask about Dad. Is he any better?"

"Yes, much better. But don't wake him up. I'll be back in a few minutes."

"Buy lots of Reese's peanut butter cups. And chocolate kisses." Sara shook her head. "I can't believe you spaced out Halloween!"

"Well, honey," Lee said, "I've had a lot on my mind."

* * *

Sara knocked on the bedroom door. "Mom? Dad? Are you decent?"

Lee was sitting in the chair beside the bed, watching the early news on television with Nick. "I'm afraid so," she called. "Come on in. We're just—" She broke off as the door burst open and a wild-haired apparition waltzed in.

"Well, what do you think?" Sara struck a dramatic pose in the doorway. "Is this a killer outfit, or what?"

Lee stared, not trusting herself to speak. Sara's brown curls had been transformed into long spikes that stuck out from her head like spokes on a broken wheel. Her eyes were outlined with thick black eyeliner and her mouth glistened with purple lipstick. She was dressed in a black denim mini-skirt and turtleneck sweater. She weaved toward them in high-heeled boots, carrying a black leather jacket over one shoulder.

Nick gasped. "What the hell..." He started to cough, "...are you supposed to be?" he finally managed to finish.

Sara looked at him, an exasperated expression on her face. "Dad, I'm a punker!"

"A punker?"

"Right. Isn't it just too wild?"

"You almost gave me a relapse, young lady," Nick said. "You certainly aren't going out of the house like that!"

"Dad!" screeched Sara.

"Nick," Lee explained, "it's Halloween."

"Oh, for heaven's sake." Nick leaned back against his pillow. "What a relief." He chuckled. "Halloween. I completely forgot. Where are you going, sweetheart?"

"Over to Wendy's for dinner. Then to the Halloween dance at school."

"Well, okay. But be in by eleven. And be careful." Nick spoke in an eerie voice. "Remember, goblins are on the prowl tonight. And witches. Don't let the witches catch you, little girl."

Lee's throat tightened. "No," she echoed in a small hollow voice. "Don't ever let that happen."

Sara laughed and kissed them good-bye, leaving purple smears on both their cheeks.

* * *

It was a quiet Halloween night. The Lindsay house was too isolated to attract random trick-or-treaters. The only visitors were several groups of small neighborhood children escorted by their parents. Nick, still looking pale and drawn, went to bed before nine. Lee settled herself on the sofa in the family room to wait up for Sara.

She spread a wool afghan over her legs and glanced at a stack of magazines on the coffee table. Picking up the latest issue of **Writer's Digest**, she turned to an article titled "The Effective Interview." I could offer some advice on that subject, she thought ruefully. Don't drink any funny tea, and keep your clothes on. She yawned. Halfway through the article, her eyes began to close and she fell into a deep sleep.

* * *

He lay with his back to her, his naked shoulder silhouetted against the glowing fire. She pressed against him under the soft furs, running her hand down his hip, caressing the hard muscled flesh of his thigh. He awoke and turned toward her with a soft, welcoming murmur. Her heart swelled with pride. He had chosen her. He had elevated her above the others. She ran her finger over the strange red sign on his cheek. He was a child of the gods. They had marked him as one of their own.

He buried his face in her neck, then began to gently massage her breast. She clung to him, flushed with sweet, hot pleasure. He moved on top of her, his long hair falling like a black curtain around her face.

* * *

"Mom? Mom, wake up. I'm back."

Lee jerked awake and stared at her daughter with uncomprehending eyes. "What...? Oh, Sara. You frightened me. Did you just get home?"

Sara sat down beside Lee on the sofa. "Yep. You must really be pooped to fall asleep in here. Why didn't you go on to bed?"

"Daddy went to sleep early and I didn't want to disturb him. So I thought I'd wait up for you in here. How was the dance?"

"It was a total blast. And guess what? I won a prize for my costume." She held up a stuffed, black corduroy owl. "I think I'll call him 'Spooky'. Isn't he a hoot?"

Lee closed her eyes. "He sure is, honey," she said, suppressing a faint shudder. "A real hoot."

Chapter 22

"Nick, I don't think you should go into work today." Lee studied his face as he spread jam on a piece of toast. "You're still awfully pale."

"I'm okay," he said, reaching for a napkin. "Can't miss the meeting this morning." He bit into the toast, scanning the front page of the newspaper. "Those damned politicians are at it again, trying to cut our research budget."

"Here, take these," Lee said, handing him an assortment of vitamin pills. "You need extra vitamin C now." She refilled his orange juice glass. "And wear your heavy jacket. It looks like we might get some snow today."

"Yes, dear. Doctor Zimmerman is right. You make an exceptional nurse."

"And you make an impossible patient. More toast?"

"No time. Gotta run." He gulped his juice and leaned over to kiss her cheek. "I'll try to get home a little early tonight."

Sara came rushing into the kitchen, dropping a stack

of books onto the snack bar. She poured a glass of orange juice and looked at Nick in surprise. "What are you doing out of bed, Dad?"

"He's going back to work," Lee said. "I tried to talk him out of it, but he thinks he's irreplaceable."

"I am. Nice to see your hair back to normal, Sara," Nick said, waving at them as he left the kitchen. "I'll see you two mother hens tonight."

After Sara left for school, Lee walked into the family room and opened the draperies on the sliding patio doors. Dark clouds stretched across the horizon to the west and obscured the distant hills to the north. There was no doubt about it, winter was on its way. Sighing, she rested her forehead against the cold glass. She had half-hoped Nick would change his mind about working today, so she would be unable to go to Cavado. Now she had to make the decision. What in hell is wrong with me? she wondered. Why am I even considering seeing Juan again? I should go to the office. Annabel must be buried in paperwork by now.

She climbed the stairs and walked down the hall to her bedroom, arguing with herself. This whole situation is insane. It's dangerous, and it's wrong. How can I do this to Nick? How can I do it to myself? I must be crazy. I'm obviously crazy because I know I'm going back to Cavado. I have to see Juan again. Just one more time. But seeing him today will clarify things. I'll find a way to break this off.

She walked into the bathroom and turned on the shower. Stripping off her robe and nightgown, she stood motionless under the hot water, letting it beat on the top of her head and cascade down her face and body. She didn't even bother to envision the golden light.

* * *

Dressed in a sweater, denim skirt and boots, Lee hesitated in the entryway. I can still change my mind, she thought, continuing to fight with herself. I don't have to go. She opened the coat closet and put on her leather jacket. But I am going. God help me—I can't seem to stop myself. She grabbed a pair of gloves and, as an afterthought, wrapped Sara's red woolen scarf around her neck.

* * *

Occasional snowflakes were swirling against the windshield when she pulled into Juan's barren front yard, parking her car beside his pickup. I should turn around and drive away, she thought, while there's still time. Why don't I? Why can't I? She was still sitting in the car staring miserably at the small adobe house when the front door opened, and Juan stepped out.

He stood shirtless in the doorway, his arms folded across his bare chest, and watched her get out of the car. His amulet flashed silver against his dark skin. Lee saw a slight smile play across his lips. He's making me do this, she thought as she walked toward him. Somehow, he's making me do this.

He ushered her into the house without speaking, and closed the door. As before, the only light came from candles flickering in corners of the room. Juan unwound the scarf from her neck and tossed it onto a nearby chair. Then he removed her jacket. When he slid his hands under her sweater, she jerked away. "Don't touch me," she said, turning her back to him.

He ignored her words, resting his hands on her stomach, then sliding them up to cup her breasts.

"I mean it!" She pushed his hands away and turned to face him. "I didn't come here for...that. There are things we have to talk about."

"Later," he said, holding her face in his large brown hands and kissing her lips. "There will be time for that later." Before she could reply, he was kissing her again.

With an effort, she extracted her mouth from his. "I mean it, Juan," she said, breathing hard. "I don't want you to..." Her words trailed off as his lips grazed her temple, and his warm tongue began tracing the curve of her ear. Once again, his hand was beneath her sweater, sliding under her bra, gently squeezing an erect nipple. She felt warm wetness between her legs as her traitorous body responded to his touch. Socorro's expression, "spirit-sucker," echoed in her mind. That's what he is, she thought. He's stolen my spirit. His black magic has destroyed my will.

He pulled her to him, the hand under her sweater pressed hard against the small of her back. His other hand slid up the side of her throat to lightly caress her cheek. Suddenly his strong fingers gripped her chin, tipping her head back and forcing her to look into the dark depths of his eyes. She stared up at him, unable to speak. Candlelight played across his face, accenting the sharp hollows under his cheekbones and the soft curves of his lips.

A feeling of detachment enveloped Lee, like a warm, thick fog. Her ears began to ring. As she closed her eyes, she wondered if she was dreaming. Could she make herself wake up? She jerked, blinking her eyes and trying to twist her chin out of his grasp. "No," she pleaded. "Please. Let me go. I...I can't do this."

"Don't fight me, *querida*," he said, tightening his grip on her chin. His thumb pressed hard into her cheek. "It's not wise to fight me. Didn't your husband's sickness teach you that?"

Lee's blood turned to ice as his words registered in her mind. "What?" she whispered. "What did you say?"

"I said that you should know better than to fight me." Juan's mouth curled into a cruel smile. "Your scientist has apparently recovered. The next time he may not be so fortunate."

Lee stared at him, momentarily stunned. Then an image of Nick's feverish face flashed through her mind, and she wrenched her face free, pushing against his chest with all her strength. "You son of a bitch!" she screamed. "Let me go!"

"Never, *mi vida*." Juan yanked her back into his embrace. "Never."

Lee sunk her teeth into his bare shoulder. When he pulled back in surprise, she slapped him hard across the cheek. "Take your hands off me," she warned, drawing her arm back to hit him again.

He grabbed her arm and bent it behind her back. With her free hand, she struck at his face, raking her fingernails across his cheek. Half-lifting her off her feet, he forced her backwards until she was pinned between his body and the closed door. He held her arms in a viselike grip. "You were always a fighter," he said, bending his head toward hers. This time his mouth was not gentle.

Lee bit his bottom lip, tasting blood, then twisted her head to one side against the rough wooden door. She heard him chuckle, deep in his throat. "Yes, yes," he whispered, his voice muffled in her hair. "It was often like this with us. Biting and scratching. You remember, don't you? You made love like a mountain lion."

She felt the hardness of his erection against her and squirmed frantically. "You crazy—"

Her words were cut short by the pain of his sharp slap. "You will remember," he said as he picked her up and carried her, yelling and pounding on his chest with her fists, into the other room. "I will make you remember."

He flung himself on top of her, on the buffalo skin rug. The weight of his body knocked the breath from Lee, turning her scream into a gasp. "The memories are coming back," he said, "I can feel it in your body." His mouth moved across her neck and still-stinging cheek. Then he began to chant in her ear—the same harsh, guttural sounds he had spoken during the awakening ceremony.

"No! Damn you! No!" She twisted beneath him, pulling his hair and beating on his shoulders. Juan's chanting continued, changing in pitch as his breath came faster. At some point she realized that her skirt was up around her waist. Then she felt her panties being yanked down. As his hand moved between her legs, she cried out, uncertain as to whether the sound sprang from the fear and outrage she felt—or from her sudden and shocking desire. He unbuttoned his Levi's with one hand and thrust into her.

The sounds she made in the moments that followed sounded completely alien to Lee's ears. And her cry when she climaxed—high-pitched and savage—seemed to rise from somewhere in the very depths of her soul.

* * *

Afterwards, Juan held her close, stroking her hair and face. "*Te amo,* Tarena," he whispered, "I love you." Rigid and numb with shock, Lee could not reply. She felt divorced from time—torn between two realities and disconnected from her body. When he held a cup of sweet-tasting liquid to her lips, she swallowed it mindlessly. Sometime later, she was vaguely aware of Juan undressing her—tugging off her boots, removing her sweater, bra and skirt. Then he covered her with a blanket.

* * *

She awoke to a vague awareness of warm fur beneath her naked body. Her eyes opened with a start, scattering dream images of unknown, but somehow familiar scenes and faces.

She sat up in a panic. I'm back here in Cavado! And Juan. Oh, God, he forced me.... Where is he? I've got to get away from here! She threw off the blanket and stood up, looking frantically for her clothes. Then she saw them, lying under her purse in a neat pile on the sofa.

Shivering, she pulled on her panties and skirt. She had just fastened the front clasp of her bra and was putting her arms into her sweater when something caught her eye on the shelf above the sofa. Something sitting there, beside green and yellow gourds and tied stalks of dried purple flowers. Resting on top of a grey and white pelt was a small animal's head, with white bone showing through patches of torn fur. One pointed grey ear hung loosely, peeled almost off the skull. Lee pulled the sweater over her head and moved closer. She stood on tiptoe and stretched up to take the terrible object off the shelf.

She knew, even before she touched the soft, familiar fur beneath the skull. Her mind reeled as she felt the poor torn ear and touched the grey and white whiskers still clinging to the muzzle above the small, sharp teeth, now exposed in a silent scream. Mister!

Lee clutched the torn head to her chest as she sank to her knees, her anguished wail echoing in her ears. Nightmare visions filled her mind. Mister running for his life while relentless dark wings and sharp talons drew steadily closer. Then ripping pain and gradual oblivion. Poor Mister. Poor, sweet kitty. "No, no, no," she cried aloud, rocking back and forth on her knees.

The door burst open, and Lee had a glimpse of Juan's scratched cheek and startled expression as he stared down at her, kneeling on the wooden floor. Her grief-stricken wail turned into a scream of rage, and she scrambled to her feet. The small head fell to the floor.

"You!" she screamed. "You murdering bastard! Why? Why did you have to kill Mister?" She grabbed her purse, swinging it toward him by the straps. Her screams rang in her ears. "You killed Socorro too, didn't you? And then you tried to kill Nick! What are you? What the hell kind of monster are you?"

Juan ducked, raising his arms to protect his head. "*Querida*! What—?" Lee grabbed a heavy pottery jar from a nearby table. She crashed it down on his head and ran past him out the door.

She ran heedlessly barefooted over sharp, snow-covered rocks and locked herself in her car. The fact that it was snowing hard finally registered. How long had it been snowing like this? How long had she been in there?

Lee gasped with horror as Juan staggered through the open front door, his forehead smeared with blood. She searched her purse for what seemed like an eternity while he stumbled toward her. Keys! Where were the damn car keys? Everything seemed to be happening in nightmarish slow motion. Her fingers finally closed around the keys.

Juan pounded on the car window, yelling her name. Snowflakes coated his hair and mixed with the blood that trickled between his eyes. The key wouldn't turn. It was stuck in the ignition. Then, miraculously, it turned, and the engine started. Lee threw the car into reverse, knocking Juan off to the side. She slapped at the steering column, searching for the windshield wiper switch while the car careened down the dirt road through a thickening curtain of snow. Finally, she hit the right lever and the front and rear windshield wipers began to move.

In spite of them, it was hard to see. How far had she driven? She must be almost to the main highway. She brushed at her tears with the back of her hand. Then her heart almost stopped when she glanced in the rear view mirror. Juan's pickup was behind her—gaining fast.

She pressed the accelerator, speeding past the service station and sliding onto the paved highway. Her breath came in loud sobs as she fought to control the car on the icy road. Something silver flashed through the snow ahead. She rubbed at the fogged windshield, clearing it enough to see a car stalled in the road, directly in her path. She screamed and jerked the wheel sharply to the right.

There was an unreal sensation of skidding, bumping, rolling, and then flying, while a blurred white world spun outside the windshield. This must be a dream, she assured herself. Just a terrible dream. I'll wake up in a minute and be home in bed. Then reality arrived in a bright red flash of pain and everything went black.

* * *

Lee floated through a silent darkness, safe and peaceful. She tried to think, to understand where she was, but her thoughts kept sliding away. It didn't matter. Nothing really mattered.

A voice floated toward her from a great distance. Someone was calling her name. The voice was familiar. Growing louder. But whose? She tried to answer but

was unable to make a sound. The voice was closer.
"It's all right, *mi vida*. I'm here. I'm here beside you."

The darkness lifted and she saw him, striding toward
her through swirling grey mists. She felt a flash of
recognition. He was here. He was here with her...Juan.
But that wasn't really his name. He had another name.
Why couldn't she remember? Black hair hung over his
shoulders and down his bare chest as he moved toward
her. Then his arms were around her, his breath warm
against her cheek. "Take strength from me," he whispered in her ear. "Don't let go. Don't leave me, Tarena.
Don't leave me."

Tarena? Who is he talking to? Her thoughts were
interrupted by chanting. Sounds and words that were
unfamiliar, yet some part of her knew their meaning—
and their power. She almost remembered... something.
Something important. But the memory melted away as
shadowy forms appeared, whirling through the darkness
around her. His voice broke once more through the dark
fog. She strained to hear, to follow the words that faded
in and out.

"Hear me, Raven, messenger to the spirit world.
Enter the great void. Implore the Guardians to spare this
woman...for the sake of your brother who loves her..."
More words, growing fainter.

She tried to move, to turn her head. A sharp pain
shot through the left side of her chest. No, she tried to
say. You're hurting me. Please, don't...hurt me. For an
instant she remembered his real name and tried to speak
it. Then it slipped away, and she felt herself being
lifted, floating higher and higher, as the black fog
receded and she spiraled upward toward the light.

Chapter 23

*P*ain pulsed through her head, forcing her awake. She opened her eyes and found herself in a strange room. Nick was at her side, his eyes bloodshot and full of concern.

"Where am I?" Her voice was little more than a hoarse whisper.

"Just lie still, babe. You're okay. You're in the hospital."

"Hospital?" She moaned from the pain of jerking her head. "How did I get here?"

"Don't you remember the accident?" Nick stroked her right arm. Her left hand felt heavy, as if it were weighted down.

Lee's puzzled frown turned to an expression of horror as her memory began to return. She'd been in Cavado with Juan. He'd been so brutal. He'd forced her—raped her! And Mister. Oh, God, what he did to Mister! She groaned, squeezing her eyes shut at the thought of her shocking discovery.

"It's true! Oh, no! It's really true!"

"Lie still, honey. What's true?"

Nick's voice was blotted out by the memories that flooded Lee's mind. She was running through falling snow to her car...sliding along the winding dirt road...Juan's pickup in her rearview mirror, coming closer and closer...the terrifying sight of a vehicle blocking the road ahead and then...nothing.

"He was after me. Coming closer and closer—"

"Who? Who was after you?"

"Oh, Nick. It's horrible! He killed Mister. And Socorro, I'm sure he killed her too. And he made you sick. He—"

"Lee, who on earth are you talking about?"

"Juan Mascareñas. He's a *brujo*, Nick, a witch! Socorro was right. I didn't want to believe it. I tried not to believe it, but it's true. The raven—my nightmare about the raven—" She tried to raise her head and groaned in pain. "My head hurts."

"Lie still." Nick leaned over her to ring for the nurse. "Don't talk," he said. "The nurse will be here in a minute. You hit your head. But you're going to be fine. Just fine. Hold on."

"You have to believe me, Nick. Someone has to believe me! He used black magic." She broke off, as pain jolted through her head followed by a wave of nausea.

Nick rang the buzzer again. Moments later, she heard murmured voices and felt the sharp jab of a needle in her arm. The last thing she heard was Nick's voice speaking urgently. "Nurse, she's saying crazy things. Where's Doctor Zimmerman? Get him in here!"

* * *

The room came slowly into focus. Nick was sitting in a chair across from her bed, his eyes closed. When she made a hoarse moaning sound, he was instantly at her side.

"Lee? I'm right here."

"I'm in the...hospital?"

"You were in an accident. Don't you remember?"

267

Helpless tears spilled out of the corners of her eyes and ran along the sides of her ears. "Yes," she whispered. "I remember." She raised her right hand and touched something smooth where her hair should have been. "What's on my head?" she asked in alarm.

"Bandages. You hit your head pretty hard." Nick reached for a tissue and blotted her tears. "But you're going to be just fine."

"What time is it? How long have I been here?"

"It's a little after eight. You've been here about five hours."

The door opened and Sara came in. Her face lit up when she saw Lee. "Mom, you're awake. Are you gonna be okay?" She began to sob. "I was so scared."

"Oh, baby. Don't cry." Pain vibrated through Lee's head with each word.

"How you do feel?"

"My head hurts. And my arm. What's wrong with my arm?"

"You broke your wrist," Nick explained. "And you got a nasty knock on the head. But you're going to be okay."

"It hurts when I breathe."

"You also have a cracked rib. But, thank God, none of your injuries are life-threatening. You were incredibly lucky, Lee. The car rolled several times."

The door opened and a nurse entered the room. "I'm glad to see you're awake, Mrs. Lindsay." She wrote something on a chart which she attached to the foot of the bed. "Doctor Zimmerman will be in shortly. Any pain?"

"Lots. My head," Lee whispered.

The nurse nodded. "The doctor will order something for that." She stuck a thermometer in Lee's mouth and glanced at Nick and Sara, standing together by the bed. "No more talking, now. Just lie quietly until the doctor gets here. I'll be back soon." She left, leaving the door open.

Lee wiggled the thermometer around between her dry

lips. Her mind was racing, trying to remember what she'd said to Nick earlier. Her efforts were interrupted by Dr. Zimmerman's walking through the door.

"Well, hello, Lee. Welcome back. I have to say, you are one lucky lady. You gave us quite a scare." He walked over to Lee's bed, plucked her chart and bent to peer into her eyes. "Pupils back to normal. That's good." He removed the thermometer and glanced at it. "Does your head hurt?"

"Does it ever," she whispered.

He wrote something on her chart. Sticking his pen in the top pocket of his white coat, he looked down at her. "That's to be expected. You have a concussion and a pretty impressive cut above your left temple. Your left wrist is broken and you also have a cracked rib. Not to mention a minor cut on your chin and numerous contusions. Do you remember the accident?"

"It was snowing. There was a car stalled in the road. I tried to miss it. That's all I remember."

"You don't remember being in the ambulance, or in the emergency room? Doctor Gonzales said you were semi-conscious but disoriented."

"No," she said, closing her eyes. "I don't remember anything after seeing the car in the road." She felt exhausted. If only the pain in her head would let up.

"Any more nausea? You vomited in the ambulance and again in the emergency room."

"No," Lee whispered.

"What's today's date?"

"Friday. The first of November."

"What's your phone number?"

"999-6538." Lee stared at Zimmerman in alarm. "Am I going to be okay?"

"You're going to be fine. Your head injury isn't as serious as we feared it might be. Still, I'd like to keep you here for a few days just to be on the safe side. I'm afraid you'll have a lot of soreness and pain around that cracked rib for several weeks. As I said, you also have extensive bruising over most of your body. It'll look worse before it looks better, but don't be alarmed." He smiled down at her. "You're going to be good as new."

"What about my wrist?"

"A simple fracture. It should heal nicely in five to six weeks. Now, I'm going to give you something to help you sleep and send your cheering section home. They can come back to see you tomorrow."

Nick and Sara took turns kissing her cheek. "Sleep tight, Mom," Sara whispered. "You're going to be okay. The doctor said so. See you tomorrow."

Nick touched Lee's shoulder. "I'll be here first thing in the morning."

She lay very still after they left, trying not to cry from the pain in her head. After a moment, the nurse reappeared and pulled up Lee's hospital gown. She felt a cold swipe of wet cotton, followed by a quick sting in her hip. "Now then," the nurse said, "you'll be feeling better in no time. Take a few deep breaths for me. That's right. I know it hurts, but you don't want pneumonia setting in. Just a couple more real deep ones. Good. Now, just push that buzzer by your right arm if you need anything tonight." She left the room.

A wave of drug-induced relaxation washed over Lee, dulling her pain, and she sank gratefully into a soft, black cushion of sleep.

* * *

Another nurse came into the room early the next morning to take her temperature and blood pressure. Lee groaned when she tried to lift her head. The left side of her rib cage throbbed and her body felt like one giant bruise.

"Can I go to the bathroom?" Lee asked as the nurse cranked her bed up into a semi-sitting position.

"Doctor Zimmerman wants you to stay in bed until he examines you later this morning. I'll bring you a bedpan in a minute."

"I'd also like to brush my teeth."

"I'll bring you a basin and toothbrush."

"My purse. Is it here?"

"Let me check." She opened the door to the small closet by the bathroom. "Yes, here it is, right beside your coat."

Lee started as she saw a heavy sheepskin jacket hanging in the hospital closet beside her blood-splattered sweater and denim skirt. She immediately recognized it as Juan's. She had an image of him standing in the doorway after she had discovered Mister's head. He had been wearing a sheepskin jacket. She remembered how he had looked as he pulled at the locked car door and pounded on the car window. Yes, she was certain. He had been wearing that jacket yesterday afternoon.

"Here you are." The nurse handed Lee her purse. "I'll be right back." She walked out, closing the door behind her. Lee's mind raced. She didn't think she'd had her own jacket when she ran away from Juan. Or even her boots. She remembered stepping on sharp stones as she ran barefoot through the snow to her car. No wonder the bottoms of her feet felt so sore. But what was Juan's jacket doing here? She remembered his pickup following closely behind her through the snow, just before she saw the car blocking the road ahead. She squeezed her eyes shut, trying to think. Juan must have been there with her, after the accident. She remembered jerking the steering wheel and skidding off the road. But nothing else. Except...a dream. A dream about flying or floating. And Juan. Yes, Juan had been in that dream. He had been talking to her, holding her. And he had been chanting. And praying. Praying to...a raven? There had been something about a raven.

Lee pressed her palm to her forehead. If that was just a dream, what about the jacket? She must have been wearing it when she was admitted to the hospital. She closed her eyes. How could she possibly explain all this to Nick?

The door swung open. "Now you're in business, Mrs. Lindsay," the nurse announced cheerfully. "Here's a bedpan, a toothbrush, and a mirror. Let me get you a basin and some fresh water."

"Thank you." Lee fought to keep her voice steady. "Oh, Nurse? That jacket in the closet isn't mine. I would appreciate it if you'd take it out of here."

* * *

Nick arrived sometime later. He bent to kiss her cheek. "How're you feeling? You sure look better than you did last night."

"I must have been a sight then. The nurse brought me a mirror a little while ago. I look like the bride of Frankenstein with this bandage around my head. And my eyes look like I got into Sara's Halloween make-up."

Nick gently touched her left upper arm. "You have some impressive bruises there, too. And on your other arm also, as a matter of fact." He frowned. "They almost look like finger marks."

An image of Juan, dragging her across the room and shoving her against the door flashed through Lee's mind. She pushed it away. "I must have bruises all over my body. You said the car rolled several times."

"At least three times. That must have been terrifying. Do you remember it at all?"

"Not really. Just blurred impressions."

"How's your head?"

"It still hurts. But it's better. Where's Sara?"

"I left her sleeping. She's just wiped out, poor kid. Went to pieces when I phoned her yesterday. She had Kevin drive her here to the hospital." He hesitated. "I have to admit I was pretty shook up myself."

Lee reached out with her right hand to touch his cheek. "I'm sorry," she whispered. "You look so tired."

"I didn't get much sleep last night. I finally took one of those pills of yours around two this morning."

Lee braced herself. She'd decided to tell Nick that she'd returned to Cavado to interview someone else for another article. It was a weak story, but the only one she could think of. She prayed that he would buy it, that he would never learn the truth about her relationship with Juan. The truth would end their marriage. Nick would never understand or forgive her. "Nick," she began, "I know you must have some questions—"

"Well, I think I have some idea now what happened."
Her heart almost stopped. "You do?"

He pulled a chair up beside the bed and sat down.
"You said some pretty strange things when you came to
after the accident. About Juan Mascareñas being a
witch and killing Mister and someone else named
Socorro. You even said that he'd made me sick. I
didn't know what to make of it. I assumed you were just
out of your head." He paused. "But then Jim Mallory
called this morning. He wanted to talk to you about the
autopsy report on a friend of yours named Socorro Hall.
I realized that's who you'd been talking about when you
first regained consciousness. I told Mallory about your
accident. Then I said I wanted to know what the hell
was going on. We had quite a conversation."

Lee held her breath, feeling cold dread seep through
her body.

"Of course, Mallory wouldn't tell me much of
anything. Professional ethics and all that. But, after I
told him what you'd said about Mister and Socorro, he
opened up a little. He admitted that he was worried
about you, that you'd been under a lot of stress. I got
the impression that he was already aware of your theory
about Mascareñas being a witch."

"Oh, Nick. I know how crazy it sounds."

"I just don't understand. Why didn't you talk to me
about it?"

"I couldn't. Because it does sound so crazy. I didn't
want to upset you. I don't know, I just thought—"

"You just thought you'd go back out there and poke
around. See if you could gather some evidence. Isn't
that right?"

Lee swallowed hard. She reached for a tissue,
stalling for time to assimilate what Nick had just said.

"That's what happened, isn't it? You were going to
do a little investigative reporting."

"Well, I..." She stopped as tears of relief filled her
eyes. Not trusting herself to speak, she nodded her head.

Nick sighed and shook his head. "I guess I don't have to tell you how foolish that was. Not that I believe that charlatan was responsible for anything but upsetting the hell out of you. But he certainly did that. You haven't been yourself since you went to Cavado weeks ago. I just had no idea how much that idiotic ceremony had affected you. Where did Socorro Hall fit into all of this?"

"She owned Galería de Canyon Road."

"That's one of your advertisers. Did I ever met her?"

"I don't think so. I didn't really know her myself, until a couple of weeks ago. We became friends while you were in Alaska. She...she died last week. She was a friend of the Mallorys, and he suggested that I talk to her about the awakening ceremony. Because she was an Indian, Doctor Mallory thought she might be familiar with that particular ceremony. Socorro was also a psychic." She hesitated as Nick's eyebrow shot up. "And she was convinced that Juan was a *brujo*, a sorcerer."

Nick shook his head. "Mallory doesn't believe in any of that psychic crap, does he?"

"No, of course not. He just thought—"

"I'm surprised that he'd get you mixed up with someone like that. He knew you were already upset about the witch doctor. Christ, he should have known better than to involve you with another fruitcake."

"Nick, please," Lee said with a tired sigh. "Socorro was a wonderful person. In fact, she was one of the nicest..." Her voice broke.

"Okay, okay." He patted her leg. "I don't want to upset you. I'm just trying to understand what happened. So you went back to Cavado yesterday. Did you confront Mascareñas with any of this?"

"Well, not exactly. I...I got scared and ran out. I even left my jacket there. By then it was snowing hard. The road is quite narrow and winding up there. And a car was stalled right in the middle of it. I tried to miss it. Apparently, I did miss it, but I ran off the road. That's all I remember."

"I understand that the man whose car had stalled ran to a nearby filling station and called the police. You were lucky. If it had happened farther down that God-forsaken road there's no telling how long it would have been before someone had come along."

"Yes, I was lucky."

"By the time the ambulance arrived, a passer-by had gotten you out of the car. Good thing you didn't have a spinal injury. He could have made it much worse. Anyway, he disappeared before they could get his name."

Lee closed her eyes.

"You're too tired to talk anymore," Nick said. "I'd better go and let you get some rest." He stood up. "Honey, Mallory said that he felt he should see you again. I think so, too. In fact, I asked if he could come by here for a little session, as soon as you're feeling up to it. Is that okay?"

She nodded.

"I'll give him a call. Now you take it easy. I'm going to work for a while, to catch up on a few things. It shouldn't take long. I won't have the usual interruptions because it's Saturday." He bent to kiss her cheek. "We'll have to replace your car. You might give some thought to what you want."

"I loved my Subaru. We should probably get another one. Can we talk about it later?"

"Sure. I'll be back with Sara this afternoon. You'll be feeling better then."

"I hope so. One more thing before you go. I want an alarm system installed in the house. I'm worried about Sara staying there alone while I'm here."

He nodded. "That's something we should have done before now. I'll make the arrangements this afternoon. Oh, I almost forgot," he said, reaching into his pocket and removing a small envelope. "The nurse gave me your jewelry last night. They took it off when you came in." He spilled the contents into his hand. "Earrings, watch, wedding ring..." He stopped, frowning. "Where on earth did you get this thing?" Lee's heart sank as Nick held up Juan's silver amulet, its crystal eyes glowing red as blood.

Chapter 24

Lee was lying propped up after a lunch of soup and crackers, watching snowflakes hit the second story window of her hospital room. She turned her head at the sound of a soft knock. The door opened slightly, revealing a familiar round face. "Hi. Feel up to a visitor?"

"Hello, Doctor Mallory." She pulled the sheet up to cover her wrinkled hospital gown. "Come in."

"I've been quite concerned about you." He stood beside her bed, arms folded across his chest. "How are you feeling?"

"Not as bad as I look. And a lot better than I did when they brought me in here."

"No roommate?" he asked, indicating the empty bed beside hers.

"Not so far, thank goodness. I'm in no mood for small talk with a sickly stranger. But I am glad to see you. Nick said you might be coming by."

"Yes, your husband and I have had several conversations." He pulled a chair close to the bed and sat down, crossing his short legs. "Nick answered when I called your house yesterday morning to give you the results of Socorro's autopsy. Actually, I had tried to call you on Friday."

Lee laughed, a short, bitter sound. "Well, I was a little out of touch on Friday."

"Do you want to talk about it?"

"You don't usually make house—or rather, hospital—calls, do you? Especially not on a Sunday afternoon."

"Not usually. But, I actually was, as they say, 'in the neighborhood.' Another patient of mine was admitted a couple of hours ago. Besides, under the circumstances, I felt you and I should talk as soon as possible."

"I appreciate your coming." She took a deep breath, then grimaced as pain shot through the left side of her chest. "I really need to talk to you. But first, tell me about Socorro. What did the autopsy show?"

"She had a stroke. A massive cerebral hemorrhage caused by an aneurysm, a weak spot in an artery." He shook his head, looking sad. "It was a congenital time bomb just waiting to go off."

"That's all they know? An artery just happened to blow, for no apparent reason?"

"It happens. A defect like that can go completely undetected for years and then, with no warning—boom."

"That's not what happened to Socorro."

"Lee, I know you've had trouble accepting —"

"I'm convinced that her artery had some outside encouragement to blow."

"You still suspect Juan of using witchcraft?"

"It's more than a suspicion! He as good as admitted that he caused Nick's illness. He was gloating over it. And he killed my cat." Lee began to cry. "That *brujo* bastard killed poor Mister."

"You'd better tell me exactly—"

"And that's not all! He raped me. He held me down on that damned buffalo skin rug and raped me. I fought him, Doctor Mallory. I really did. I tried to get away.

278

But he just picked me up and..." She broke off, unable to finish the sentence.

Mallory's expression was grim. "My God, Lee. I'm so sorry." He was quiet for a moment, waiting for her sobs to subside. "Have you told anyone else about this?"

"No. Of course not. How could I?"

"I see your point. But you need to talk about it now. Do you feel like doing that?"

Lee nodded and blew her nose.

"I want you to tell me everything that happened in Cavado on Friday. Just take your time, and go through all the events that led to your accident."

Mallory sat riveted in his chair as Lee recounted Juan's comments about Nick's illness, the ensuing struggle, and their violent sexual encounter on the buffalo skin rug. She broke down, choking with the horror of the memory, as she described her grisly discovery of Mister's head. "It was just sitting there, on the shelf. All mangled and torn. And his fur was rolled up in a neat little bundle." Taking several deep breaths, she forced herself to continue. "Then Juan came bursting in. He'd been outside, doing God-knows-what. I hit him over the head with something heavy, a pot of some kind, and ran to the car. I didn't even stop to get my boots or jacket."

Mallory nodded, encouraging her to continue.

"Before I could get the car started, Juan came after me. His head was bleeding. I remember blood running down his forehead. He was yelling and pounding on the car door—thank God it was locked—and snow was coming down—I couldn't find my car keys—"

"Slow down, Lee. You're doing fine. Just take your time."

Lee closed her eyes and tried to relax against the pillow. Her heart was pounding. After a moment, she continued. "I finally got the car started and took off down the dirt road. I thought I'd gotten away. But just before I got to the highway, I saw his pickup in the rear view mirror. I stepped on the gas. That's when I saw the car stalled in the road. I swerved to miss it—it all happened so fast—the next thing I knew, my car was sliding over to the shoulder of the road. And then it was rolling, over and over."

Mallory stood up and poured Lee a glass of water. She took a long swallow and handed it back to him with her good hand. "Thanks."

"Okay," he said, returning to his chair. "If you're up to it, I want to go back over this, one piece at a time."

Lee nodded.

"Juan implied that he'd caused Nick's illness. Do you remember his exact words?"

"He said, 'It's not wise to fight me. Didn't your husband's illness teach you that?' Then he said, 'He got well, but next time he may not be so lucky'. Or something very close to that."

"Is there any way he could have known that Nick had been sick?"

Lee hesitated. "Yes. I told him, on the phone, the day before."

"So, all he did was try to take the credit for it. That doesn't take any supernatural abilities."

"I...I guess you're right. But he was so threatening, so convincing."

"He's a con artist, Lee. And a very good one. Now, you said that you struggled with him."

"I went to pieces after he said that about Nick. I started screaming, hitting him. He grabbed me, and I tried to get away. I remember biting his shoulder and scratching his face."

"Go on."

"He dragged me across the floor and slammed me up against the door. I know at one point he slapped me. Then he picked me up and took me into the other room—where he pinned me down on that rug and..." Her voice broke. "I can't talk about that any more right now."

"That's okay. You're doing fine. Let's go on to your

discovery of the cat."

"Mister."

"Isn't it possible that you were mistaken about that? I mean, didn't you tell me that Juan has that place of his filled with animal skulls and bones? Can you really be sure that what you found was Mister? Couldn't it have been another cat who had been run over on a road somewhere?"

Lee shook her head, then groaned and shut her eyes, dizzy with a burst of pain. "No! I'm telling you, it was Mister."

"But he's been missing for how long? Close to three weeks? And you said yourself the remains were in pretty bad shape." He hesitated. "Lee, this situation is traumatic enough, without your jumping to erroneous conclusions."

"I'm not jumping—"

"Now, let me finish. He had just attacked you. You were undoubtedly in shock. Now, isn't it just possible, given those circumstances and a dimly lit room, that you jumped to the wrong conclusion? That you mistook a dead stray for Mister? Isn't that possible?"

"When you put it like that, of course I have to admit it is possible. But I'm telling you, down in my gut, I know that it was Mister."

"Juan knew that you were coming to see him Friday, didn't he? You said you called him the night before. Do you really think he would have carelessly left the carcass of your pet cat lying around for you to find?"

"Who knows what a *brujo* might do? I think he's capable of anything. And he's made me crazy." Her shoulders shook with sobs.

"Lee, let me assure you again, you aren't crazy."

"You don't know, Doctor Mallory. There's some-thing you don't know. And I...I don't know how to talk about it."

"Try."

"It's about the rape. I guess I'm not even sure if I should be calling it a rape."

"What do you mean?"

"I mean, what exactly is the definition of rape?"

"Did Juan force you to have sexual intercourse?"

"Yes."

"That's rape."

"Even if I ended up responding to him?"

"Technically, that doesn't make any difference. But emotionally, it's a loaded issue. And one that can cause you a lot of problems if we don't work it through." He was quiet for a moment, obviously deep in thought. "Before we tackle that, though, I'd like to go back and sort through your earlier feelings about Juan."

She looked down at her clenched hands. "I've spent sleepless nights trying to do just that. I don't understand what happened between us. But I do know that I've been absolutely obsessed by him. Whether it's witchcraft or just a powerful sexual attraction, I've certainly been under his spell."

She met Mallory's concerned eyes. "Can you explain it to me? Can you tell me how I could have been so terrified of Juan and yet so attracted to him at the same time? I mean, for weeks now, I've suspected this man of having supernatural powers, of being some sort of character out of a horror story. I've even thought he might be guilty of murder! And yet, I've gone to meet him and, despite my best intentions, I've had sex with him, repeatedly. You can't tell me that's not crazy behavior!"

"Well, it's certainly ill advised. I'll admit that. But I wouldn't go so far as to call it crazy." He pulled out a package of mints. "Care for one?"

Lee shook her head no.

"Let me tell you how I see your attraction to Juan," Mallory continued, unwrapping the mint and popping it into his mouth. "He's obviously a strong, charismatic personality. And from what you've said, I gather that he's not bad looking. There's something dark and dangerous about him, with his shaman mystique. And a dangerous aura, for some reason, is often very sexy."

He sucked thoughtfully on the mint. "Now, let's combine those qualities with the fact that he managed to break down your normal barriers and establish a high degree of intimacy with you within minutes of your first meeting. As I told you weeks ago, the man is obviously a first-rate and utterly unscrupulous manipulator. He drugged and no doubt hypnotized you right off the bat. Then he played on your belief in reincarnation, setting you up for the seduction." He leaned forward in his chair. "Don't you see? That's a terrific line. 'Hey, we were lovers before. This can't be wrong. It's just history repeating itself'."

"That makes me sound so gullible."

"Not really." Mallory studied her for a moment. "I want you to try to look at yourself objectively for a minute. You're, what, forty years old? And because you grew up in a chaotic, dysfunctional home, you trained yourself early to keep a tight rein on your emotions. Watching your father's alcoholic rages taught you to equate passion with danger. Am I right?"

Lee shrugged, not saying anything.

"So you put a lid on those normally powerful teenage sexual impulses. You pushed them down somewhere deep inside of you. But suppressing feelings doesn't make them go away. They just simmer in the subconscious until someday, when conditions are right, they explode to the surface. That's what happened when you met Juan."

"But why? Why with him?"

"Because he's passionate and unpredictable, qualities that would appeal strongly to you on an unconscious level. Look, I remember you telling me once that you were still a virgin when you met Nick. Isn't that right?"

She nodded.

"And, if my memory serves me, you married him several months later. You threw yourself into a busy, productive, well-ordered life. Now, eighteen years later, here you are, married to an exceptionally intelligent but—by your own description—not especially passion-

ate man. Add to that the fact that he's an admitted
workaholic who's out of town half the time. That must
get lonely. Frankly, I think you were ripe for an affair.
Enter Juan—sexy, domineering, and more than a little
mysterious. He's clever enough to sense your suppressed sexuality. And he manages to blow your caution
all to hell.

The fact that he comes from a completely different
culture just works in his favor. The whole thing is so
bizarre, so off-the-wall, it seems more like a fantasy than
an affair. Your relationship doesn't seem *real* enough to
be wrong. After all, you aren't meeting some ordinary
guy in a Holiday Inn. You're meeting a mystery man in
an isolated hideaway and making passionate love by
candlelight on a buffalo skin rug! Wow, Lee, that's
straight out of every woman's secret fantasy."

Lee stared into space, a slight frown on her face.
"What are you saying?"

"I'm just saying that it isn't difficult to understand.
You don't have to convince yourself that supernatural
spells are involved in order to justify your attraction to
Juan."

"And that's what you think I've been doing—
convincing myself that Juan is some kind of sorcerer, in
order to give myself permission to have an affair with
him?"

"Doesn't it make sense?"

"Yes, damn it, it makes perfectly logical sense. But I
know there's more to it than that." She hesitated.
"Something very strange happened while Juan was
forcing himself on me. I...I don't know if I can explain
it to you."

"Give it a try."

"While we were struggling, he kept saying things
like, 'Yes, that's how it often was with us, biting and
scratching'. I remember that he said that I 'made love
like a mountain lion'. Doctor Mallory, he certainly
wasn't talking about this lifetime. I hate to admit this,
but by the time he threw me down on the buffalo skin, I

was excited—sexually I mean. And during the act itself, which was fast and brutal, I truly felt like I was someone else. Like my body didn't even belong to me. Juan was whispering strange words in my ear—some kind of chant—and I just went wild. I had the most incredible orgasm of my life." She took a long, shuddering breath. "Afterwards, I felt the most terrible emptiness. I was numb, literally unable to speak or move."

"You were in shock."

"I have a vague memory of Juan undressing me and giving me something to drink. Then I slept. When I woke up, I don't know how much later, I felt like I was myself again. Juan was gone, outside, I guess. I was terrified, afraid he would never let me leave. As I was frantically putting my clothes on, I looked up and saw Mister's head."

"Lee, he drugged you after the rape. You must have been disoriented when you woke up. That's another argument against its having been Mister's head."

When she didn't respond, he continued. "Let me just say that, given the strength and complexity of your attraction to Juan, I'm not at all surprised that you responded sexually to him."

"Even when he was forcing me?"

"As I said earlier, he lifted the lid on your suppressed sexuality. And he used those romantic past-life references to fan the fire."

"What about my feeling like I was no longer myself?"

"It's called disassociation. And it's a common defense mechanism during a traumatic occurrence. After all, Lee, you were being raped." He paused for a moment. "Have you considered bringing charges against him?"

"No! I couldn't do that. The most important thing right now is to protect Nick from all this. How could I accuse Juan of raping me without everything being revealed? I mean, what the hell was I doing there in the first place?"

"Okay, I agree that it wouldn't be in your best interest. But Juan has proven now that he's more than just a backwoods con artist. He's dangerous. You can't afford to let him confuse you with any more supernatural or past-life nonsense."

"But that's just it, Doctor Mallory. I'm not convinced that it is just nonsense. What about my dreams? They're so realistic, like I'm really living them. And I'm someone else in those dreams! There's something else I haven't told you, something that's really been haunting me."

"Don't hold anything back, Lee. Let's hear it."

"Okay. I remembered a dream, or what I assumed was a dream, when I woke up here in the hospital. I must have had it after the accident, while I was unconscious. Juan was holding me, chanting and praying. Calling on a raven spirit for help. Asking the Great Spirit to spare me. And we weren't alone. I saw shadowy forms moving all around us."

Mallory watched her intently. "Go on."

"Only it wasn't a dream, I know that now. Because when I arrived here at the hospital, I was wearing Juan's amulet." She reached into the drawer of the night stand and took out the amulet. "He must have put it around my neck after the accident." She handed it to Mallory.

"Interesting piece of jewelry," he said, examining it. "Quite old from the looks of it. This is an antique chain."

"Look at the stones. Juan said that they were a rare crystal, found only in the mountains of northern Mexico. When I repeated that to Socorro, she said that her grandmother used to talk about a legendary red crystal that had miraculous healing qualities. There was something about Aztec priests using it."

"Socorro knew all of those old stories. I'm surprised that she took that one seriously."

"She said she wasn't sure the healing stones even existed. She was just curious about this amulet. But she never saw it. At least, not as far as I know. Unless..."

"Unless?"

"I guess we'll never know whether or not Socorro went to Cavado the afternoon before she died."

"But you think maybe she did?"

"I'm afraid that she did."

"Lee, even if Socorro saw Juan, even if she confronted him—the fact remains that she was killed by an aneurysm. Not by the Cavado con man." He handed the amulet back to her.

"But how can you be so sure that Juan is just a con man? I was wrapped in his sheepskin jacket when they brought me here. And I was wearing his amulet."

"What does any of that prove?"

"I think it proves that Juan is sincere in his beliefs. Don't you see? There was no reason for him to be doing all that chanting and praying, unless he was sincere. It couldn't have been some sort of show for my benefit. After all, I was unconscious, or almost, anyway."

She held the amulet in her palm, staring at it. "Who knows? Maybe the crystals worked. Doctor Zimmerman said he was amazed that the impact I suffered to my head didn't have more serious consequences. Apparently, the cut on my temple was an impact split—the kind you get when you hit your head really hard. Everyone agrees that it was a miracle I escaped with such comparatively minor injuries. I wasn't even wearing my seat belt, and the car rolled several times." She dropped the amulet back inside the drawer and closed it. "Maybe my injuries were actually much worse and Juan healed them before the ambulance arrived."

Mallory shook his head. "You don't really believe that, do you?" he asked.

She didn't answer for a long moment. "I don't know what to believe anymore."

"What about Nick?" Mallory said, changing the subject. "You haven't told me how you handled this with him."

"Fortunately, he'd already jumped to the conclusion

that I went back to Cavado to gather evidence against Juan. I was more than happy to go along with that. The only thing I had to lie about was the amulet. I said I had no idea where it came from." She looked away.

"So everything is okay between the two of you?"

"I think so, as far as Nick's concerned. He's upset with me for being foolhardy, but the truth would never occur to him. And I certainly don't intend to ease my conscience—or end my marriage—by confessing it. I just want to put this behind me and get on with my life. Do you think I'll ever be able to do that?"

"Yes. But it's going to take some time. And it's going to take all the strength you can muster where Juan is concerned."

"What do you mean?"

"I suspect you'll be hearing from him any day now. He won't want to give you up."

"He doesn't have a choice. It's over!"

"I certainly hope you mean that."

"Trust me, Doctor Mallory. I've never meant anything more."

Chapter 25

Bloody, mutilated cats were everywhere—littering the floor, sprawled in tortured positions on chairs and table tops, stacked like firewood against the wall. Lee pushed the furry bodies aside with her feet in her frantic scramble for the door. It was locked. She rushed to the window. It wouldn't budge. Pounding on the glass, she yelled for help. A man materialized out of the darkness beyond the window. She stood frozen as he moved closer, his feet seeming not to touch the ground. When he was inches from her, his smiling face pressed against the glass, she began to scream.

The ring of the telephone jarred Lee awake. She rolled over in her hospital bed, hurting her cracked rib and knocking the box of tissues to the floor. She fumbled for the telephone and finally succeeded in pulling it onto her chest. "Yes? Hello?" She was answered by a faint hum of silence at the other end of the line. "Hello?" She was about to hang up the receiver when she heard the familiar voice.

"Are you alone? Can you talk?"

Lee's mouth went dry. "No! Never—"

"Don't hang up. Please. Tell me how you are. It has been so hard, *querida*. So hard to be separated from you."

Lee squeezed her eyes closed. "Stop...just stop it."

"Stop what? You sound so strange." There was a pause. "Is there much pain?"

"Yes," she angrily spat the word into the receiver. "There is much pain. There has been much pain since the day I met you. Now leave me alone. Get out of my life. I don't ever want to see or hear from you again!"

"Why are you angry with me?" His voice sounded genuinely puzzled. "You must explain your anger."

"You really are crazy. I don't have to explain anything to you!"

"You still don't understand—?"

"You're the one who doesn't understand," she interrupted, her voice shaking. "I want you out of my life!" She slammed the receiver onto the bed beside her leg. Then she pulled it back by the cord and replaced it on its cradle. She lay exhausted on the bed, staring at the white ceiling, as tears ran down the sides of her face and made small stains on the pillow.

* * *

A short time later, the door opened with a muffled squeak, and Lee opened her eyes to see Nick peeking into the room. "Hi," he said. "I thought you were asleep." He stood above her for a moment, staring down with a concerned frown on his face before he bent to give her a quick kiss.

"I napped earlier, but I woke up a little while ago. I was just resting." She licked her lower lip. Her cheeks felt hot and tight with dried tears. "Would you hand me my makeup kit? Sara brought it last night. I think she put it in that drawer. She obviously thought I needed it. I must be quite a sight."

"You're a sight for sore eyes to me," Nick said in a tender voice. He opened the drawer of the bedside table and handed her a small leather case. "Are you still in pain?"

"No, not really," she said, avoiding his eyes. "Only when I move." Or think. Or remember, she silently added. She flipped open the clasp and looked into the mirror. Her eyes were red and swollen, and the skin under her right eye was an impressive shade of blue. Her entire face looked blotchy and bruised. "Lipstick certainly wouldn't improve this situation," she said, snapping the case shut.

"You've been crying, haven't you?"

She nodded, her eyes blurring with fresh tears. "I can't seem to stop blubbering. Do you see a box of tissues on the floor?"

Nick bent to retrieve them, pulling one out for her before sitting in the chair beside the bed. He sat silently as she wiped at her eyes and blew her nose. When he spoke, his voice was hesitant. "Honey, I don't know if this is a good time to bring this up or not. But I've been thinking about something."

She dropped the damp tissue into a wastebasket by the side of her bed. "What?"

"Well, you know that I'm several years overdue for a sabbatical." He shifted in his chair. "Remember how we've talked about both of us taking a year off and going someplace where I could teach physics? Some-place far away from Santa Fe. A complete change of scene."

"Yes, of course. But I thought that's all it was. Just talk."

"Well, I think we ought to do it. George Washington University has an opening for a guest professor in my field. I talked to them this afternoon."

"George Washington? As in Washington, D.C.?"

He nodded. "I think it might be a good thing for all of us. It would be broadening for Sara, a real change from Santa Fe High. You could take a well-earned break from the magazine to concentrate on your writing, or even finish your master's degree at GWU. You used to talk about going back to school. Annabel and the staff could get along without you for a year. What do you think?"

"I think this is very sudden. I don't see how I could just leave the magazine for that long. And what about your experiments?"

"Morrison can keep them going. He's been my right hand for years. And I can always fly back for a day or two if there's an emergency. The truth is, I could use some time off from the program. I'm beginning to feel a little burned out. I think you are, too."

"I admit that the idea is tempting. Actually, very exciting. But I just don't see how I could leave."

"Sure you could, babe. That's one of the advantages of owning your own business. You can't be fired."

"But what about Sara? She won't want to leave her friends, especially Kevin."

"I think she'd adjust quickly. Besides, it would only be for two semesters. She'd be back in the middle of her junior year."

"Wait a minute. You're talking about making this move right away? Couldn't we at least wait until next summer?"

"GWU needs someone next semester. One of their physics professors had a heart attack last week and took a year's leave of absence. It's great timing for us. Sara could begin school there the first part of January. Kids do that sort of thing all the time. For Sara, with her outgoing personality, it'd be a breeze."

"I don't think it'd be quite that easy for her. Then there's the house. We couldn't just go off and leave it empty."

"We'd rent it, and rent a place there. One of those fancy apartments."

"I don't know what to say. I'm a little surprised."

"I think it might be just what you need," he said, leaning forward in his chair to stroke her arm. "Mallory said—"

"Mallory? You've talked to Doctor Mallory about this?"

"Well, yes I did. We just—"

"Wait a minute. Why would you talk to him about this before you mentioned it to me?"

"I called him this morning, and it just came up. We're both concerned about you. You've been going through a rough time lately." He paused, staring down at the floor for a moment, before looking up again to meet her eyes. "I hope you know how proud I am of what you've done with that magazine. You've worked your butt off for years, running a business and a home— not to mention raising a great daughter. And I know it hasn't been easy. Especially with my traveling. Mallory suggested that a rest and change of scenery might be just what you need right now."

"Let me get this straight. You talked to Mallory, then called GWU and they just happened to have an immediate opening?"

"That's how things happen in this business. I don't have to remind you that I spend a lot of time in Washington. I have contacts at the University. Tom Loree—he's head of the physics department—is willing to pull the necessary strings. They've been looking for someone with my experimental background."

"Nick, you love your work here. Teaching would be a big change."

"It would be good for me. Good for all of us." He reached for her hand. "It's true that my work is important to me. But you've always been more important. You and Sara. I just assumed that you knew that. Your accident has shown me how much I've taken for granted."

Lee turned to face him, looking into his anxious blue eyes. She was again struck by how tired he looked. Deep lines creased his forehead and slashed vertically between his brows. Puffy bags lay under his eyes. She pulled his head toward hers and kissed him lightly on the lips. "I love you," she whispered. "I really do."

Nick's grin erased years from his face. "Promise you'll think about Washington. Just imagine. The

Kennedy Center. Long afternoons wandering through
the Smithsonian." He wiggled his eyebrows. "Eating
soft-shelled crabs in one of those ritzy Georgetown
restaurants."

"You silver-tongued devil."

"I think it's time for you to get some rest now." He
stood up, pushing the chair back. "Besides, I have a
date. I promised Sara I'd get home early and take her to
the Zia Diner for dinner. We'll both be back to see you
tonight. Now, no more tears. Deal?"

"Deal."

He blew her a kiss and left, closing the door behind
him. Lee spent the rest of the afternoon weighing the
pros and cons of spending a year far from Santa Fe.
There was no contest. The pros won. She reached for
the phone and dialed Annabel's private number.

* * *

Lee could tell from Sara's face when she walked
through the door several hours later that Nick had tried
to enlist her support for the proposed move. It was also
obvious that he hadn't succeeded. Sara's eyes were red
and swollen, her expression guarded.

"I have some good news," Lee said, striving for an
upbeat tone. "Doctor Zimmerman said I can go home
tomorrow."

"Hey, that's terrific," Nick said, putting his arm
around Sara's shoulders and hugging her close. "Isn't it,
princess?"

"Yeah." Sara touched the cast on her mother's wrist.
"How long do you have to wear the cast and the bandages and all?"

"Well, the cast stays on for five to six weeks.
Zimmerman says the rib will be painful for awhile, but
as long as I don't take up bungee jumping, I should be
okay. You guys will have to put up with me looking
like this until the stitches come out next week."

"That'll be tough, Mom." Sara teased, making an
obvious effort. "We'll have to keep you locked in the
guest room. Leave food outside your door."

They all laughed, breaking the tension. Lee looked at her husband and daughter, noting the strong family resemblance. Although everyone remarked on Sara's resemblance to Lee, she definitely had her father's nose and smile. Lee felt a surge of love for them. Her family, the center of her world. She took a deep breath. The craziness with Juan was finally over. It was all behind her.

"Sara and I have been talking about my taking a sabbatical," Nick said, interrupting her thoughts. "She was a little upset at first, but I think she understands that it would be a good experience for all of us. Probably our last chance to do something like this as a family. Before we know it, our baby girl will be off to college."

"Now, let's not rush that," Lee said, watching Sara. "Honey, how do you really feel about the idea?"

"Well, I don't know. It scares me. I mean, I don't want to leave my friends and all." She glanced at Nick, then looked down at the floor. "But I guess it wouldn't be so bad. After all, we would be coming back."

"Sure, we would," Nick interjected.

"But I'll bet Wendy will try to snatch Kevin up the minute I leave."

"Hey, you'd have so many new boyfriends you wouldn't have time to worry about Kevin." Nick looked at Lee. "Well, babe. What's your vote?"

"I talked to Annabel this afternoon. She encouraged me to go, reminding me that she had taken off for nine months when Milt had his heart attack. She even had the nerve to say that they could manage fine without me. Strangely enough, I had the feeling that you had already talked to her, Nick."

"Guilty as charged." He grinned. "So, is it settled then?"

"It really does sound wonderful—"

"Great! I'll call GWU in the morning. And I'd better contact a realtor about renting our house. We could rent it furnished. Just store the valuables, take a few essentials: clothes, computers, books."

"My TV, stereo, and posters," Sara added.

Nick laughed. "Well, maybe just a few posters. We'll want to travel light and rent something furnished in Washington. After all, this is going to be an adventure. Let's keep it as simple as possible. Tell you what. I'm going back there for a meeting next week. I can find us an apartment then. And check into the schools." He smiled, looking from Lee to Sara. "Now, let me see some real enthusiasm."

They glanced at each other before bravely returning Nick's smile.

* * *

The telephone rang as Lee was finishing her breakfast the next morning. She stopped a spoonful of cereal halfway to her mouth, and let the phone ring twice more before reaching for the receiver. "Hello?"

"Don't hang up, *querida*. You must speak with me."

Lee pushed the tray away, feeling her last bite stick in her throat. "You still don't get it, do you? I don't want to talk to you—ever again."

"Then just listen. Let me tell you how it is with me. I don't eat, I don't sleep. I think only of you."

"Stop it! I don't want to hear it. I told you—"

"I know what you told me. But you're wrong. You can't end it between us. You belong with me."

"No, I don't belong with you. Look, I don't know what kind of power you've had over me. But it's over. It ended last Friday."

"I can't lose you. I can't let that happen." His voice grew harder. "*¿Comprendes?* Do you understand?"

"You're the one who doesn't understand! I'm leaving. My family and I are moving away."

"Moving away?" He sounded stunned. "What do you mean, moving away? Where do you think you're going?"

"That's none of your business."

There was another long silence. When he finally spoke, his voice was so thick with anger that she almost didn't recognize it. "Understand this, Lee. You aren't going anywhere. I won't let you go."

"You can't stop me. You can't—"

He laughed, a mirthless sound that sent chills through Lee's body. "You think not? You think I can't stop you? Then you are very mistaken. Do you think I saved you—brought you back—only to let you leave me?"

"What do you mean, you 'saved' me?"

"It's not over," he said, ignoring her question. "You'll see, *querida*. It will never be over between you and me." The line went dead.

Lee replaced the receiver, trembling with shock and fear. Mallory was right. Juan wasn't going to give up easily. Still, she hadn't anticipated his anger or his threats. How did he plan to stop her from leaving? Would he tell Nick about their affair? She tried to imagine the scene between the two men—Juan insisting on a prior, past-life claim to Lee and her husband's outraged reaction. When angry, Nick could be pretty formidable himself. And even if Juan told Nick he'd slept with his wife, Nick wouldn't believe him. Maybe Juan was just bluffing....

Her thoughts were interrupted by Dr. Zimmerman's striding through the door. "Hi there. How're we doing this morning?"

"I'm ready to go home. The nurse said you had to give the final okay."

"Let's change that bandage on your head." He cut away the tape and peered at the stitches above her temple. "Looks good," he assured her. "You'll only have a thin scar. And that'll be hidden by your hair when it grows out. The cut on your chin was superficial. No stitches. The bruises are still impressive, but they'll fade soon. Still having headaches?"

She shook her head. "A slight one yesterday. But it's gone this morning."

"How's the rib?"

"Still really sore," she admitted. "But I'm learning to be cautious in my movements."

"Good. No belly dancing for a few weeks."

"Oh, well, there goes my new career."

He smiled. "I want to see you in my office early next week. I'll remove the stitches then." He taped another bandage on her head. "You can take shallow baths. Just be careful not to get the tape or the cast on your arm wet. I'm afraid you're going to have to live with that cast for awhile longer. It's going to cramp your style at work, isn't it?"

"It'll give me an excuse to sit back and play boss."

"Okay. I'll sign the papers springing you from this joint. Is Nick picking you up?"

She nodded. "He went into work early this morning. But he's planning to take off as soon as I call him."

"Good enough. Remember to call my office and schedule an appointment for Monday or Tuesday."

"I will. Thanks for everything."

He waved and was gone.

* * *

Nick had left instructions to be called out of his meeting when Lee called, and his secretary put her through immediately.

"I'll wind things up here and hit the road," he said. "Be there in about an hour."

"Don't forget to stop by the house and grab something for me to wear home. Just a jacket, Levi's, and some kind of top that will fit over this cast." She hesitated. "And bring my old brown boots. Somehow, the emergency room staff managed to misplace my new ones."

She hung up the phone, realizing that she was fast becoming a pretty smooth liar. No wonder, she thought bitterly. As Mother always said, practice makes perfect.

Chapter 26

"Yes, Annie, I'm taking it easy. But it sure feels strange to be sitting around the house instead of coming into the office. I'll try to enjoy it. Thanks for dropping the packet off. This issue looks great. Nice cover. How many subscribers did we pick up this month? Oh, good. Listen, I've got to go. There's a man here installing a burglar alarm, and he needs to talk to me. Thanks for calling. I'll get back to you later."

She hung up the receiver and turned off the telephone ringer. Better let the answering machine screen the messages in case Juan tries to call. Of course, he might leave a message, one that Nick could overhear. He'd called before when Nick was at home. And now that he was angry, there was no telling what he might do. Well, she would just have to take that chance. She wasn't about to leave herself open to another conversation with him.

* * *

Lee was resting on her bed and looking through magazines when Sara came home from school.

BRUJO

"Hi. Aren't we burglar alarmed yet? No sirens went off when I unlocked the front door."

"Not yet. This is a big house. It'll take a couple of days to get the system installed. How was school?"

"The usual. Everyone is really knocked out that we're leaving. I think Kevin is super sad." She grinned. "He said he'd write to me every night. Oh, here, I picked up the mail." She tossed a pile of envelopes and fliers on the bed and left the room.

Lee shuffled through assorted bills and advertisements. She opened a large manila envelope from the office, stuffed with correspondence Julie thought Lee should see. One return address immediately caught her eye. Luis Tafoya, Rio Arriba County Sheriff's Department, Española, New Mexico. She ripped the envelope open and removed a Xerox copy of a newspaper clipping from the *Albuquerque Journal*, dated June 18, 1962. Attached was a one-sentence note:

"Mrs. Lindsay—Thought you might be interested in this old clipping re: Juan Mascareñas. Regards, L. Tafoya."

Lee stared at the picture of a pretty, smiling young woman. Underneath was the caption: Susan Michelle Miller, age 19, reported missing in Mexico.

The story was brief:

A missing persons report has been filed on Susan M. Miller, a sophomore anthropology major at the University of New Mexico. When last seen the California native was reportedly en route to Chihuahua, Mexico, in the company of another UNM student, Juan Mascareñas of Cavado, New Mexico. Neither Miller nor Mascareñas has been heard from since April 13.

Miss Miller is described as five feet, seven inches tall, 120 pounds, with long blond hair and blue eyes. Her sudden departure baffled family and friends.

"Susan said they were leaving for a week to ten days," said the missing woman's roommate and long-time friend, Jessica Manning. "I was surprised because it was the middle of the semester. Susan has always been a serious student and very reliable person. It's not like her to just take off and disappear like this. Everyone is terribly worried."

Mascareñas, a sophomore psychology major, is described as six feet tall, 170 pounds, dark hair and brown eyes.

Anyone with information concerning the whereabouts of Miller or Mascareñas is asked to contact the Albuquerque Police Department.

After rereading the article, Lee studied the picture. Although it was a photocopy of a black and white picture, there was no denying the obvious. Large eyes, small upturned nose, oval face with a slightly squared jawline. A blond with blue eyes. Even their height and weight matched.

Lee replaced the article in the envelope and slipped it into her nightstand drawer. Her hands were shaking. The resemblance was remarkable. Twenty years ago, Susan Miller could have been her twin.

* * *

Nick came home from work Friday night with a wide smile and a surprise for Lee. Parked in the driveway with a huge pink bow on the windshield was a new cream-colored Subaru station wagon.

"I didn't know when you'd feel up to shopping for a new car, so I decided to spare you the hassle," he said. "A station wagon will come in handy for the trek to Washington. Well, what's the verdict? Did I do good?"

Lee put her arms around his neck and hugged him as hard as her sore rib would allow. "You did just great." She gave him a long kiss. "I love you. I hope you know how much."

Nick beamed down at her. Then his expression grew serious. "I've never doubted your love, babe. We've been through a few rough spots in the last eighteen years, but we've always been a team. And I wouldn't trade that for anything."

Her chest tightened and she buried her face in his shoulder. "Neither would I," she said, trying to control the quiver in her voice. "Not for anything."

* * *

The weekend passed quietly. Nick was delighted with the intricate alarm system and patiently instructed Lee and Sara in its use. "Remember," he repeated, "the police are automatically alerted when the alarm goes off."

"Jeez," Sara sighed, "that thing's a computer. You need a Ph.D. to understand it."

"Or a father with a Ph. D. to explain it to you," Nick said.

"I hope the renters can figure it out."

"I'll write out detailed instructions. By the way, have you heard anything from the realtor—what's her name?"

"Katherine. She called yesterday to say that she's working with a young couple who sound perfect. They're going to be in town in a couple of weeks. She'll bring them over then."

"Great. I'll see what I can find for us to rent in Washington next week."

"How long will you be gone?" Lee felt a pang of anxiety at the thought of Nick's being out of town again.

"I leave on Tuesday and get back Saturday night. It'll be a busy trip. I've got back-to-back meetings scheduled for Wednesday, but that'll leave me Thursday and Friday to look for an apartment and find a school for Sara."

"I still can't believe that we're going," Lee said.

"You're not having second thoughts, are you?"

"No. I'm really eager to go."

"Good. I was thinking that we should plan to leave

the Saturday before Christmas. Just as soon as school's out. Christmas in Washington. Doesn't that sound terrific? They go all out with decorations back there. You'll see. It's going to be great!"

* * *

Lee was standing in her closet early Monday morning, trying to decide what to wear. It had to be something that would fit over her cast. She had a list of errands to run this morning, before her appointment with Dr. Zimmerman. And she was determined to spend the afternoon at the office. There were a few problems to be ironed out. Her year in Washington would require a little reorganization. They'd have to hire another editor. She agreed with Annabel that Julie should be promoted to office manager. And that meant that they would have to find another receptionist.

She struggled to remove a loose-fitting dress from its hanger with one arm. The rib was feeling a lot better, and today she would get the bothersome stitches removed from her head. Then she would just have the cast to cope with.

"Mom?" Sara called, running up the stairs. "I'm leaving for school now. Kevin just honked."

"Okay, honey. Have a good day. And wear your down jacket. It's chilly outside."

"I know. Oh, that reminds me. Have you seen my red wool scarf? I thought I left it in the downstairs coat closet, but I haven't been able to find it."

"Your scarf?" Lee froze, remembering. The last time she went to Cavado, the day of her accident, she had worn her heavy leather jacket. And because it was cold, getting ready to snow, she had wrapped Sara's red scarf around her neck! She'd completely forgotten about the scarf, had never given it another thought. Oh, my God, she thought frantically, I left it at Juan's! Along with my jacket and boots.

"Mom?" Sara was standing at the closet door, staring at her. "Are you okay?"

"What? Oh, yes. I was just remembering.... I

borrowed your scarf the day of my accident. I'm sorry. I forgot about it. I guess it got...lost."

"Don't worry about it. It's no big deal. I can wear my blue one." She gave Lee a quick kiss on the cheek. "Gotta run. See you after school."

Lee's knees felt weak. She walked out of the closet and sat on the edge of the bed. "He has it," she whispered to herself. "Juan has Sara's scarf!" She felt clammy fear crawl across her skin as she was hit with another realization. The scarf was monogrammed with Sara's initials. She had given Juan both the motivation and the means for revenge.

Chapter 27

*S*ara's scarf! How could she have forgotten about it?
If only she hadn't worn it to Cavado.

"Lee?" Annabel's voice penetrated her thoughts.

"I'm sorry. What?"

"I asked if you like the Glad Rags Boutique ad
layout. Honestly, you act like you've already left us.
You hardly said a word during the staff meeting. Are
you all right? Did your visit to the doctor go okay this
morning? You know, I still get chills when I think of
you wrecking your car out on that road. It's an absolute
miracle that you weren't killed."

"I know. I was very lucky. And the doctor said I'm
doing fine now. I just have a lot on my mind."

"Well, I don't doubt it. Getting ready to spend a year
in Washington! I'm green with envy. The shopping
there! Kiddo, you're gonna think you've died and gone
to heaven. I spent six solid hours in Loehmann's when
we went back to Washington for Milt's thirty-fifth high
school reunion. That's where I bought my cashmere
coat and that red sequined dress I wore to our office

Christmas party last year. Well, let me tell you, I almost lost my mind in that store. Milt finally dragged me out, kicking and screaming...."

Sara should be home from school by now, Lee realized, glancing up at the clock on the wall. I've got to remind her to reset the alarm when she's there alone. She reached for the telephone. "Excuse me for a minute, Annabel. I just remembered that I need to call Sara."

The phone rang and rang. No answer. Feeling something close to panic, Lee sprang to her feet. "I have to go," she said. "There's something I have to check on."

"What? Where?"

"At home. Listen, the layout looks great. I'll call you later." She grabbed her purse and hurried out the door.

* * *

Lee pulled into the garage and jumped out of the car. When she opened the door to the house some part of her mind registered the fact that the burglar alarm was off. "Sara!" she yelled, running down the hall and up the stairs. "Sara, where are you?" She flung Sara's bedroom door open.

Sara was lying across her bed, telephone in hand. She looked at Lee with startled eyes. "What is it, Mom? Why are you freaking out?"

Lee sagged against the door frame in relief. "I called you twenty minutes ago but you didn't answer. I knew the school bus should have come by then."

"I didn't ride the bus. Kevin brought me home and we stopped for a coke. What's the matter? I thought you were going to be at work all afternoon."

Lee sat on the bed and put her arms around Sara. "Oh, baby," she said, "when I didn't know where you were, I just got scared. I don't know what I'd do if anything happened to you."

"Why should anything happen to me? I don't understand. I just stopped for a coke. I've done that before, and you've never minded."

"I know. But from now on, let me know when you're going to be late. Okay?"

"Okay. Sure. Uh, I'm on the phone, Mom."

"Oh. I'm sorry. Finish your conversation. I think I'm going to lie down and rest for a little while." She walked into her room and collapsed on her bed. After a few seconds, she got up and reset the burglar alarm.

* * *

"So, Doc Zimmerman said you were healing nicely?" Nick had just gotten home from work and was laying out shirts, ties and underwear, starting to pack for his trip the next morning.

"Yeah." Lee was lying across the bed, watching him. "I guess the rib will be sore for awhile yet. But it's nothing I can't live with. Makeup covers the cut on my chin. And look, there's only a hairline scar at my temple."

He peered down at her. "I can't even see it."

"I combed my hair so that it doesn't show. Is there anything I can do to help you pack?"

"No, just lie there. You look bushed. Sara and I can fix sandwiches for dinner."

"I am tired. I guess I wasn't in shape yet for an afternoon at work. I think I'll go to bed early. I could really use a good night's rest."

* * *

She awoke in the darkness, sweating and breathless. It had been a familiar and terrifying dream. She had been falling from a great height, grabbing frantically at empty air. She'd managed to force herself awake just before smashing into the rocks below.

She shuddered. It was the first nightmare she'd had since she was in the hospital. Were they starting again? She tried to calm her breathing, to force her muscles to relax. The Indian man—the one with the birthmark like Juan's—was in the dream again. But this time their relationship was different. He was no longer her lover. Instead, he was an angry, threatening presence. Trying to force her into doing... something. Some ceremony she didn't want to perform? The memory flitted across a dark corner of her mind and out. But the anxiety and adrenaline remained. Lee threw the covers back and sat on the edge of the bed. This has got to stop, she thought. Before I go nuts. Maybe I should take a sleeping pill. I feel so wired, I'll never get back to sleep on my own. She got out of bed and walked into the bathroom. The shades were up on the bathroom window. After swallowing a pill and turning off the bathroom light, Lee paused to look outside. It was a bright night. The moon, only days away from being full, reflected off the light snow that had fallen earlier, casting an eerie luminescence across the midnight landscape. From the hills beyond the house came the lonely yelping cry of a coyote, answered by the barking of a neighbor's dog.

The sounds triggered thoughts of Mister, and brought a heavy sadness to Lee's heart. Maybe Nick was right. Maybe she should get another cat when they got to Washington. Mister could never be replaced, but a kitten might help fill the void that he left.

She was about to turn from the window when a slight movement caught her eye. Just beyond the house, beside a large *piñon* tree, something was moving. Lee leaned her face closer to the window, straining for a better look. What she saw made her whole body tighten in terror.

A man stepped away from the tree and stood clearly silhouetted in the moonlight. The set of his powerful shoulders, the arrogant angle of his head left no doubt as to his identity. It was Juan! For a long moment he seemed to gaze toward the darkened window where she stood, locked in fright. Then he moved back behind the tree.

Lee held her breath while her blood roared in her ears. For a moment she thought she might faint. What was Juan doing out there, skulking around in the middle of the night? Maybe she should wake Nick. Or set off the alarm to scare him away. Before she could decide what to do, Nick opened the bathroom door.

"Babe? Are you all right? I heard you get up."

Something inside Lee crumbled. It was time to let the chips fall where they may. "There's a man out there," she whispered, almost choking on the words. "Hiding in the trees."

"What? Where?" Nick pressed his face against the window. "I don't see anyone." He turned away from the window and grabbed his robe off the hook on the bathroom door. "You stay here. I'm going out to look." He slipped loafers on his bare feet and hurried down the stairs. Lee was right behind him.

"Go back upstairs," he said over his shoulder.

"No!" She hesitated for only a moment. "Nick, I know who's out there."

He stopped at the bottom of the stairs, staring up at her. "Who?"

"Juan."

"The medicine man? What makes you think so?"

"I recognized him! Nick, he could be dangerous. We should call the police."

Nick zipped a down jacket over his robe and turned off the alarm.

"No! Nick—please!" She grabbed his arm. "Don't go out there!"

"Lee! Let go," he said, prying her hand loose. "I'll be fine. Stay here and lock the door behind me." He left through the sliding glass door that led to the outside patio. Lee locked the door and leaned against it, watching Nick move around the side of the house and disappear behind the *piñon* trees. Her heart was thundering in her chest. Oh, dear God, what would Juan do to Nick? She knew what he was capable of doing. She gripped the door handle as she stared through the glass.

Something moved behind one of the *piñones*. She drew back, holding her breath. Suddenly a bird—black, with a huge wingspread—flew out of the tree and over the top of the house. Lee heard a loud ringing noise in her ears, just before her knees buckled and she slumped to the floor.

The next thing she knew, Nick was banging on the door. His face looked deathly pale in the moonlight. "Lee! Lee!"

Fighting a wave of nausea, she pulled herself to her knees and unlocked the door. In an instant Nick was beside her. "Are you all right? What happened?"

"I...I guess I fainted. Oh, Nick, you're safe."

"Of course I'm safe. I circled all around the house but didn't see anyone. What made you—"

"But he was there. I saw him. Then he flew away."

Nick stared at her. "Flew away?"

Lee started to cry. "It sounds crazy. But I did see Juan, when we were upstairs. Then a huge raven flew out of the tree."

"Are you saying that you fainted because you saw a raven?"

"You don't understand. The raven was in the tree! The same tree that Juan was hiding behind. The raven —"

"Babe, ravens are common around here. I see them all the time." He helped her to her feet. "Come on, let's go upstairs." With his arm around her waist, he half-carried her up the stairs.

"Easy now," he said, helping her into bed. He peered down at her with a worried look. "Do you feel sick?"

"Yes."

"Let me get a wet cloth for your head," he said, going into the bathroom and turning on the light. He came out holding the bottle of sleeping pills. "How many of these did you take?"

"Just one. I had a bad dream and—"

"Are you sure you only took one? Maybe you took one and then forgot and took another one. That could easily happen. They're pretty strong."

"I only took one, dammit!"

"Well, it obviously hit you hard. You're still weak from your accident. It's going to take awhile for you to recover completely." He took the pills back into the

bathroom. Lee watched him reset the burglar alarm
before getting into bed. "I don't want you to take any
more of those pills while I'm gone," he said. "You
clearly had some kind of reaction to them tonight. I'm
just glad you didn't hurt yourself when you passed out."
He yawned. "I've got to get some sleep, babe. Big day
tomorrow." He kissed her cheek and rolled over.
Before long he was snoring softly.

Lee lay awake, staring at the ceiling and trying to
deal with what had happened. No wonder Nick thought
she was drugged out of her mind. She had insisted that
Juan was lurking outside, and then passed out cold at the
sight of a bird. There was no way to make Nick understand. Any rational person knows that a man can't turn
into a bird. She couldn't say anything about this to
anyone, not even Doctor Mallory. Not if she wanted to
be considered sane. But she knew what she'd seen.
Juan had been out there. And he'd be back.

Chapter 28

Lee was in her study the next afternoon, staring at
the newspaper picture of Susan Miller. She was haunted
by the girl's face, so like her own. Luis Tafoya had said
that she had never been heard from again after she went
to Mexico with Juan. Mexico. Juan had wanted to take
Lee to Mexico, too. Dear God, what happened to Susan
Miller down there? Juan swore that she had left with
another man. The police believed him. Was that the
true story? I doubt it, Lee thought, folding the piece of
paper. But I guess I'll never know for sure.

Glancing at the clock, Lee realized that it was almost
time for Sara to get home from school. She disarmed
the alarm system and hid the clipping in the back of her
desk drawer.

She heard the front door open and Sara calling from
downstairs. "Mom? Where are you?"

"Up here," she answered.

Sara ran up the stairs and burst into the room.
"Mom, it's the neatest thing!"

"What?"

"It must be someone's pet. It's totally tame."

"Sara, what are you talking about?"

"A really huge black bird—I guess it's a crow—but it's the most colossal one I've ever seen! Perched on the courtyard wall, just sitting there as calm as anything. I opened the gate and walked right up to it and it still didn't fly away. It just cocked its head from side to side and went 'Kraaak Kraaak'—but kind of soft, like it was talking to me."

In a flash, Lee was out of the room and down the stairs. She ran through the family room and yanked open the front door. The courtyard wall was empty.

"Where?" Lee demanded urgently, as soon as Sara caught up with her. "Where was it? Was it a raven?" She grabbed Sara by the shoulders, ignoring a stab of pain in her side. "Answer me!"

Sara stared at Lee, perplexed. "What's with you, Mom? Why are you freaking out? I mean, it was just a bird!"

* * *

Sara looked worried during dinner that night, watching her mother out of the corner of her eye. Lee did her best to make conversation and appear normal, but she knew that Sara wasn't fooled. She wondered if she'd ever feel normal again. At eight o'clock she rechecked the already locked doors and windows and activated the alarm system. Command, Instant. All set. Then she gave Sara a goodnight kiss and went straight to bed.

* * *

A deafening sound pierced the night, catapulting Lee out of bed and into the hall before she realized what she was doing. Sara ran out of her room to join her, face pale with fright. "What's happening? What is it?"

"It's the burglar alarm!" Lee grabbed Sara's arm and pulled her into the master bedroom. Then she locked the door behind them and ran to examine the alarm control panel on the wall. A numbered flashing red light indicated that the downstairs sliding patio door had been opened. The high-pitched siren continued to scream.

"Mom? What should we do?"

"I don't know! Nothing. We're going to stay right here until the police arrive." The bedside clock told her that it was just after midnight. She hurried into the closet and felt behind Nick's ski boots. Sara gasped when she saw a pistol appear in Lee's hand.

"A gun? I didn't know we had a gun! Oh Jeez, are we going to have to shoot somebody?"

"I hope not. Maybe the siren scared away whoever was trying to get in."

"The police will be coming, won't they? Do you think they're already on their way?"

"They'd better be."

Within moments a police car pulled into the driveway. Sara cheered.

Lee put the gun in her nightstand and slipped into her robe. "Now you stay here while I go downstairs and let them in."

"No way. I'm not staying up here by myself." Sara hurried down the stairs behind Lee.

A policeman stood at the front door. Lee saw his partner in the driveway, shining a flashlight into the darkness on the side of the house. "Come in," she said, clutching Sara's hand. "It's the patio door that went off. Through there—through the kitchen. Shall I turn it off now?" She pointed toward the downstairs control panel. "The siren, I mean."

"Yes, ma'am, please. Then I want you two to stay right here, by the door. Where are the light switches for the kitchen?"

"Right there on the wall. By the bookcase." She punched in the numbers that would deactivate the system. The instant silence was almost shocking. She felt a draft of cold wind just before light from the family room flooded the foyer, exposing an open sliding patio door. Lee stared at it in horror. She knew she'd locked that door. In fact, she'd checked and rechecked all the doors in the house before going to bed.

"Looks like you forgot to lock up, and someone just

slid it open," the second policeman said, coming in through the open patio door. He stayed with Lee and Sara while the other policeman went quickly from room to room, checking the house.

"But I didn't forget! I know that I locked it."

"There's no broken glass, or sign of forced entry."

"But, officer, I'm telling you, I locked that door!"

He shrugged. "Well, anyway, I'm sure whoever it was is long gone by now. Probably just a kid looking for quick drug money."

The other policeman reappeared and shook his head. "There's no one in the house, ma'am. We'll check the grounds again before we leave. But I think you're safe now. Usually all it takes to spook these characters is just the sound of the alarm. Whoever tried to break in is probably half-way to Albuquerque by now." He gave Lee and Sara a reassuring smile. "That patio door is locked for sure now. And all the outside lights are on. I'm sure you won't be bothered again tonight. Just turn your alarm back on after we leave. Good night now."

"Good night. Thank you." Lee locked the front door behind them and reactivated the alarm system. Then she hurried upstairs with Sara.

"Can I sleep with you tonight, Mom?" Sara looked very young and shaken.

"Sure. To tell the truth, I'd appreciate some company myself."

They got into bed and Lee turned out the light. "Mom?" Sara's voice was a nervous whisper. "Who do you suppose was trying to burglarize us?"

"You heard the policeman. Probably just some kid with a drug habit planning to steal a television or a VCR."

"Do you really think you locked that patio door?"

Lee stared up into the darkness. "Well, I thought I did. But I must have been mistaken. Anyway, we're all locked up now. Sleep tight, sweetie."

Sara rolled over and was soon asleep. But Lee lay awake until dawn, staring at the red lights on the alarm control panel—her frantic thoughts swirling around a red woolen scarf, Sara's "colossal crow," and a locked patio door that had been opened without any sign of forced entry.

* * *

Lee returned from the grocery store the next morning to find a police car parked in front of her house. The burglar alarm was screeching, shattering the silence of the otherwise peaceful neighborhood. She pulled to a stop at the end of the driveway and bolted from the car. A young police officer was just coming around the north side of the house.

"What's going on?" Lee called, rushing up to him.

"Are you the owner? Mrs. Nickolas Lindsay?"

"Yes."

"We got a call from your alarm service that the system was triggered. I've checked all the doors and windows and everything is locked up tight. It's probably just a malfunction."

"The alarm went off last night," Lee said, shouting over the noise and doing her best to stay calm. "Someone opened the patio door after the alarm was set."

"An attempted break in? In that case, I'd better do a thorough check of the inside of the house. I'll need the key to the front door."

"Just a minute." Lee ran to the car and got her key chain out of her purse. She handed it to the officer and started to follow him toward the house.

"Wait out here, ma'am," he said.

Moments later he stuck his head out of the front door. "The downstairs seems secure. How do I disarm the system?"

Lee gave him the code. "Can I come in now?"

"You'd better wait outside until I check upstairs."

Before long he was back. "No signs of forced entry," he said. "Everything's locked tighter than a drum. Had to have been a malfunction. Is it a new system? Sometimes it takes awhile to get the bugs out."

"Officer, please. Will you come with me to check all

the rooms?"

"I just did that."

"Did you look under the beds and in all the closets?"

"Well, no. But I rechecked all the doors and windows. As I said, there's no sign of a break-in."

"Please."

"Of course. I won't leave until you feel safe."

"Then you might be here for a long time."

"Ma'am?"

"Never mind." Lee went in the front door and followed behind the police officer as he went from room to room, searching every possible hiding place.

"Do you notice anything missing or out of place?"

"No."

"Okay." He paused at the front door. "I think you can relax now, Mrs. Lindsay. There's no one in your house."

"If I seem unduly nervous it's because my daughter and I are alone this week," Lee explained. "And I did see a prowler several nights ago. Then last night, someone tried to break in."

"Would you feel better if we kept an eye on the property for the next few days? I can arrange to have one of the patrol cars drive by and check things out a couple of times during the day and at night. That's usually enough to discourage anyone who's watching the place."

"I'd really appreciate that."

"You won't know they're there unless something doesn't look right. Call if you have any more problems."

"Thank you." Lee closed the door behind him and locked it. Moments later, she remembered that the back seat of the car was filled with groceries and reluctantly went back outside. Not until the car was parked inside the garage, and the garage door closed and locked, was she able to breathe normally again.

* * *

Sara seemed unusually subdued when she returned from school that afternoon. She disappeared into her room and closed the door. Lee, noting the absence of the rock music that normally blared from behind her daughter's bedroom door, decided to investigate. When she opened Sara's door, she found her lying on her bed, surrounded by her menagerie of stuffed animals.

"What's the matter?" Lee asked, sitting on the edge of the bed.

"I don't know. I just don't feel very good. My head hurts, and I feel sort of...wobbly."

"Wobbly?" she felt Sara's forehead. It felt warm and slightly damp.

"Yeah. You know, kind of weak. And a little dizzy when I climbed the stairs."

"When did this start?" Fear stirred in the pit of Lee's stomach.

"Around noon. In fact, I only had a Pepsi for lunch. Everything in the cafeteria looked yucky to me."

"Are you hungry now? I could fix you some soup."

Sara wrinkled her nose. "No thanks. But would you get me something for my headache? It's really killing me."

Lee fought a rising panic as she hurried into the bathroom. She's getting sick! she thought. Sara's getting sick—just like Nick did. Stop it, she told herself, opening the medicine cabinet and shaking two aspirins into her hand. Calm down. Sara just has a headache, that's all it is. Please, God. Let that be all it is. She filled the water glass and hurried back to Sara's room.

* * *

Sara napped on and off for the rest of the afternoon. She refused to eat, turning down even a bowl of her favorite ice cream. By eight o'clock she was in a deep sleep. Lee felt too anxious to go to bed. She decided a hot bath might help her to relax.

She meditated in the tub, trying to unwind. Allowing her mind to float, she visualized a beach in Hawaii, on the island of Kauai, that she had visited with her parents when she was a teenager. It was one of those rare times when her father was on the wagon, and her parents seemed almost happy together. She remembered thinking Kauai must be the most beautiful place on earth. What was that beach called? Poipu. That was it. Poipu Beach. White sand, warm turquoise water, palm trees, red and orange bougainvillea clinging to a high lava rock wall.

Lee felt some of the tension seep from her body. She could almost smell the odor of plumeria blossoms and feel the warm humid air against her skin. Maybe Nick would take her back to that beach. As soon as his sabbatical was over. A real family vacation. Sara would love it. She smiled, visualizing the three of them walking together on the warm beach.

* * *

Lee got out of her bath and into a flannel nightgown, feeling almost drowsy. She checked on Sara, who seemed to be sleeping peacefully. Her forehead felt cooler. Sara would be better in the morning, she told herself.

All the doors and windows were locked. The alarm was set. Lee did some neck rolls, trying to ease the knotted muscles in the back of her neck. Bed was going to feel good, she thought, as she pulled the heavy quilted bedspread back.

Lee reeled back and stared at the pillows, not believing what she saw. She must be hallucinating! She closed her eyes, and opened them again. It was still there! The cat's skull she had found in Juan's bathroom. The skull that was unmistakably Mister's. Hand clamped over her mouth, she staggered into the bath-room—barely reaching the toilet before she vomited.

Afterwards, long after she had no more tears to cry, Lee lay on the bathroom floor. She couldn't make herself go back into her room and face what was in there. Thank God Sara was asleep. Sara! She pushed herself up to a sitting position. Sara could wake up and come looking for her. She had to make sure Sara didn't see what was left of Mister. Oh God, Juan was a monster. He was clearly capable of anything. She remembered Socorro warning her not to underestimate Juan. Well, she had. And it had cost her dearly. She would never make that mistake again.

She forced herself to face the question she had been avoiding. Juan must have left the skull here while she was at the store this morning. And, in doing so, he had triggered the alarm. But how did he get in without breaking a window or forcing the lock on a door? Could he possibly have a key? He could have made an imprint of her keys while she slept in Cavado. Then an even worse thought gripped her. Maybe he didn't need a key. Maybe a *brujo* just used magic to come and go as he wished.

She forced that thought from her mind. Getting to her feet, she made herself walk into her room and over to her side of the bed. She picked up the partially fur-covered skull and held it for a moment to her chest. Then she walked straight to the closet and gently placed the skull on the top shelf, behind her beige suede purse.

She reached along the right side of the shelf until her hand felt the pistol. Holding the gun in front of her, she walked through the house, rechecking all of the windows and doors. Satisfied that everything was as secure as she could possibly make it, she went into Sara's room.

She felt her daughter's forehead. A little warm, maybe a slight fever. Yet she couldn't bring herself to leave. She put the gun on the floor, just under Sara's bed. Then she got into the bed, inching close to Sara's slender body. Not allowing herself to think, she stared into the darkness. Finally, her eyes began to close.

* * *

It was just past midnight when Sara started scream-ing. Lee jerked awake. "What is it? Sara, what's wrong?" As she fumbled for the light on Sara's nightstand, she smelled it. Sweating oil!

Sara was sitting up in bed, staring blindly, her face twisted in terror. She screamed again. "No! Get away! Mommy! Mommy, help!"

The smell grew stronger. Frantic, Lee cradled her daughter's thin frame in her arms. Sara felt very hot. "I'm right here, baby," she said. "Mommy's here." Was the smell real? Lee no longer had any doubt that it was.

"Don't let it bite me!"

"Sara, wake up. You're having a dream, honey. Please, wake up!"

Sara twisted violently in Lee's arms. "The crow! It's after me!"

Lee blood turned to ice. Now there could be no doubt. It *was* Juan. In some way—some impossible way—he was causing Sara's sickness. Just as he'd been responsible for every terrible thing that had happened in the past month—Socorro, Mister, Nick's illness, her accident, and now—now the son of a bitch was after Sara! She remembered his angry voice on the phone when she had spoken to him in the hospital. *"You think I can't stop you from leaving me? Then you are mistaken. You are very mistaken."*

"Mom?" Sara's eyes, wide and glassy, were now focused on Lee. "Why are you in here with me?"

"You were having a nightmare. Come on, I want you to sleep with me in my room."

Lee helped Sara out of bed. The odor seemed to follow them as she led Sara into her own room. Fighting to stay calm, she gave Sara two more aspirins and tucked her into Nick's side of the bed.

Hurrying back down the dark hall, Lee grabbed the gun from under Sara's bed. When she returned, she locked the door behind her, taking care to hide the gun in the folds of her nightgown. But there was no need for such caution. Sara's eyes were closed.

Lee slipped the gun into her nightstand drawer, within easy reach if she should need it. Then she rechecked the windows, balcony door and alarm panel.

Everything seemed secure. But she didn't dare count on it.

"Mom?" Sara's voice sounded weak and fretful.

"I'm here, honey," she said, getting into her side of the bed. She slid close to Sara and gave her a hard hug. "Go back to sleep. No more bad dreams. Nothing's going to hurt you." Anger flared into a red-hot rage inside Lee, overshadowing her fear. "I promise," she whispered fiercely into Sara's hair. "I'll never let anyone hurt you."

After Sara had fallen into a fitful sleep, Lee lit the pottery candle Socorro had given her. Then, figuring more must be better, she gathered three more candles from the bathroom shelf. When the room was illuminated by candlelight, the odor suddenly disappeared.

Lee climbed back into bed, her mind racing. What could she do? Go to the police? She had no evidence against Juan, no proof that he'd done anything at all. Bitter tears of helplessness rolled down her cheeks. She felt so alone. If only Socorro were here. She'd know how to fight back. But Socorro couldn't help her. Never again. Juan had seen to that.

By dawn the wax candles had burned completely down, and Lee had come to terms with what she had to do.

* * *

Sara was still asleep early the next morning when Lee dialed Juan's number. He answered on the third ring.

"¡*Hola!*"

"All right, you bastard," Lee said in a toneless voice. "You win. I'll come back to Cavado. But stop what you're doing to Sara. Do you hear me? Stop it right now."

There was a short silence at the other end of the line. "I will be expecting you," he said softly. Lee imagined his smug smile. "Come alone. Don't try to trick me, *querida*." He paused. "Did you like my little surprise?"

She clutched the countertop with her free hand.

"You're evil. Or crazy. I don't know which."

"There is much you don't know. But no matter. *Los ojos se abriran*, your eyes will be opened. I will be expecting you tomorrow. Come early."

Lee replaced the receiver, backing away from the phone as though it were a snake. For a moment she thought she was going to be sick. She sat at the kitchen table, taking deep breaths until the nausea passed. He'd been waiting—like a spider in his dark little den—confident that she would call, knowing that he had given her no choice. She forced herself to her feet and turned on the burner under the tea kettle. Juan would be in for a surprise. Tomorrow, she'd be calling the shots. He'd undo his filthy black spells, she'd see to that. If it was the very last thing she did. Filled with grim resolve, Lee stood in the kitchen, willing the water to boil.

* * *

Sara's temperature remained high. Then, in the late afternoon, she awoke from a nap, her condition dramatically improved. In fact, her fever was almost gone and she was hungry.

Light-headed with relief, Lee hurried into the kitchen to fix tea and toast. It had worked. Juan was satisfied that he'd won. Now he could afford to let up on Sara. The ruthless bastard. How could she have let him even touch her? Much less make love—but that was in the past. She had returned to her senses, at last. The spell was finally broken.

Chapter 29

"*A*re you sure you're well enough to go to school?"

Sara nodded. "I have to, Mom. I have an exam on *Macbeth*." She gathered her hair into a ponytail and sighed. "Why couldn't Shakespeare have written in plain English? Without all that 'forsooth' and 'henceforth' business. I get a kick out of the witches though. They're cool. We had to memorize one of their scenes." She started to chant: *"Round about the caldron go. In the poisoned entrails throw. Toad that under cold stone—"*

"Terrific," Lee interrupted. "You'd better hurry. It's getting late. I called the school yesterday, so you shouldn't need a note."

Sara continued: *"Days and nights has thirty-one; Sweltered venom sleeping got; Boil thou first in the charmed pot."*

"I hear Kevin honking outside. Wear your down jacket."

Sara gave her a quick kiss and started down the stairs, still chanting: *"Double, double toil and trouble;*

Fire burn and caldron bubble. Eye of newt and toe of frog...'"

"Good-bye! Good luck on the test." Lee hesitated, wanting to call Sara back and hug her close, tell her again how much she loved her. But she had to let her daughter go. She couldn't weaken now. "I love you, baby," she called out. "See you after school."

The front door closed, and Lee walked resolutely into the bathroom. She ran a brush through her hair and automatically applied a quick smear of lipstick. Then she stopped and stared at herself in the mirror. Grabbing a wash cloth, she rubbed at her lips. No need for makeup this morning, she thought grimly. This is no social call.

She opened her closet door and collected what she needed, trying to block the thought of Mister's head, resting out of sight on the top shelf. Poor Mister was beyond her help. What mattered now was Sara and Nick. It was her fault that they were in danger, and she was the only one who could save them.

She dressed quickly in a pair of loose-fitting jeans, a flannel shirt and boots. When she opened her jewelry box to get her watch, she saw the amulet. Holding it for a moment, she wondered briefly about the role it might have played in her recovery. Amulets were supposed to offer protection from harm. Well, she certainly didn't want it, whether it had magical power or not. She didn't want any reminders of Juan. He'd understand that when she threw his family heirloom in his face. She dropped the amulet into her shirt pocket and walked to her nightstand. Steeling herself, she reached inside and transferred the handgun to her purse.

* * *

Fear for the safety of her family blocked all other feelings as Lee drove along the now familiar road that led to Cavado. She didn't want to use the gun. Maybe she wouldn't have to. But one thing was certain: Juan had to be stopped. He wasn't going to hurt Sara or Nick again, not while she had life left in her body. A few short weeks ago, she wouldn't have believed that something like this could happen in her world. But she had been drawn into another world—a world of passion and danger—the first time she had looked into Juan Mascareñas' eyes.

She rounded a curve and saw the gas station ahead. The accident must have occurred right about here, she realized, looking across the narrow road at the rough terrain beyond. She imagined her car sliding off the road and rolling over and over, through *piñon* trees and over the rocks. It's really a miracle that I wasn't.... She didn't let herself finish the thought.

Too soon she was there, in front of Juan's shuttered adobe lair. Not allowing herself to hesitate, she got out of the car and walked up the dirt path, clutching her purse.

The door opened before she could knock, and Juan materialized from the darkness within. "So," he said. "The time has finally come." His eyes were merciless as they locked onto hers. Terror gripped her and Lee knew, too late, that she'd made a terrible mistake. Even with her gun, she was no match for him. She had no defense against the sheer force of his personality. As she turned to run, he seized her arm and pulled her inside.

She noticed a strong odor that burned her eyes. Before she could react he held a small, smoking bundle of what looked like dried weed beneath her nose. She coughed and tried to pull away, but he held her in place. Smoke filled her lungs, choking her. Her eyes closed as the room began to spin. She felt her knees buckle and heard her purse hit the floor. "No!" she screamed, the sound echoing in her head. At that moment, everything went black.

* * *

At first she thought that she was dreaming again. The cave, lit by the soft glow of candles, had a surrealistic quality about it, which was somehow familiar. She was lying on soft fur, naked from the waist up. She lifted her left arm, heavy with the weight of the cast, and touched soft suede covering her hips. Instantly she was wide awake, and the cave became a room. She was back in Cavado! And she was lying on the buffalo skin rug, dressed in the bottom half of the ceremonial outfit she'd worn before. She tried to sit up, gasping as pain shot through the left side of her ribcage. She fell back, dizzy and nauseated.

"Lie still." Juan's voice seemed to come from nowhere, startling her. "The sickness will soon pass." She raised her head and saw him sitting in a dark corner, his face hidden in shadows. He appeared to be naked, except for the glint of silver around his neck. "Thank you for returning my amulet," he said. "It fell from your shirt pocket when I undressed you."

"I feel so sick. What did you do to me?" Her voice sounded hoarse, and it hurt her throat to talk.

"I did what was necessary. To prepare you." When he stood and walked toward her she saw that he was wearing a loincloth. He dropped to one knee, looking down at her. Lee gasped when she saw that his face was painted with white streaks, in a distantly familiar zigzag pattern.

"It is time for the final ceremony," he said. "It is time for us to go through the spirit door together."

Lee screamed. Before she could make another sound, his hand clamped over her mouth and nose, cutting off her breath. "No more of that," he said. "Do you understand?"

She nodded, frantic for air. He removed his hand. "Now it begins. Our journey into the spirit world. There you will find your true identity. You will regain your lost powers."

He stood and picked up his black gourd rattle from a nearby table. Shaking it in a circular pattern, he moved counterclockwise around the buffalo skin rug where she lay. Lee tried to think. The final ceremony! A journey into the spirit world? What does that mean? What's going to happen to me? But even as she asked herself the questions, something within her knew the answer.

Once through the "spirit door" with Juan, she wouldn't be coming back. At least not as she knew herself, as Lee Lindsay, Sara's mother and Nick's wife. She would be changed—rejoined with the medicine woman Juan wanted her to be again.

"The sacred circle is cast," he said, standing over her and stretching his arms toward the ceiling. "The space between the worlds has been created." Overwhelmed by fear, Lee fainted.

* * *

When she came to, she was lying on her side and Juan was kneeling beside her, fastening a necklace around her neck. It was a leather cord threaded through a small wooden bird-like figure, dressed in red and covered with tiny black feathers.

"Ye-na-lo-he," Juan whispered, "Guardian of Those Who Fly. Remember, I promised that she would accompany you into the spirit world. Now, sit up."

"Please," she begged, "Don't make me do this. I'm afraid."

"I know you are." His voice was suddenly gentle. "That's why you must do it, *querida*. To regain your courage. There was a time when you knew no fear." His eyes shone with a distant memory. "You were a woman of strong medicine who feared no one, not even me, when..." He broke off, an expression of anguish on his face.

"Juan," she pleaded, "this is crazy. I know you believe I was someone else. But even if I was, I'm not now. I don't want to be that person. I want to be me. I want to live the life I have now." Tears ran down her cheeks. "Please, just let me go."

"Enough! No more talk." He held a bowl of hot liquid to her lips. "Drink!"

She turned her head to one side. "No! I won't! I won't drink—"

He grabbed her hair and yanked her head back. Then he held the bowl to her mouth again. "You will drink it," he hissed. "Or I will pour it down your throat."

Lee choked down a small swallow. It was bitter with an almost sweet aftertaste, unlike anything she had ever tasted before.

"Drink it all." He gave her hair another yank.

When the bowl was empty, Juan released her hair. "It pains me to hurt you," he said. "But you leave me no choice."

"Is this what you did to Susan Miller? Did it 'pain you' to hurt her, too?"

A strange expression—part shock, part outrage—distorted Juan's face. "What did you say?" He gripped her shoulders. "What do you know of that? Of Susan?"

"Just that you took her to Mexico." Lee fought a wave of dizziness. "She...she never came back."

"It was a long time ago. I was young. My deep memories were hazy. I mistook her for you."

"For me?"

"But I soon realized that I had fooled myself." He gazed past her, his eyes narrowed to slits. "She had only wanted to use me, to research my people and their ways. We were in Hermosillo when she left our room one night. I found her later in a bar, dancing with another man, some gringo. I left her there. And I never saw her again." He was quiet, lost in the memory for a moment. Suddenly he refocused on Lee. "*Basta, ya no mas.* Enough about that. It is of no importance. Now, the time has come. Lie back down on the sacred buffalo skin. Don't be afraid. I will be with you on the journey. But first we must purify ourselves with the sweating oil."

Lee closed her eyes as the room seemed to tilt. When she opened them again her vision was blurry. How could she have been so stupid? She thought she could force him into...into...what was she going to do? Oh yes, the gun! She was going to threaten him with the gun. She was going to make him return Sara's scarf. And Nick's sweater. A familiar sickening smell interrupted her scattered thoughts. Then she felt him rub the sweating oil across her breasts and midriff, up under her skirt and down her legs. She closed her eyes helplessly when he began to chant.

He held her tightly while they both sweated beneath a heavy wool blanket. Lee had snatches of dreams of a shadowy female figure with the face of a bird. She tried to force herself awake, to organize her thoughts. What did he say about Susan Miller? Something about thinking that she was me. But that was twenty years ago. He didn't even know I existed then. Crazy. He's crazy.... Her thoughts trailed off and she drifted, carried by the soothing rhythm of Juan's chanting.

"Drink the water of remembrance," he said, propping her head up and putting another bowl to her lips.

Lee was so thirsty she drank it all before his words registered. "What was that?" she asked. Her queasy stomach forced her to lie back down.

Juan ignored her question. He sat cross-legged near her prone body. Beating on a small drum, he began singing repetitive lyrics in a foreign tongue. The sounds ricocheted through Lee's head, evoking emotions too complex for her to identify.

For a while nothing happened. She strained to stay alert, to keep an eye on Juan, but something was wrong with her eyes. Everything was growing darker. She heard a ringing in her ears and felt a soft sensation of upward movement. Then she was floating, drifting through darkness into lighter swirling mists.

She raised herself into an upright position and found that she could walk. Not walk, exactly, but move as she wished, trailing a thin shining cord. She understood that the cord was connected to her body, which was still lying on Juan's buffalo skin rug. This is what I did as a child, she thought, I floated out of my body. But I never went this far. She stopped, realizing that she wasn't alone. Other shapes moved through the mists, hovering near her. I know this place, she thought, I've been here before. After my accident. And he was here with me. Juan. No, not Juan. His name was....

Then he was beside her, as he had been for so long in

her dreams. His black hair hung down his chest and over his shoulders, and the medicine mark of the scarlet spider clung to his cheek. Recognition came to her in a rush. "Kamulko." Her voice was a dry whisper. "Shape Changer."

He smiled. "You remember. My Tarena, She Who Talks To Animals."

At that moment a terrible memory flooded into her mind—Kamulko's furious expression as he faced her on the edge of a high rocky precipice, the horror of realizing what he planned to do.

You killed me," she blurted. "You pushed me from the top of Sacred Mesa."

"No, Tarena. It was an accident. You lost your balance and fell, don't you remember? I moved fast, but was unable to save you."

"Liar!"

"My grief was unbearable," he continued, as though she hadn't spoken. "I followed you into the spirit world shortly after your passing. Ah, but none of that matters now. We are together again. At last. In new bodies. The sacred vows cannot be broken."

"You broke those vows when you perverted the Power, when you abandoned all that you had taught me about how it should be used. You used your magic against your own people. You betrayed us. And when I tried to stop you—"

"You pushed against me and slipped. Your crippled foot could not sustain you. I would never have harmed you."

"You cannot deceive me, Kamulko. I had become too great a threat to you. You had taught me too well and my power was too strong. You could not allow me to live."

"No, no! It broke my heart to lose you—"

"You lost me long before I fell to my death. But you refused to accept it. It was not what you had planned. You always had to have your way, taking what you wanted, whatever the cost to others. You misused your gifts. And you continue to misuse them in this life. You work black magic against my family. I am Lee now."

"You are also Tarena, High Medicine Woman. She Who Talks to Animals."

His words released another flood of long-forgotten memories. She heard the voices and saw the faces of those she had loved in another lifetime. Those she had tried to protect from Kamulko's ruthlessness.

Something shifted and swelled within her. Her two selves merged. Although she was still Lee, part of her was once again the medicine woman called Tarena. The veil between lifetimes lifted and she saw her situation with stunning clarity. History was repeating itself. Once again, she must do battle with her ancient lover and enemy. She must fight for her identity in this present lifetime, and—even more important—she must fight for the lives of Sara and Nick. Kamulko meant to destroy them and reclaim her, body and soul. She must get back! She must return to Lee's body!

As soon as she had willed it, she felt herself being sucked back through the mists and the darkness. Down...down...then a sensation of impact and heaviness. She was lying on the dark fur, shivering. Her body felt cold and weak. Juan was beside her, slumped over the drum with his eyes closed. In his open hand lay the small black statue of a raven.

A dizzying pain clutched at her head, but Lee forced her reluctant body into a sitting position. There was no time to lose. Juan might return to his body at any time. But she couldn't leave without Sara's scarf and Nick's sweater! As long as Juan had them, her family would be in danger from his malevolent spells. He would show them the same mercy he had shown Socorro. And Mister. She had to find the articles of clothing. That was why she had come! But first she had to find her purse—and the gun. She had to have the gun before Juan returned to his body. Where had Juan put her purse? She prayed that he hadn't looked inside.

Crawling to the sofa where her clothes lay in a pile,

she rummaged clumsily until her fingers touched the smooth leather of her purse, hidden beneath her coat. The gun was still there. With a wary glance at Juan's motionless body, she got to her feet.

The room tilted and whirled. Lee took a deep breath, fighting for equilibrium as her eyes searched the dark corners of the room. Then she saw it. Sara's scarf was on top of a table, coiled like a red woolen snake around a canine skull. She staggered forward and snatched it, knocking the skull to the floor. It rolled toward the center of the room, toward Juan.

He jerked violently and opened his eyes. Surprise flashed across his face when he saw her. He laughed. "A gun? You brought a gun? You surprise me, Lee. There is more of Tarena in you than I suspected." He sat up and looked at her with an amused expression. "When will you learn, my love? You're no match for me. You never were."

"Don't be too sure of that. And don't call me your 'love'. You never loved me—in this life or any other. You have no idea what the word means."

"Ah, Tarena, you are lecturing me again. After all this time." He wiped at the white streaks on his cheeks, smearing them. Then he held out his hand. "Give me the gun."

She shook her head. "I found Sara's scarf. Now give me Nick's sweater. I mean it. Or I'll—"

"You'll what? Shoot me? I don't think so."

"You won't hurt my daughter again. Or my husband. I won't let you destroy my family."

His face twisted with an old bitterness. "Your family?" he sneered. "I don't want to hear any more about your precious 'family'. You belong with me. Were your eyes not opened to that on our journey?"

"My eyes were opened, all right. I saw you for what you really are, the ruthless *brujo* that you've always been."

"Give me the gun." He held out his hand.

"Stay back!" She steadied the gun with both hands.

"Don't make me use it."

"¡*Demelo*! I said give it to me." His eyes blazed with anger as he sprang to his feet and lunged toward her. Lee jerked to one side, her scream lost in the sharp crack of the pistol discharging.

He was thrown backward, staggering. Lee saw a bright red bubble of blood burst from a small hole in his chest just below the silver amulet. He covered it with his hand. "No," he said in a shocked voice. "You can't have done this." His eyes fastened on hers with an expression of great sorrow. "Tarena," he whispered. "My Tarena." Then he crumpled face down on the buffalo skin rug.

Lee sank to the floor, the gun in her hand. She had no idea how long she sat there before Tarena's voice in her head began issuing orders. *"Go! Run from this place! Now!"* Scrambling to her feet, she dropped the gun back into her purse. She shoved her bare feet into her boots, pulled on her coat, grabbed her clothes and Sara's scarf, and started toward the door.

"Wait! Find Nick's sweater!" She whirled and ran into the small room containing the portable toilet.

The sweater was there, splattered with a dark, dried substance and nailed outstretched to the wall. A part of her mind noted that it was a north-facing wall. *"North,"* Tarena's voice whispered, *"the direction of winter. The direction of death."*

Lee ripped the sweater from the wall and ran from the room. She averted her eyes from Juan's body as she headed for the front door, but not before she saw a pool of blood, seeping through the dark buffalo fur and spreading slowly across the wooden floor.

Chapter 30

*L*ee clutched the steering wheel and raced along the narrow, twisting road. All that mattered was getting back to Santa Fe. Home to Sara and sanity. After what seemed like an eternity, she was finally in her own driveway. She parked the car in the garage and stumbled into the house.

Not until she removed her coat and saw that she was still wearing only the leather ceremonial skirt, did the terrible reality of what had happened hit her. She recoiled at her reflection in the bathroom mirror—oily, disheveled hair, wide staring eyes in a shockingly pale face. And around her neck, hanging between her naked breasts, was the feathered fetish. She yanked it off and worked furiously to untie the knot in the leather cords that held the skirt around her waist. When it fell to the floor, she sank naked to her knees on the bathroom carpet and let the tears come.

Lee's hysterical sobs were soon replaced by feelings of panic. I killed Juan. I shot him and left him lying there. But I didn't have any choice! He was trying to

take the gun. I had to stop him. I had to save Sara and
Nick. He planned to destroy them, I'm sure of that. It
was self-defense. But how could I prove that? Who
would believe any of this?

My God, I could go to prison! A band tightened
across Lee's chest at the realization of what that would
do to Sara and to Nick. She scrambled to her feet,
fighting for breath. I can't deal with this, she thought
frantically. Rushing to the medicine cabinet, she
swallowed a tranquilizer. Then, for good measure, she
gulped down another.

* * *

By the time Sara got home from school several hours
later, Lee was in bed and under chemical control. The
draperies were closed and a cloth lay across her swollen
eyes.

"Mom? What's wrong?"

"I guess I caught your bug. Don't turn on the light,
honey. I have a terrible headache. How are you feeling?"

"Fine. I feel great, completely well. But now you've
got it. Bummer. You've sure been sick a lot lately.
Can I get you anything?"

"No. I just need to lie here for awhile. Are you sure
you're okay?"

"Yeah. I had this really killer headache until third
period. Then—it was weird—all of a sudden, right in
the middle of the English exam, the headache just
disappeared and I felt fine." She hesitated. "I think I
screwed up the last question on the test, though. We had
to discuss the use of imagery in *Macbeth*. We were
supposed to list three main images—they were blood,
water and darkness. But the only one I could remember
was blood—"

"Sara," Lee said, cutting her off. "Don't worry about
it. You're well again. That's all that matters." She
paused, fighting to steady her voice. "That's absolutely
all that matters."

* * *

Lee forced herself to watch the early local news on television that night. But there was no mention of Juan's death. They haven't found him yet, she thought, pacing back and forth in her bedroom. The tranquilizer had worn off and panic was threatening once again to overwhelm her. What should she do? Who could help her? If she told Dr. Mallory what she'd done, he'd insist that she turn herself over to the police. There would be an investigation. A trial! She couldn't let that happen. She had to stay calm until she could decide what to do. Hurrying into the bathroom, she swallowed another pill.

In bed, two hours later, Lee was still wide awake. She spent most of the night tossing and turning, reliving the terrible hours in Cavado. Especially the split second just before the gun went off. Did she pull the trigger deliberately? Or did Juan's lunge toward her cause the action? She didn't really know. On the other hand, she asked herself, what if she hadn't shot him? Would Juan have let her go? Would any of them ever have been safe again? Alone in the darkness, Lee knew the answer. Not a chance.

* * *

She woke suddenly. It was still early and the house was quiet. The horror of the previous day rushed at her. With a great effort, she suppressed her anxiety. There was something she had to do, something that couldn't wait any longer. Feeling stiff and sore, she pushed herself out of bed. She opened the closet door, reached behind her purse, and felt the stiffened fur.

Stifling a sob, she wrapped Mister's head in her favorite silk scarf. Then she emptied a shoe box, lined it with a white hand towel and placed the pitiful bundle inside. As an afterthought, she added Mister's collar and his catnip-filled cloth mouse, which had been hidden out of sight in her nightstand drawer. She dressed hurriedly in heavy sweats and tennis shoes. A peek into Sara's darkened room satisfied Lee that her daughter was still asleep.

She crept down the stairs and disarmed the alarm

system. Carrying the small make-shift coffin and a shovel, she climbed the hill behind her house. It took longer than she'd anticipated to dig a hole in the hard, frozen ground. Finally, it was deep enough. Lee knelt and gently lowered the shoe box inside. "Good-bye, little buddy," she whispered, her voice choked with tears. "I'm sorry, so terribly sorry that you had to pay for my weakness. Both you and Socorro. But the *brujo* didn't get away with it, Mister. And he'll never hurt anyone again."

Using her hands, Lee gently filled the hole with dirt. She placed three large rocks over the slight mound, the only marker she dared to leave. Neither Sara nor Nick must ever know about the little grave—or its gruesome contents. That would raise too many questions, questions she could never answer. Weak with grief and exhaustion, Lee made her way back to the house.

There was nothing about Juan in the morning's paper. Nor on the Saturday night local news. Waiting for Nick to get home, Lee was almost sick with apprehension. Why hadn't Juan's death been reported? He was, after all, a well-known person around Cavado. On the other hand, an unexplained shooting in a remote mountain village might not make the Santa Fe paper. Cavado probably didn't see a policeman for weeks at a time. And it was common knowledge that the residents of those little mountain villages took care of their own problems, avoiding the police whenever possible. But if the local *curandero* was found murdered, especially if he owned most of the town, surely the authorities would be notified. It would probably be in tomorrow's paper.

She rushed into the bathroom, intending to take another tranquilizer. Nick mustn't see her in this condition. But as she opened the medicine cabinet, an inner voice told her to stop. *No more pills.*

Lee closed the cabinet door. Glancing into the mirror, she gasped. Staring back at her was a dark-skinned woman's face, her strong features framed by long straight black hair. An instant later, the image faded and was gone. Lee stepped closer to the mirror, raising a hand to her pale cheek. I must be seeing things, she thought, her heart pounding in her chest. Probably a result of all the pills I've taken. Or lack of sleep.

But deep inside, Lee knew better. As the moments passed, she became aware of a profound shift in her consciousness. Hallucination or not, the image had given her an unexpected surge of strength.

I can get through this without pills, she realized. I must. What did Socorro say about drugs separating us from our inner knowing? She was right. I have to remember that. I have to stay connected to myself— whoever that really is.

Lee forced herself to do some yoga exercises, while concentrating on deep breathing. After a few minutes she felt much calmer. No one can connect me to Juan's death, she thought, standing at the sink. She ran cold water and splashed it on her face. No one even knows that I saw him yesterday.

Unless...unless the guys at the gas station had seen her drive by! Her stomach knotted at the thought. No. They wouldn't recognize her new car. And besides, they'd never suspect her. She didn't have a motive, at least not one that most people would believe. The only person who knew about her connection to Juan was Doctor Mallory, and that was privileged information. Besides, even he didn't know that she'd returned to Cavado.

Suddenly, she had a terrible thought. Socorro's uncle, the Deputy Sheriff! If Juan's body was found, he would certainly remember Lee's call and all of her questions about the Mascareñases.

Calm down. Think this through. Tafoya had been told that she and Juan had a little "run-in." That could mean anything, perhaps a misunderstanding related to the article she had written. Hardly a motive for murder.

Lee took a deep breath, assuring herself that she was safe. Sara and Nick were safe, too. Her family was still

BRUJO

together. What was it Socorro had said? Only the death of a spirit-sucker could free his victim. Only the death.... Lee closed her eyes and buried her face in her hands. Then, after a moment, she lifted her head and squared her shoulders. She had done what she had to do. Now she would have to learn to live with it.

Lee brushed her hair back. Nick would be home soon. She frowned at her reflection in the mirror and opened her makeup drawer, wishing that the circles under her eyes were all she had to conceal.

* * *

"I'm back!" Nick came up the stairs, lugging his suitcase. Lee flew into his arms.

"Let me put this down," he said, laughing. Then he gave her a long kiss. "Boy, am I glad to be home," he said.

"I'm glad to have you home." She kissed him again.

"If I'd known I was going to get such a great reception, I'd have hopped an earlier plane."

"How was your flight?"

"Not bad. No crying babies this time, believe it or not. I had my laptop computer with me and actually got some work done."

"Do I hear Dad?" Sara came out of her room and down the hall to give Nick a hug. "Well, did you find us a neat apartment?"

"I sure did. Better than neat. Large rooms and a great view of the Potomac River. Plus, it's in a very good school district. Come on," he said, with an arm around both Lee and Sara. "Let's go downstairs. I'll fix myself a drink and tell you all about it."

* * *

That night in bed, Lee put her arms around Nick. Pleading the effects of a twenty-four-hour virus, she resisted his sexual advances. "I just want to be held," she said.

"Happy to oblige," Nick said, holding her close. Within moments, Lee was fast asleep.

* * *

340

Socorro's face, serene and smiling, looked even more beautiful than Lee remembered. Her voice was gentle and comforting. "Be at peace, Lee," she said. "All is exactly as it should be."

"Socorro! Is it really you? I thought you were dead."

"My earth walk has ended," Socorro said. "But let that be no cause for grief. Death is only an illusion, a transition. Trees do not grieve that they must drop their leaves and rest through the winter. They know that spring will soon return and with it another season in which to grow. So it is for all of us."

"He killed you, didn't he? Juan killed you. And he was going to kill Sara and Nick. I had to stop him, Socorro. That's why I went back there. That's why I took the gun. I thought I could scare him, and get back the scarf and sweater. But he lunged at me and the gun—Oh, God!—the gun went off and then Juan was lying there with blood all around—" She broke off, sobbing.

Socorro nodded. "Don't you see, Lee? It is all part of the dance."

"What dance? I don't understand."

"The dance between you and Juan began long, long ago. It has played out in different ways, many different times. All earth walks are a circle. It is all a learning."

"But how do I live with what happened, with what I've done?"

"I will help you. Close your eyes."

Lee heard the sound of drumming. Then Socorro was singing in her sweet, soft voice. At first the words sounded strange, although the melody was familiar. As Socorro sang, the sounds washed through Lee like warm, soothing water.

"Your spirit knows the song," Socorro whispered. "Let it come back to you. Rise above your pain and sing your healing with me."

Lee began to sing, hesitantly at first, stumbling over the words. Gradually, her voice grew stronger and her *tongue slipped easily around the strange sounds.*

For what seemed like hours, she sang with Socorro, their voices blending together in a song as old as time. Lee felt her grief began to release, and to be replaced with a feeling of great peace and love."

The drumming died away. "I must leave you now," Socorro said.

"No. Please, don't go. I need you—"

"My work here is finished now. Yours is not. You still have much to learn. And much to teach. Walk in beauty, my sister."

Lee felt the touch of a warm hand on her forehead. She watched as Socorro's face faded into a soft, golden light. Slowly, the light disappeared.

* * *

Lee opened her eyes. Her cheeks were wet with tears.

"Socorro," she whispered.

Nick rolled over to face her. "You okay, babe?"

"Yes. I'm fine."

"You were making a humming sound in your sleep. Having another dream?"

"No," Lee said, smiling in the darkness. "I don't believe that was a dream."

Chapter 31

"*L*ee? Hi, it's Jim Mallory."

"Doctor Mallory. Just a moment." Lee put her hand over the telephone receiver. "Thanks, Julie. Just leave those articles on my desk. I'll get to them sometime this morning." She waited until Julie left her office.

"Hi," she said, hoping that she didn't sound as guarded as she felt.

"I had a few minutes between appointments and thought I'd check up on you. I see you're well enough to be hard at work."

"This is my first week back. It's been quite an adjustment after being out of the office for so long."

"I'll bet. How's it going?"

"Very busy. I have a lot of loose ends to tie up before we leave for Washington."

"When's that?"

"In two weeks."

"That soon? You really must be busy. Well, you're obviously on the mend physically. How are you doing otherwise?"

343

She hesitated for just a moment. It would be such a relief to go into Mallory's office and tell him everything, to share the horror of her last trip to Cavado. But how could she do that? How could she risk telling anyone? "I have my ups and downs," she said. "But I'm doing pretty well, all things considered."

"Is Juan giving you any trouble?"

"No," she answered carefully. "I haven't heard from him in some time."

"That surprises me. But I'm very glad to hear it. Well, if I don't see you before you go, have a great year in Washington. I think the change will be good for you."

"I'm counting on that. Thank you for calling. And for all the support you've given me."

"You bet. Be good to yourself, Lee. It's time to put all of this behind you."

"That's what I'm trying to do. I really am. Good-bye, Doctor Mallory."

Lee hung up the phone and hurried to close her office door. Leaning against it, she fought for composure. Hearing Mallory's voice had cracked the fragile wall of control she had managed to erect during the past three weeks. Put it all behind her? Would she ever be able to do that?

There were so many unanswered questions. She still waited and watched for some word about Juan in the newspaper or on television. But there had been nothing. Not a single word. Sometimes she found herself wondering if it had really happened. She had certainly been drugged, both by that terrible smoke and by whatever he'd forced her to drink. Maybe the entire ceremony—her journey to the spirit world, her fusion with Tarena—and even the shooting were just a drug-induced hallucination.

As much as she would have liked to believe that, she couldn't. Nick's sweater and Sara's scarf had provided tangible evidence of her last moments in Cavado. They had remained hidden in the back of her closet for almost a week until a strong impulse had made her burn them, along with the bird fetish necklace and ceremonial skirt, in the outdoor barbecue pit. Immediately after she scattered the ashes behind the house, a wind had come up and blown them away.

I can't afford to kid myself, Lee thought, returning to her desk. The unbelievable did happen in Cavado. Several times.

But why didn't Juan's death make the news? Could it be that she only wounded him? He was wearing his amulet when she shot him. Maybe the healing crystals.... Was it possible? Was he recovering in Cavado and plotting some diabolical revenge? She had to know!

Before she could stop herself, Lee picked up the phone and dialed Juan's number. As the phone rang, she held her breath, half expecting to hear his abrupt, *"¡Hola!"* She let it ring for almost a full minute. No answer. Trembling, she replaced the receiver.

Of course he's not there, she thought. I killed him. I shot him in the chest. Dear God, there was so much blood. Suddenly, sick to her stomach, she bolted out of her office and down the short hall to the bathroom. She locked the door and turned on the water in the sink to cover the sound of her vomiting.

Afterward, she splashed water on her face, and smoothed her hair back from her forehead. As she looked into the mirror above the small sink, Lee remembered the image she had seen in her bathroom mirror, the night after the shooting. An image of Tarena? A message from her Higher Self? Lee couldn't know for sure. But the memory soothed her and gave her strength.

I need to guard my light, she thought, returning to the privacy of her office. Sitting at her desk, she closed her eyes and envisioned her spirit body, as Socorro had taught her to do. She soon found herself humming a strange, soothing tune. For just an instant, she could have sworn that she heard Socorro's voice, singing along.

Chapter 32

"Grab your parasol, Scarlett darlin'," Nick said, rinsing out his coffee cup in the kitchen sink. "The wagons are loaded and ready to roll."

Lee managed to return his smile as he headed for the garage. The time had come. A truck carrying the items they would need during their stay in Washington had just left. They were to follow in the two family cars.

She hoped the renters would take good care of everything. They had impressed her as a trustworthy young couple, eager to lease the furnished home while they were designing and building their own dream house.

Walking into the family room, Lee was torn by conflicting emotions. It was hard to leave the magazine that she had spent so many years establishing, even though it was in good hands. She planned to stay in close touch with Annabel and be involved in any major decisions. Still, she knew she would miss the daily interaction, the frustrations, and the excitement. Just as she would miss the beauty and special charm of Santa

Fe. But she was ready to go.

"Mom, I can't possibly live for a whole year without my posters," Sara said, bursting into the room and interrupting Lee's thoughts. "Can I put them in the back of your car?"

"Sure. Oh, and don't forget your hairdryer. I saw it on the counter in your bathroom."

"Oh, jeez, that reminds me. Kevin's picture! I almost forgot Kevin's picture!" Sara ran back up the stairs.

Lee put on her jacket and took a final walk through the house and out onto the master bedroom balcony. The sun had risen just above the mountains, warming the early morning sky to a delicate salmon hue. It promised to be a beautiful day. She leaned against the stucco wall, trying to memorize the snow-spotted landscape that stretched west to the Old Taos Highway. Her eyes lingered on the hills and shadowed *arroyos* where Mister used to hunt and play. She bid him a silent good-bye, feeling sure that his spirit still happily roamed the area.

Her thoughts turned to the medicine rocks that Socorro had placed around the house. It would be a comfort knowing that they were here, guarding the property while she was gone.

Just then, a lizard with a ragged stump where its tail used to be darted up the wall, close to Lee. She observed the tiny reptile, damaged but undefeated, carrying on in spite of its injuries. A courageous spirit. I'll remember the lesson, Socorro, she silently pledged. I'll remember everything you taught me.

"We'd better get going," Nick said, walking up behind her. "It's almost seven o'clock. We really lucked out with this good weather. Let's hope it holds." He put his arms around her. "You doing okay?"

She nodded. "I'm just saying my private goodbyes. Did you leave instructions for the renters about the alarm system?"

"Everything's taken care of. Sara's already in my car. I told her she can drive me to Albuquerque. Then

347

when we head east on I-40, she can ride with you, if you want company. Now that she has her learner's permit, she needs to get in some practice on the road."

"I agree. But I'd rather you drove through town. Let her practice on that nice straight stretch to Albuquerque."

"Okay, babe. Let's get started. We have a long day's drive ahead of us." He took her hand. "Take it easy on your wrist. You just got the cast off last week."

"It's feeling stronger all the time. I'll manage fine."

"We'll meet you in Albuquerque for breakfast." They walked through the bedroom and down the stairs. "How about the Marriott? It has a nice coffee shop and it's right next to the freeway."

"Fine. I'll meet you two there in about an hour." Lee walked out the front door, and turned to watch Nick lock it behind them. She got into her car and waved to Nick and Sara as they pulled out of the driveway. Then, after a long last look at the house, she fastened her seatbelt and drove down the dirt road into town.

She turned off the radio, wanting to be alone with her thoughts as she drove south. Soon she was out of the city limits and Santa Fe was receding into the distance through the rear view mirror. As she neared the top of the long slope of La Bajada Hill, Lee impulsively pulled over to the side of the road. She turned off the ignition and got out of the car, walking around to the rocky shoulder of the highway.

She stood motionless, captivated by the panoramic view Squinting against the early morning brightness, she scanned the snow-covered Sangre de Cristo mountain range that stretched far into the distance. Santa Fe shimmered below, nestled in the foothills and bathed in cool pure light. I'll be back, she thought. This will always be home to my heart.

Her eyes were drawn to the north, to where Cavado lay hidden. An image leapt, unwelcome, into her mind. She saw Juan's face bending toward her, his dark eyes intent with passion. Then it was replaced by another, even more vivid image—Juan lying motionless on a bloody buffalo skin rug. She shut her eyes tightly, forcing the memories away.

When she opened her eyes moments later, Lee saw an enormous raven circling above her. She watched it glide gracefully through the air, sleek black wings parallel to the ground. In the next instant the bird turned and landed on a branch of a *piñon* tree not five feet away. Stretching on its perch, it screeched—a hoarse, croaking "Kraak!"—and beat the air furiously with powerful wings.

The hair rose on the back of Lee's neck as her rationality was invaded by something far older, a mindless primordial terror. "Juan?" she whispered. "Is that you?"

The raven fixed her with a fierce, unblinking gaze.

"No, it can't be! This is crazy. You're just a bird. Juan's dead!" Suddenly she heard Socorro's voice warning, *"Never underestimate a spirit-sucker, Lee. They don't die easily."*

At that moment, Lee's reality seemed to shift. The thought of her brave, dead friend ignited an ancient anger deep within her. Fed by long buried memories of injustice and betrayal, it blazed into a powerful rage that dissolved her fear. *"Keep your distance, Shape Changer,"* she heard herself warn in a strong voice that no longer sounded like her own. *"Or I will use the Power against you. I will call on the Grandmothers to curse you, to trap you in that black shape."*

The raven shrank back. It cawed once more—a terrible anguished sound—and flew into the air.

She watched the bird fly northward until it dwindled to an insignificant dot in the clear morning sky. For a long moment she stood there, her heart pounding. She felt confused, like a visitor in her own body. Finally, she made her way back to her car and locked herself inside.

What just happened? she wondered. Was that Tarena? For a while there, I was absolutely certain that raven was really.... Without daring to finish the thought, she turned the key in the ignition, shifted into forward and, after a quick backward glance, sped over the hill.

A few miles down the road, Lee began to feel more like herself. Better, in fact, than she had felt in a long time. She felt centered deep within herself and lighter, as though a heavy darkness had finally disappeared.

It could be that my imagination ran wild back there, her rational mind argued. Maybe that was only a raven. A common raven. She found herself smiling. But then again, maybe not. Maybe *She Who Talks to Animals* had worked a little magic of her own.

Watch for Upcoming

Books from

**Route 66
Publishing, Ltd.**

Now Available

Auschwitz 1940-1945

An English language guide to the museum located at the most notorious of the Holocaust's concentration camps. Fifty eight black and white photos illustrate the atrocities inflicted by the Nazis on more than four million victims.

"*Auschwitz 1940-1945* is a passport to the camps. It documents the degeneration of mankind."
Phillip Reiss, Holocaust Museum

Coming Soon

A series of illustrated Indian tales designed for young readers

An New Age mystery thriller

Auschwitz 1940-1945

"*Auschwitz 1940-1945* is a passport to the camps.
It documents the degeneration of mankind."
Phillip Reiss, Holocaust Museum

Look for this book at your local bookstore or use this page to order

Please send me _____ copies of *Auschwitz 1940-1945* (ISBN 0-9644293-1-4) at $8.95 each.

I am enclosing $_____, for _____ copies of the book, which includes $2.75 per book ordered for postage and handling. Send check or money order; no cash or COD's.

Visa/Mastercard #_____
Expiration date _____
Signature _____

Ship to:
Mr./Ms._____
Address_____
City/State/Zip _____
Telephone (_____)_____

Send order to:
Route 66 Publishing, Ltd.
Attn: Order Dept.
P.O. Box 25222
Albuquerque, N.M. 87125

Please allow 4-6 weeks for delivery.
Prices subject to change without notice.

BRUJO
Seduced by Evil

"Compelling and powerful! After reading **BRUJO**
I knew I had to produce it as a movie!
Richard Polak, Cinestage Productions
Los Angeles, California

**Look for this book at your local
bookstore or use this page
to order.**

Please send me ___ copies of **BRUJO,** *Seduced by Evil*
(ISBN 0-9644293-0-6) at $6.95 each.

I am enclosing $___, for ___ copies of the book, which
includes $2.75 per book ordered, for postage and han-
dling. Send check or money order, no cash or C.O.D.s
please.

Visa/Mastercard #_____
Expiration date _____
Signature _____

SHIP TO:
      Mr./Ms._____
      Address_____
      City/State/Zip _____
      Telephone (___)_____

Send order to:
Route 66 Publishing, Ltd.
Attn: Order Dept.
P.O. Box 25222
Albuquerque, N.M. 87125

Please allow 4-6 weeks for delivery.
Prices subject to change without notice.